For Kristina

puppy reader!

Leighton

World Cities, City Worlds

World Cities, City Worlds

Explorations With Metaphors, Icons And Perspectives

William Solesbury

Matador
9 Priory Business Park
Kibworth Beauchamp
Leicestershire LE8 0RX, UK
Tel: (+44) 116 279 2299
Fax: (+44) 116 279 2277
Email: books@troubador.co.uk
Web: www.troubador.co.uk/matador

ISBN 978 1783060 085

British Library Cataloguing in Publication Data.
A catalogue record for this book is available from the British Library.

Printed and bound in the UK by TJ International, Padstow, Cornwall
Typeset in 11pt Aldine401 BT Roman by Troubador Publishing Ltd, Leicester, UK

Matador is an imprint of Troubador Publishing Ltd

For my children Eliza, Jack and Tara, world travellers

'We shall not cease from exploration
And the end of all our exploring
Will be to arrive where we started
And know the place for the first time.'

T S Eliot, *Little Gidding*

Contents

1. Introduction: making sense of cities   1
   Putting cities in the frame
   Metaphors, icons and perspectives
   Real and imagined cities
   Origins

2. Living together: cities as communities   18
   Hong Kong 2002
   Identities
   The ideal city
   City states
   Cosmopolis
   Neighbourhoods
   Social capital

3. Legacy: Venice past and present   36
   Riva degli Schiavoni 2005
   No ordinary city
   La Serenissima
   Earth, water, air and fire
   Backstage
   Ancient and postmodern

4. Conflict: cities as battlegrounds   51
   Madrid 2009
   Cities under threat
   Walls and ghettos
   Riots and revolutions
   The personal and the political

5. Transformation: Mumbai's many worlds   67
   North Mumbai 2010
   Full-on
   India's powerhouse
   Old and New Mumbai
   The social mosaic
   Underworld and overworld
   In transition

6. Images and narratives: artists' cities   85
   Marrakesh 2004
   Subjects and settings
   Low life
   Soundtracks
   Fantastical cities
   Cities of memory

7. Energy: novelty and excess in New York   101
   Seventh Avenue 1998
   We love New York
   Outwards and upwards
   New people
   New enterprises
   New places
   Governability
   9/11

8. Transactions: cities as marketplaces   119
   Lima 1995
   Markets and malls
   City economies
   Boom towns
   Livelihoods
   Shelter
   The (i)n(f)ormal city

9. Space and time: analysts' cities   140

St Petersburg 2008
Mapping the city
Urban geometry
Travellers' tales
Old and new cities
Globalisation and cities
Close-up and distant views

10. Metamorphosis: Tokyo's renewals and reinventions   157
Venus Fort 2011
Looking west
Four traumas
Low city, High city
Technology and touch
Transience

11. Efficiency and order: cities as machines   174
London 1970s, London 2000s
Increasing tempo
On the move
Support systems
Engineering cities
Hardware and software

12. Variety: the contradictions of Paris   191
Montparnasse 2003
1789 and all that
The avant garde
Quartiers
The boulevards
Americans in Paris

13. Power: rulers' cities   205
Berlin 1990
City fathers
New capitals
Monuments and makeovers

Public works
Command and control
Love and fear

14. Modernity: Los Angeles' rise and fall   226
    Beverly Hills 2000
    Mobility
    Five and a half ecologies
    Angelenos
    Hooray for Hollywood
    LA's dark side

15. Growth and adaptation: cities as organisms   241
    Hanoi 2007
    Body parts and functions
    City growth
    Evolution and complexity
    Sustainability
    Designing with nature
    Resilience

16. Getting by: city life   258
    Stellenbosch 2001
    Surprises and secrets
    Assaults on the senses
    In the streets
    Life skills
    Consumers and citizens

17. Postscript: cities as Heaven and Hell   273

    Notes and references   275
    Image sources   287
    Thanks   289
    Index of cities   290

1.

Introduction: making sense of cities

Putting cities in the frame

Imagine you have been kidnapped, blindfolded, driven some distance and then released by your captors in a strange place. How would you know, when the blindfold came off, that you were in a big city? Probably a busy atmosphere would be the first impression – traffic and people on the move, bright lights, noise. Then you might note that it was all buildings, roads and pavements, little greenery, clearly a man-made place. Walking along, the variety of it might strike you next, with many kinds of faces in the crowds, all sorts of things going on, big and small vehicles. Before long something novel – odd behaviour, offbeat conversation or bewildering graffiti – could jolt you. Then, if you walked long enough, you would sense that this place seems to have no limits in time or space – it stretches as far as the eye can see and it keeps going twenty-four hours a day. These sensations – seen, heard, smelled – would tell you incontrovertibly that you were in one of the world's cities. But which city? One you know? Even the one you live in? One you've read about, seen on TV or in film or photos? Or one you don't recognise at all? Other clues will help you here: the language people speak, maybe their looks and clothing, the street names, the adverts, a familiar monument or building, the livery of the taxis – black, it's London! Yellow, it's New York! Green?!

We experience, characterise and understand cities in many ways. Most basically, we have to find ways of relating to a city where we live or visit. We need help to get by in our daily lives. As visitors we can buy tourist guides to direct us to the sights, the hotels, the restaurants. As residents we may have the A–Z map and the transport timetable. But our need for guidance will be subtler than that; we need to know a particular geography and temporality, when as well as where to find what or who we may need. We must acquire a working knowledge of the many transactions needed for our shopping, work, housing, recreation, health and welfare. Beyond these tangible qualities of cities, we also

1

need to grasp its intangible customs and practices: the appropriate forms of address, how to cross the road without mishap, the degrees of trust to be accorded to people and institutions, whether and how to queue, when to be extra mindful of personal safety. It is these things that city outsiders – whether newcomers or visitors – take longest to learn, struggling with them long after they have mastered the bus routes or shop opening hours.

If we are in the work of managing cities we need other kinds of understanding. As city politicians or bureaucrats we need to know how the city functions – its economy, its community, its environment – and what drives changes there: the boom and bust of city economies, the sources of community friction, the decay and renewal of its infrastructure. As professionals in healthcare, education, engineering or architecture we need an understanding of how actions we might take will succeed or fail in our particular city. As business leaders we need to grasp the opportunities that the city offers and the limits it imposes on our enterprise: the local markets for goods and services, the local supply of labour and capital, the efficiency of energy, telecommunications and transport systems. In short we need models of how the city works through which we can analyse trends and patterns and test our decisions and actions.

Others of us are observers of the city. As journalists we observe and report, offering our interpretations of what is going on. Researchers seek to understand the city through the prism of particular disciplines – as political scientists, economists, geographers, sociologists, even as psychologists. Over the last two centuries academics have developed paradigms to explore how the experience of city life has shaped people's values and behaviour. Artists are also observers who through their images and narratives provide us with visions of the city. City worlds have become a particular inspiration in a whole range of media – painting, photography, fiction, poetry, music, film and video – since cities became so large and have absorbed within them so much of social life.

So, as residents and visitors, as politicians, professionals and entrepreneurs, as journalists, researchers and artists, we need help in describing, analysing, designing, governing, living and working within cities. We need guides or models or paradigms or visions – let's call them frames. My dictionary[1] offers two definitions of 'frame.' One is the everyday definition as a 'structure that surrounds a picture, door, windowpane or similar', that is, what you look through or pass through from one position to another. But the dictionary also offers a second definition of 'frame' as 'a basic structure that underlies or supports a system, concept or text' and says it is short for 'frame of reference'. This captures my use of the term. I am exploring frames of reference to help us make sense of cities – not just particular cities but cities in general and also cities of the past as much as of the present and cities across the world.

For there are continuities and discontinuities between historic and present-day cities. Clearly such activities and places in cities as airports, general hospitals, energy or recycling plants and metros did not exist before recent times. On the other hand, other activities and places have always existed in cities – dwellings, workshops, roads, theatres, temples and churches. There are also some extraordinary analogues between ancient and modern cities. The crowds watching gladiator contests in the Roman Colosseum would be at home watching football or a rock concert in today's Wembley Stadium. Travellers were similarly accommodated in the *caravanserai* in Islamic cities, the *han* in central Asia, the *choultry* in India, the *gostiniy dvory* in Russia, or in the English coaching inn as in the modern motel – with a simple room, secure storage for their goods and somewhere to park their transport, whether camel, horse and cart or car. Today's live/work spaces (to adopt the property agent's term) for homeworkers with desk space and internet connections are essentially similar to the artisan's accommodation in many pre-industrial cities. And, of course, café life has gone on forever.

Equally there are similarities and differences between the cities of today's global North and South. Industrialisation and immigration have been features in the histories of both, as have poor housing and tough working conditions and, in the longer run, improved health and welfare and higher incomes. But it is wrong to see them as at different stages on a common development trajectory with, say, Mexico City now where Manchester was in 1850. For there are important contextual differences. Most importantly the new cities of the South have come into a world in which the North and its cities are already globally dominant, in part from their historic colonialist exploitation of the South. They are latecomers and as such the terms of international trade and aid are frequently stacked against them. Their economies may also be weak, dependent on natural resources or farming, with low labour costs that immiserate their population their main competitive advantage, and their governing elites can be corrupt and exploitative. All the while they still act as magnets for immigration from the countryside swelling their populations. But, despite these differences, it is hard to distinguish sharply between the present-day cities of the global North and South. All combine similar elements, though in different proportions, to create their own specific characters. So, most cities in the South have airports. shopping malls, business centres, freeways, high-rise luxury apartments. Equally, many cities in the North have street sleepers, shanty towns, sweatshops and rundown public services. In a globalised world the city has become a global phenomenon. Framing cities helps us understand both the history and the geography of cities.

Metaphors, icons and perspectives

In this book I explore three particular ways of framing cities – through metaphors, icons and perspectives. Metaphors use differences to express similarities: thus we might describe a journey as hellish, chaotic, nightmarish or, on the other hand, as a dream. Icons capture certain essential qualities: in this way film stars, product brands or buildings are often described as iconic. Perspectives are shared ways of seeing or understanding things: exemplified in phrases like 'Muslims believe…' or 'In our experience…' What metaphors, icons and perspectives have in common is that they provide analogies, points of comparison that illuminate both similarities and differences. The use of analogies is an important way in which we get to understand the world around us. We take something familiar as a means of understanding something new, thereby building on what we already know. That is how we commonly learn. With the help of analogies we pick out patterns and recurrences, form concepts that abstract them and express these concepts in language.

Metaphors, icons and perspectives are all forms of analogy that can be richly expressed in words and images. We have in our minds a mental lexicon of these kinds of analogy that we constantly draw upon. So we might look at a building and think 'Art Nouveau' (or 'Jugendstil' or 'Liberty style' in other languages and cultures). We might see and smell some food and recall the occasion, even the companions, when and where it was last experienced. Or we might agree with a friend that the demands of our workplace are turning us into zombies. There is similarly a lexicon of analogies – as metaphors, icons and perspectives – which can capture thoughts and feelings that help us make sense of cities. These city analogies are what this book is about. They are drawn from both real cities and imagined cities, from across the world and through history.

Take metaphors first. In the past linguists often drew a contrast between literal and figurative language. Literal language tells it how it is, coolly, logically, precisely, appealing to reason: it is the language of science or the law. Figurative language, in contrast, is colourful, less precise and uses various tropes – like simile, metaphor, metonymy, synecdoche – to achieve greater descriptive power, sometimes an emotional impact: it is the language of fiction, poetry or speech. Literal language was judged superior. Modern linguistics takes a different view. It sees the whole range of tropes as basic to the way language and thought work. We can see many applications in accounts of cities. Simile makes explicit comparisons – as with 'driving in Shanghai is like a rollercoaster.' With metonymy, a name, often a place name, stands for the object – such as the US examples of Wall Street, The White House, Hollywood. Such metonyms often survive change in the reality on which they rest, thus Fleet Street still signifies the British press though no newspaper offices remain there. With synecdoche a part stands for the whole or vice versa, as when football teams are described just by their home towns – Chelsea v Milan, Barcelona v Eindhoven.

Metaphor is the most common trope. My dictionary describes it as 'a figure of speech in which a word or phrase is applied to an object or action to which it is not literally applicable. Fowler's *Modern Usage* notes that 'our vocabulary is largely built on metaphors; we use them, though perhaps not consciously, whenever we speak or write.'[2] Here, for example, is a description of Jakarta in Indonesia with the metaphors italicised:

> 'People come to the city *above all* for the sake of livelihood, to labour, in an effort to *make good* the *felt* deficiencies in the rural areas, the *decay* of self-reliance, the *ruined* subsistence. Many migrants *discover* at the end of their journey that *industrial life* is an ambiguous and often *treacherous liberator*. But they learn other *lessons* too. Even the poorest communities *create* informal *networks* and *bondings* to *defend* themselves. In Jakarta workers in the formal and informal *sectors*, slum dwellers, if they are to *create* a decent life for themselves, must do so in some of the most *hostile* conditions, against some of the most *repressive* social *forces* on *earth*; their *triumphs*, however partial and temporary, are the more inspiring for that.'[3]

You might dispute whether some of the italicised words are metaphorical. If so, it is because they have become 'dead metaphors', that is, ones that are in such common usage that they go unnoticed.

Metaphors work through juxtaposing two superficially unlike components

– which linguists call 'term' and 'analogue' – so that their separate meanings interact to create a new understanding, as in 'The Royal Palace (term) is the heart (analogue) of the city.' The effectiveness of metaphors depends on the power of the analogy. If too weak, then the metaphor may not work at all or may just fail to excite the imagination. 'The Royal Palace is the centre of the city' would have this lesser power. 'Heart' offers us more meaning than 'centre' – it implies not just the Royal Palace's geographical centrality (as the heart lies in the centre of the human body), but a functional role (the heartbeat on which life depends) and maybe also an emotional attachment (the heart as a symbol of love). How well such a metaphor works for us will depend strongly on prior knowledge – in this case, that we know the palace is home to a ruler, we have a grasp of the role of the heart in the human body, and culturally we share the association of the heart with positive emotion.

The way we think about cities is strongly shaped by metaphors. Five recur in many variations: the city as community, as marketplace, as battleground, as machine and as organism. These are 'extended metaphors', that is, they serve to structure a whole concept of the city with many dimensions and levels of meaning. It is these dimensions and levels that are explored in the chapters below. The city as community (Chapter 2) is perhaps the most common and most comforting metaphor, implying a commonality of values, identities and interests that help people to live together. But, shift to the plural – communities – and differences on the basis of location, class, income, ethnicity or religion are immediately implicit. So we also have the metaphor of the city as a battleground (Chapter 4), a place where values and interests are in contest, with enemies perceived within or without the city. Some conflicts become embodied in the structure of the city as property prices, zoning or even the building of walls and ghettos keep people in cities apart. Political battling also tends to be urban – revolutions commonly start and/or finish there, as with the French Revolution in Paris in 1789, the fall of the Berlin wall in 1989 and the collapse of the Mubarak regime in Cairo in 2011.

Then there is the city as marketplace (Chapter 8). Cities are places of multiple daily transactions, buying and selling goods and services, in street markets, supermarkets, job markets, housing markets, stock markets or on black markets. Economically they may flourish or struggle, their people winners or losers. Cities may also be perceived metaphorically as machines (Chapter 11). Modernist architects and planners embraced a rationalist, mechanical view of the whole city – 'The city of today is dying because it is not geometrical' declared the architect Le Corbusier. But this view of the city as machine has a long pedigree. It is there in new town building through the ages and round the world, it was strengthened by the development of urban networks for efficient water supply, drainage, energy and communications, and it is reinforced by the city rulers' wish for efficiency and order. Lastly, cities can be seen as organisms (Chapter 15). The body is a powerful source of metaphors for cities which are seen as having a wide range of body parts (hearts, arteries, lungs, spines) and body functions (eating up land, excreting waste). Evolutionary thought has also been influential, with a stress on the organic development of cities, recently strengthened through concern with ecological sustainability.

Metaphors like these offer more than just good description. They can give us an easily grasped overall concept of the city. They can provide us with a basis for shared understanding between neighbours, between producers and consumers, between different professions, between rulers and citizens. Metaphors can also help us to analyse problems and find solutions. This arises when the analogue used in the metaphor comes laden with an implicit diagnosis or prescription – as the machine metaphor leads us to think of ways of fixing the city's malfunctions, the organism metaphor to curing the city's ills, and the battleground metaphor to resolving its conflicts. So metaphorical thought, speech and image are pervasive in explorations of cities. But much of our use and interpretation of metaphors is tacit. Often we do not know we are speaking, reading, hearing or seeing metaphors for the city. This apparent invisibility can make them even more powerful.

Using icon as my second way of framing cities is itself metaphorical. Its original Greek meaning, once more quoting from my dictionary, is 'a painting of Christ or another holy figure, typically in a traditional style on wood, venerated and used as an aid to devotion in the Byzantine and other eastern Churches.' Many such icons are rich with gold leaf and jewels; some have myths of creation attached to them; others have supposedly miraculous properties. In all respects they are out of the ordinary. This quality has been carried over into the modern, metaphorical usage of the word 'icon' to mean, from the dictionary again, 'a person or thing regarded as a representative symbol of something.' And thereby, like the original religious icons, to serve as an aid to devotion.

The essential features of an icon are that it is recognisable and it has meaning, both widely shared. Icons are usually strongly visual, their image is what helps us to recognise them for we remember what we see more readily than what we read or hear. Images help us to imagine – note the common etymology here – more vividly. So film stars may become iconic, writers must settle for just being seminal. This visual quality is what makes cities strong candidates for iconic status, particularly when their image is unique. Before the last century the communication of such city images was rare, experienced directly or in illustration by only a few people, as travellers or art collectors. Even so, some places did acquire a status as fabled cities – Babylon, Timbuktu, Samarkand, Jericho, Constantinople. But most people had no idea what Paris or Los Angeles or Rio de Janeiro or Cairo was like. Photography, film and video – produced not just for the media but also for themselves by modern day travellers, tourists and migrants – have changed all that. In 2001 all around the world people knew Manhattan's skyline and so could grasp the enormity of the destruction of the World Trade Centre's twin towers on 9/11. It was an act of iconoclasm.

As icons, cities are more than recognisable; they also carry meaning. That meaning has several levels. Most superficially it is the general character or atmosphere of a city, its *genius loci*. More specifically it is the unique attributes of the city, its characteristic activities, buildings and street scenes, for example, the domesticity of London's low-rise, terraced housing and green squares, the neon-soaked streets of Tokyo, the dense skyscrapers of New York and Chicago. Beyond appearance, the meaning of a city is to be found in the imagined experience of being there, sharing its daily life with the locals, both its pleasures and frustrations. When the experience of a particular city – even if only in the imagination and without actually having been there – seems to capture something of a more universal experience of cities at large, then that city has become iconic.

The appropriation of city names is evidence of iconic qualities. Both Paris and Venice are strongly celebrated in this way: Budapest, Bucharest, Beirut, Saigon and Shanghai have all been deemed the 'Paris of the East'; St Petersburg and Stockholm have both been called 'the Venice of the North' and Bangkok 'the Venice of the East'. There is also Little Venice, a canalside London neighbourhood, and Venice, a district in Los Angeles built round canals. There are 'mini-Manhattans' wherever a clump of skyscrapers has sprung up. Sometimes it is a cultural or spiritual tradition that is borrowed through a city's name. Edinburgh is the 'Athens of the North' and Bogota 'the Athens of South America' because of their intellectual life; Nashville claims to be 'the Athens of the (American) South' (but that's more to do with the full size replica of the

Parthenon originally built there for a 1897 Exposition). There are multiple Romes: 'the Second Rome' is Constantinople and 'the Third Rome' is Moscow, expressing a claimed historic transfer of Christian authority from the Catholic to the Greek Orthodox and later to the Russian Orthodox Church. In some cases the names of iconic cities may become brands, used commercially to attach valued qualities to products or services, hence the many Hotels de Paris or Oxford language schools round the world. But these references are not always favourable – witness how Babylon has come to symbolise cities of excess, decadence and corruption: at various times London, New York, Las Vegas and Tokyo have all been denounced as 'the modern Babylon'.

There is something of a paradox here. For iconic cities are both unique and universal – unique enough to be recognisable, universal enough to express wider meaning. But it is this dual characteristic that identifies the truly iconic cities. In this book I explore this characteristic in the cases of Venice, Mumbai, New York, Tokyo, Paris and Los Angeles. Venice (Chapter 3) is the quintessential 'old city', ancient, elegant, a little unworldly and now largely living on its legacy. Mumbai (Chapter 5) represents those post-colonial cities of the global South progressively, and sometimes painfully, transforming itself for a new future. New York (Chapter 7) retains a crazy energy and excess fuelled by successive waves of immigration and innovation over the last two centuries. Tokyo (Chapter 10) has grown and grown at a phenomenal rate and, partly through the disasters of earthquake and war, has repeatedly renewed and reinvented itself. Paris (Chapter 12) is an extreme case of the contradictions that often characterise cities: in its politics it is both revolutionary and conservative, in its culture radical and traditional, socially it is home to the bourgeois and the bohemian. Finally, Los Angeles (Chapter 14) is, through the products of Hollywood, probably the best known city in the world and one that once represented the dream of urban modernity – rich, fast-living, glossy – but that dream has faded.

These are not the world's only iconic cities. Though, interestingly, four of them – Venice, New York, Paris, Los Angeles – featured in 2007 plans by Pinewood Studios in London to build new, permanent city scene backlots for movie making. (Also included were Rome, Vienna/Prague and Chicago). You might feel that any list of iconic cities should include Rio de Janeiro, Mexico City, Cairo, London, Rome, Damascus, Shanghai, Sydney or many others. But my chosen six serve as a sample that displays ways in which particular places come to represent urban qualities found more widely in the world's cities.

9

Perspective is my third way of framing cities. My dictionary offers as a definition: 'a particular attitude towards or way of regarding something; a point of view.' Again this is a metaphorical usage. The original use of perspective was in drawing and painting. The ancient Persians and Greeks were aware of the concept. But it was in 15th century Florence that the geometrical rules of perspective were devised to enable an approximately accurate representation on a flat surface of a three dimensional reality. To achieve this, objects are drawn smaller as their distance from the viewer increases, parallel or rectilinear lines meet at vanishing points, objects viewed obliquely are foreshortened; an associated technique is to paint distant objects with softer, cooler colours. The use of such conventions was most apparent in paintings that showed cityscapes in which the placing of buildings, statuary, figures and ground surfaces brought the three dimensions alive.

As a metaphor, perspective has come to mean reality as understood from a particular viewpoint; 'take' is a contemporary synonym. That different people often appraise the same thing in different ways is a commonplace observation. The same object may appear beautiful to one person, ugly to another; the same personality may be attractive or repellent; the same film may be exciting or dull. In making such contrary assessments, it may be that the two people are focusing on different attributes – say, the acting or the look of the film. Or they may attach different values to the same attribute – the story is judged either fresh or naïve. Such differences of perspective are something that we live with in our relations with others all the time. We also find that we have perspectives in common with others – we agree that the object is beautiful, the personality repellent or the film exciting. In fact we probably agree more often than we disagree. For perspectives come to be shared by groups of people as they engage in the same or similar acts, and use the same or similar words to talk about their ideas and experiences. Language is an important way in which such perspectives are developed and maintained. Much of what is shared in these ways is tacit, self-evident to the group but possibly incomprehensible or bizarre to outsiders.

Cities can be viewed from different perspectives like anything else. In this book four perspectives on cities are explored: those of artists, analysts, rulers and city people themselves. For Artists (Chapter 6) the city has long provided a setting for their images and narratives and sometimes a subject in itself. City life has been a particular inspiration, and found representation, in those artistic media that have developed in modern times – the novel, film, photography and popular music – to capture new sensations and express new sensibilities. Cities have also attracted the attention of analysts (Chapter 9) seeking to understand how they function. Their spatial patterns and temporal rhythms have been explored by economists, cartographers, sociologists, travel writers, geographers, historians and others. The perceptions of analysts can be very pervasive and long-lasting in their influence through their adoption by city rulers (Chapter 13) and their professional helpers. For throughout history rulers have sought – sometimes autocratically, sometimes democratically – to remould cities. It seems to be a universal and irresistible urge for the powerful to create grand urban projects which symbolise their authority in this way – Hausmann's Parisian boulevards, Robert Moses' freeways and bridges in New York, Hitler's planned transformation of Berlin into Germania, even brand new capital cities like Washington, Canberra, and Brasilia. Rulers also exert influence through regulatory and spending decisions – restricting street trading, changing permitted building densities, building transport systems, renewing whole districts.

Lastly, let's not ignore the perceptions of city people themselves, expressed in city life (Chapter 16). Less and less of the world's population now remains ignorant of the urban experience. Even people living outside cities are connected to them: maybe they have relatives there, possibly sending remittances home; they have lived and studied or worked there previously; they may trade with city enterprises; they may be city tourists from time to time; or they see or read media coverage of city events. The personal experience of everyday urban life is shared with relatives, neighbours and friends, but only occasionally recorded in any public way. Even so, it is not a perception that can be ignored. Common terms like 'street-life', 'street-wise' and 'street-cred' hint at a unique popular perspective – or take – on city life.

Real and imagined cities

In the last decade the world became predominantly urban. That is, according to United Nations statisticians, over half of the population – 3.5 billion people in total – now lives in cities.[4] Within another generation, by 2030, there may be 5 billion city dwellers, 60% of the world's population. This is a historic shift, changing a balance that had lasted for millennia when most people lived on the land and urban people were the minority. Cities are now the places in which the majority of the world's population, in all the continents, now spends its daily life – the locales of work, home life, entertainment, sickness and health, friendships, crime, learning. Cities are also the motors of national economies, places where the making of goods and the provision of services are concentrated and where innovation – new activities replacing old – occurs. They are man-made artefacts, dense with buildings and networks subject to frequent renewal. These city environments can be both a source of delight and a cause of misery, sometimes in one and the same time and place – every city in the world has its slum housing, pollution, unsafe streets as well as its civic spaces, handsome parks and charming buildings. Cities are seats of power, both political and commercial, where governments and courts sit and where corporate HQs are found and trade fairs are held. As well they often host many of a nation's cultural institutions, its galleries, theatres, museums and universities. Tourists flock to them.

This shift to an urban world fostered the growth of an urban sensibility, so that the city has become a major focus for our thoughts and feelings. City life is not just there to be experienced in its own, immediate terms. As well, the idea of the city has come to carry all sorts of other associations, both good and bad – with human inventiveness; with money, power and corruption; with poverty and deprivation; with opportunity and advancement; with a sense of shared community; or with danger, stress and isolation. Much is contradictory. An 18th century polemic about London captures this well, describing the city as:

> 'a great wicked, unweildy [sic] overgrown Town, one continued hurry of Vice and Pleasure; where nothing dwells but Absurdities, Abuses, Accidents, Accusations, Admirations, Adventures, Adversities, Advertisements, Adulteries, Affidavits, Affectations, Affirmations, Afflictions, Affronts, Aggravations, Agitations, Agonies, Airs, Alarms, Ailments, Allurements, Alterations, Ambitions, Amours, Amphitheatres, Anathemas, Animosities, Anxieties, Appointments, Apprehensions, Assemblies, Assessments, Assurances, Assignations, Attainders, Audacities, Aversions…'(and so on).[5]

All this is apparent not just in the real cities of the world, but also in the imagined cities that feature in novels, films, paintings, poetry, song and photography. Very often they present simulacrums of real cities at particular times – the 1930's Los Angeles of Raymond Chandler's detective Philip Marlowe, the street scenes of 1950's Paris by photographer Robert D'Oisneau, the modern Hong Kong of Wong Kar-Wai's movies *Chungking Express* (1994) and *In the Mood for Love* (2000). In all cases these are representations, not reproductions. Their verisimilitude varies greatly – compare Canaletto's and Turner's paintings of Venice, the former capturing the richness of the townscape through immaculate topographical detail, the latter offering bold blazes of evanescent light through which the famous landmarks are only dimly seen. Rarer are cities of pure imagination. Italo Calvino's *Invisible Cities* (1974) (of which there is more below) is a supreme example in fiction and Ridley Scott's *Blade Runner* (1982) likewise in film, though some critics maintain that the former is really Venice and the latter Los Angeles.

Both real and imagined cities may also be strongly expressive of cultural values. There is a long history of fictional urban utopias from Plato's *Republic* of 360 BC to Ebenezer Howard's *Garden City* of 1898. Particular cities are strongly associated with cultural 'golden ages' – Athens in 500 BC, Renaissance Florence in the 15th century, the London of Shakespeare at the turn of the 16th century, Vienna and Paris in the 19th century. And the shared etymology of the words 'urban', 'urbane' and 'urbanity' captures the supposed sophistication of city life, evident too in the popular contrast between the 'city slicker' and the 'country bumpkin'. The other, similarly Latin-derived terms 'city', 'citizen', 'civility' carry implications of duty and order.

Our perception of any city is bound to be influenced by real and imagined versions – our personal experience as residents or visitors and the pre-conceived views on it that we get from the news media, from novels or films, or through the accounts of our friends. So that cities are hard to see totally afresh when we confront them directly. They can confirm our prior impression and that may be a pleasure. On the other hand, the reality of some cities may take us by surprise – a different kind of pleasure or maybe a shock. This interplay between perception and reality is not just characteristic of the tourist experience of a city. It applies equally to our experience as residents, even the experience of our own familiar neighbourhood. And it applies to those whose work engages them with cities and their inhabitants – architects, social workers, teachers, refuse collectors, journalists and politicians among many others. City visitors, residents and workers all view the everyday reality of their city – making sense of it – in part through others' accounts of that reality.

To make sense of cities, to understand and use them, we need to delve below the surface of the familiar appearance of cities and the commonplace sensations of everyday city life. We need to expose the deeper explanations of why cities are as they seem. Accounts of imagined cities as well as the experience of real cities can help us to do that.

Origins

My explorations of world cities and city worlds have been a long time in gestation. My debts will become apparent throughout the text as I raid a wide variety of source material: books on history, travel, urban studies; current journalism; novels and poetry; films; travel guides and atlases; websites; art exhibitions and museums. But four works should be acknowledged for shaping my particular approach to making sense of cities.

The first is Lewis Mumford's book *The City in History* (1961).[6] This was undoubtedly on the reading list given to me as a student town planner. But at that time – occupied in the present with knocking down outworn buildings to replace them with new, shiny schemes for expectedly grateful inhabitants – I had little time for history. Later, working in government in the 1980s on urban policy, I sought some historical perspective on contemporary urban change and returned to Mumford's grand sweep through five millennia, from 'a city that was, symbolically, a world... [to] ...a world that has become, in many practical aspects, a city.' What I got from Mumford was that a city is more than the bricks and mortar that still obsess the town planner, the architect and engineer, and many rulers. Rather, it has always been a crucible for the interaction of social, cultural, economic and political influences and is as much the product of that as of city builders.

The next work is also a book, now rather forgotten: Hugh Stretton's *Urban Planning in Rich and Poor Countries* (1978).[7] Stretton, a political scientist, explored the theory and practice of urban planning in the context of different social and political systems. In the second part of the book he analysed the practice of urban planning in poor capitalist cities (his example was Bangkok in Thailand), in poor communist cities (in Cuba and Cambodia, then under the Khmer Rouge regime), rich capitalist cities (in the USA, France and Britain) and rich communist cities (in Hungary and Russia). This was an introduction to a global perspective on cities. But it was his use of metaphors in the part of the book on theories of urban planning that caught my imagination – cities as communities, cities as marketplaces, cities as battlegrounds and cities as machinery. These metaphors have structured my subsequent thinking about cities since and do so in this book.

Italo Calvino's *Invisible Cities*[8], my third inspiration, was introduced to me in the early 1990s by a young architect friend. Unlike the other two books it is a work of fiction. In it Marco Polo recounts to Kublai Khan the life of the many cities he has visited in his travels. In all, fifty-five cities are described, grouped as Cities and memory, Cities and signs, Trading cities, Cities and the dead, Thin cities and other such categories. What Calvino captures in these brief descriptions, most no more than a page, are the qualities of what we might call

---

Three of Calvino's Invisible Cities[9]

'In Chloe, a great city, the people who move through the streets are all strangers. At each encounter, they imagine a thousand things about one another; meetings which could take place between them, conversations, surprises, caresses, bites. But no one greets anyone; eyes lock for a second, then dart away, seeking other eyes, never stopping...'

'In Ersilia, to establish the relationships that sustain the city's life the inhabitants stretch strings from the corners of the houses, white or black or grey or black-and-white according to whether they mark a relationship of blood, of trade, authority, agency. When the strings become so numerous that you can no longer pass among them, the inhabitants leave; the houses are dismantled; only the strings and their supports remain...'

'Those who arrive at Thekla can see little of the city, beyond the plank fences, the sackcloth screens, the scaffolding, the metal armatures, the wooden catwalks hanging from ropes or supported by saw-horses, the ladders, the trestles. If you ask, "Why is Thekla's construction taking such a long time?" the inhabitants continue hoisting sacks, lowering leaded strings, moving long brushes up and down, as they answer, "So that its destruction cannot begin." And if asked whether they fear that, once the scaffolding is removed, the city may crumble and fall to pieces, they add hastily, in a whisper, "Not only the city..."'

'cityness'. Marco Polo says in the book 'Cities, like dreams, are made of desires and fears, even if the thread of their discourse is secret, their rules are absurd, their perspectives deceitful, and everything conceals something else...Cities also believe that they are the work of the mind or of chance, but neither the one nor the other suffices to hold up their walls. You take delight not in a city's seven or seventy wonders, but in the answers it gives to a question of yours.'[10] What this book did for me was to open my eyes to the insights that artists –

writers, painters, filmmakers and others – can bring to our understanding of cities.

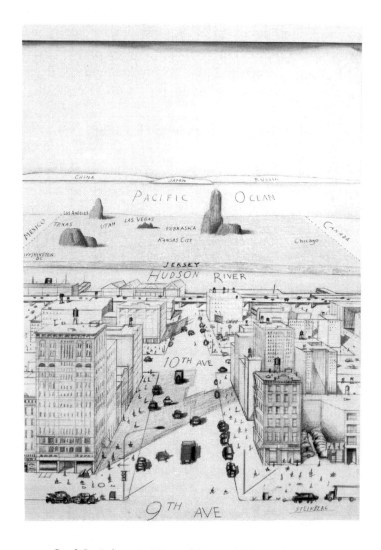

Saul Steinberg's *View of the World from 9th Avenue*

The fourth influence is a drawing by Saul Steinberg. Steinberg was born in Romania but embraced the USA, where he lived from 1942 to his death in 1999, for its images and slogans, its dark side and its comic spirit. His most famous work, *A View of the World from 9th Avenue*, was the cover for *The New Yorker* magazine of March 29th 1976. It represents a common cognitive experience:

that the perception of distance from our own part of the world tends to be on a logarithmic scale, shrinking actual kilometres as places recede. So in the cartoon, Manhattan's Tenth Avenue is as distant from Ninth Avenue as Los Angeles is from New York and the Pacific Ocean is just a wide river with Asia on the other side. It was maybe intended by Steinberg – an immigrant outsider – as a comment on native US, or even New York, insularity. But the conceit works from any point of observation. What the drawing reminds me is that we are inevitably most familiar with what is nearest home. And while I might feel that in this book I wish to treat equally the cities of all four corners of the globe, my knowledge – and certainly my experience – of them is selective. So the book is somewhat Anglo-, Euro- and global North-centric. It also has a bias towards contemporary cities, though with occasional historical excursions when they can illuminate present-day experience.

As well as these four works, my inspiration comes strongly from personal observation of cities around the world. I have lived and worked in Liverpool, Cambridge, London, Munich and Berkeley, California. I have been to most of the major European cities, sometimes for work, sometimes for pleasure. Elsewhere I have been a visitor in Bangkok, Beijing, Cairo, Cape Town, Chicago, Cuzco, Hanoi, Hong Kong, Istanbul, Lima, Los Angeles, Marrakesh, Melbourne, Mumbai, New York, Ottawa, Phnom Penh, Saigon/Ho Chi Minh City, St Petersburg, San Francisco, Seattle, Singapore, Sydney, Tokyo, Vancouver and Washington. This personal experience of cities serves as a filter through which I interpret the words and images of others. I preface each chapter with a personal anecdote from one of these cities.

So, this book takes the reader on an exploration of world cities. Like all exploration the purpose is to familiarise and learn, but what will be discovered along the way is initially unknown. Like a map or guide, the book organises its content – as chapters on my chosen metaphors, icons or perspectives – in a particular order. But you as reader must feel free to start anywhere that takes your fancy and – like an explorer – navigate your own way around. In the end, whatever route has been taken, the explorations will hopefully help you make more sense of cities.

2.

Living together: cities as communities

Hong Kong 2002. The prospect of New Year's Eve in Hong Kong arouses our curiosity. What form will local revelry take? Will people don fancy dress? Will there be fireworks? Or will it be low key, since the Chinese New Year comes later in February? We have flown in this afternoon to stay a few days with a Swiss friend who has worked here as a banker for twenty odd years. But our hopes for the celebration are dashed when he announces that he has made no plans for the evening because he knew that I would not have a dinner jacket in my luggage! Taken aback, I say "Well, let's just go into the streets and see what's happening." "Go into the streets?" he ripostes with obvious alarm. So we stay home, in his luxurious flat on the twentieth floor in Mid Levels and have a dinner of expensive bought-in delicacies and a good bottle of wine and watch the celebrations on the TV. I reflect that our friend is part of the Hong Kong ex-pat community, cosmopolitan, well-to-do, served by maids and chauffeurs – that is the community with which we as European visitors are temporarily identified. They live a life quite insulated from the many other, mostly Chinese, communities who inhabit the city. Most of whom would be taking to the streets to celebrate the New Year in their way.

Identities

In the book and film *The Wizard of Oz*, Dorothy and her dog Toto, joined by her travelling companions, the Scarecrow, the Tin Man and the Cowardly Lion, set off along the Yellow Brick Road to the Emerald City, where they hope that the Wizard of Oz will help them realise their dreams. A journey is one of the most common plotlines in fiction and a journey to the city, like Dorothy's, is a variant. Other examples are Christian's journey to the Celestial City in Bunyan's *Pilgrim's Progress* and Pip's journey to London in Dickens' *Great Expectations*. In such cases the journey is also allegorical – a political journey for Dorothy (on some interpretations), a spiritual journey for Christian, a social

18

journey for Pip. And what the travellers are seeking in the city, and maybe finding, is both an escape from their past and the discovery of a better future in a community to which they can belong. As Aristotle said in *The Politics*, 'Men come together in the city to live; they remain there in order to live the good life.' Once there, city people's sense of community has many layers. Our association can be simultaneously with the whole city, a district within it and a more local neighbourhood. The answer to the question 'Where do you live?' will usually focus on just one of these, dependent on the context in which it is asked. Some years ago I lived at 30 Redcliffe Gardens in Earls Court, London. So to a Scotsman my answer would have been 'London', to a fellow Londoner 'Earls Court', to a person from the neighbourhood 'Redcliffe Gardens'.

Each community will have features that define and reinforce its sense of self. If people identify with their city it is principally because it is their home and place of work, and maybe also their place of birth. So they describe themselves as Angelenos, Cairenes, Muscovites, Istanbullus, Glaswegians or whatever. But other city attributes reinforce that sense of identity. A few cities have shorthand names – NY and LA most recognisably, but also BA (Buenos Aires) and KL (Kuala Lumpur). Others have affectionate nicknames – New York again as the Big Apple, Rome as the Eternal City. Most cities have a symbol, maybe a coat of arms. There may be a very visible, distinctively dressed, city police force. Other institutions may be powerful identifiers – a city newspaper, magazine, radio or TV station, buses and trams, taxis, football or baseball team. Though here there may be rival claims to be the definitive voice or exclusive representative of a city. And some of these can be less rooted than they seem: in the USA baseball teams are occasionally transferred by their private owners from one city to another – usually to the fury of their fans. An iconic landmark may identify a city: the Golden Gate Bridge in San Francisco, the Opera House in Sydney, the Parthenon in Athens, the new Burj Al-Arab Hotel in Dubai, the Sugar Loaf Mountain with its Christ statue in Rio de Janeiro.

Identifiers are not just internal to the community; they may also include external links to other communities within the city and beyond. Walking up a city street you may note the language, dress and looks of the people, the style of its buildings, the activities, and think that they define that neighbourhood. But those characteristics also speak of connections beyond the neighbourhood – transport running to and from other parts of the city, shops and stalls selling imported foods, TV screens and radios carrying news and events from around the world, maybe even planes overhead coming in to land or taking off. In cities our sense of community is thus constructed from a constellation of social relations, artefacts and customs, woven together in a particular locale. The community becomes a meeting place. The urban historian Lewis Mumford argued that 'The great purpose of the city is to permit, indeed to encourage and invite, the greatest number of meetings, encounters, challenges between all persons, classes and groups.'[1]

The ideal city

Creating such a sense of community has been a common objective of the ideal cities of the utopian tradition.[2] In Plato's *Republic*, the earliest known European utopia, there are three classes: Rulers, Auxiliaries (soldiers, police, officials) and Workers; also Slaves, but they don't count. To prop up this class system the Rulers propagate the lie that these classes are physically different. There is strict censorship and no poets are allowed. Bodily and mental health are encouraged but sickly people are left to die. Breeding is strictly controlled on eugenic lines and, to eliminate families, no parent knows their child, no child their parent.

The same authoritarian streak characterises later ideal cities. In Amaurote, the capital of Thomas More's *Utopia* (1516), money and private property are extinct, all produce is kept in common storehouses, families eat in communal halls (where the food is cooked by the women on a rota), a six hour working day is the rule, leisure time is devoted to gardening, lectures and board games and everyone must be in bed by eight o'clock. In Campanella's *The City of the Sun* (1623) a priesthood rules, using the confessional to keep tabs on the city's moral health. In the early 19th century utopian designs of Saint-Simon, Buckingham and Robert Owen incentives to self expression and social improvement take the place of class-based authority. To emphasise the point, in Buckingham's *Victoria* (1849) the radial streets are called the Avenues of Charity, of Fortitude and of Concord. But a later 19th century utopian, William Morris, rejected any urban model. In his *News from Nowhere* (1890) the narrator awakes hundreds of years in the future to find that, following a civil war between capital and labour in the 1950s, the survivors have decided to recreate a pre-industrial culture. The cities have been destroyed, the railway system torn up and, where they stood, meadow and woodland now flourish; commerce no longer exists and people till the soil and band together in workshops producing beautiful objects for everyday use. Freedom prevails.

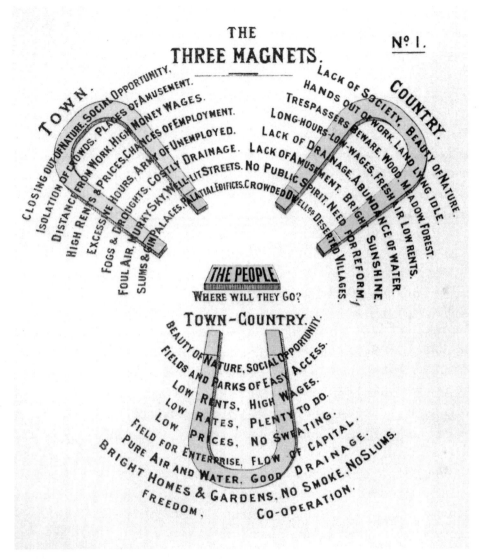

Ebernezer Howard's *Three Magnets*

It was the particular achievement of Ebenezer Howard in *Garden Cities of Tomorrow* (1902) to reconcile these urban and rural utopian traditions. This is neatly shown by his famous Three Magnets diagram where the limitations of both Town and Country are spelled out. His condemnation of the latter may now surprise us, but late Victorian rural Britain was racked by agricultural depression, lacking work and income for many and remote from the opportunities offered by towns and cities. Howard's Town-Country was the ideal compromise. He envisages his garden cities having about 32,000 inhabitants living on about 1000 acres of land with a surrounding 5000 acre Green Belt. The city is structured around handsome avenues and boulevards with, at its heart, a Central Park surrounded by a wide glass arcade, called the Crystal Palace, in which shops and libraries and meeting rooms are found. Factories, coalyards, warehouses and markets are banished to the city's fringe and connected by a circular railway. But for Howard, this was more than urban design. At the foot of the description of Town-Country in the diagram are the words Freedom and Co-operation and he had practical ideas about how these would be achieved: self-help and mutual aid featured strongly. Behind that was a business plan whereby a limited dividend company would borrow money to establish the garden city, then house owners, employers and traders would pay ground rents to them, and in time the surpluses would fund pensions and other welfare measures. For Howard, this was a social and economic system superior both to capitalism and socialism.

Howard's utopian dream of community was partly realised as new towns and cities were built around the world through the 20th century. In the 1920s German social housing agencies adopted the model in Berlin and Frankfurt. In the USA some so-called Greenbelt Cities were built as part of Roosevelt's New Deal in the 1930s. In Britain a big programme of new town building started in the 1950s, culminating in the ambitious development of Milton Keynes, a new city of now 250,000 people halfway between London and Birmingham. In the same period satellite towns were built around other big cities in both global North and South: for example, in Stockholm, Paris, Cairo, Mumbai and Mexico City. New cities to house industrial workers were also constructed in the Soviet Union and its European satellites. Nowa Huta was built adjacent to historic Krakow in Poland from 1949 onwards as a model working class city to complement the old city and correct its 'class imbalance'. What became the largest steel mill in Poland was established there, also a tobacco factory, a power station and a cement factory, in all cases with imported raw materials. The workers were housed in blocks of flats aligned along boulevards leading to the monumental Central Square. Today, when visiting Krakow, you are offered tours to Nowa Huta, in an old East German Trabant car, to see (as the tourist brochure declares) 'the sights and architecture that made Communism famous.'

Often these new cities, promoted by public agencies, were expressive of a socialist ideal of collective provision of decent housing, health and schooling from the cradle to the grave in socially mixed communities. They did not always succeed in that, often becoming where the poor and marginalised groups in society ended up living. Now around the world commercial property developers build whole new communities, for family living or retirement or as resorts. Glossy magazines and TV advertise their charms to the affluent purchaser. Howard would probably have disapproved of most of them, for little in their designs follow his prescriptions either in its architectural, social or business terms. They nevertheless represent contemporary attempts to create real ideal communities.

City states

As political communities, nation states dominate the world today. In previous centuries the world map was largely made up of empires. But throughout history there have also been city states, that is, polities consisting just of a city and sometimes its hinterland so that community, city and state become synonymous.[3] The first city states – such places as Tyre, Gaza and Carthage – were created by Phoenician maritime traders on the shores of the eastern Mediterranean in the second and first millenia BC. It was their Hellenic Greek successors, settling the islands and peninsulas around the Aegean sea, who developed the concept of the city state – the 'polis' – and ultimately exported it as an essential component of Greek civilisation around the Mediterranean. In Athens, the template for the Greek city state, the 'acropolis' – meaning 'upper city' – was the core citadel with the later lower city spreading out below. By the 5th century BC, Attica, its territory, had an area of about 2500 square kilometres and its population was 350,000. Most Greek polises were smaller to ease the participation of its citizens in civic life. In reality polises differed in their form of rule: some were democratic, others oligarchic, aristocratic or autocratic.

Later, in the 4th century BC, Alexander the Great exported the polis concept across the lands he conquered. Alexandria in Egypt is his most well-known foundation and it flourished as the new centre of the Hellenistic world, not politically but commercially and culturally. Its buildings expressed that dominance: the Pharos Lighthouse became one of the wonders of the ancient world, the Mouseion Library became a centre for Greek scholarship. There were other new Alexandrias in central Asia, Persia, Afghanistan (where Herat and Kandahar are successor cities) and in the Indian subcontinent (where one is now Karachi), all with city state constitutions and some Greek settlers. But they all subsequently lost out to the rise of nations and empires.

City states emerged again in medieval and early modern Europe. A revival of urban life was intrinsic to the 15th century Italian Renaissance, which was itself as much commercial as artistic and intellectual. Florence, Verona, Padua, Venice, Genoa, and Milan flourished. All were republics that drifted over time towards dynastic rule, as with the Medicis in Florence and the Viscontis in Milan. In northern Europe new cities were established as Germans moved eastwards on the southern shores of the Baltic. Here Lübeck, Rostock, Danzig, Königsberg, Riga and Tallinn were founded in the 12th and 13th centuries, each with their castle, cathedral and town hall. Later they and other north German cities formed the Hanseatic League of cities, more a coalition than a confederation. The seemingly democratic motto *'Stadtluft macht frei'* ('City air makes man free') appeared on their coats of arms but it was again oligarchy, in this case of the commercial class, that characterised their politics. In the late 16th century, city states also emerged in northern Holland, most notably Amsterdam. Like their Mediterranean counterparts, these north European city states succumbed ultimately to incorporation in more powerful, larger nations. A few clung on to independence longer than others: the Venetian Republic lasted until its capture by Napoleon, the Hanseatic cities of Bremen, Hamburg and Lübeck retained a semi-autonomous status in Germany until Hitler came to power. Whatever social or commercial or cultural advantages statehood had conferred on cities, they proved to be a non-viable form of polity in an increasingly less localised – if not yet globalised – world.

Modern city states have been political creations. The concept of the 'free city' emerged as an attempt to defuse or resolve competing claims, commonly at the end of wars. The free city of Krakow was created in 1815 as a remnant of the partitioned Duchy of Warsaw where Russia, Prussia and Austria agreed to share influence; it lasted until 1846, when the Austrians seized it. In 1919 Constantinople was a candidate for such status but it did not happen; similarly Jerusalem in 1947. But Danzig, with its mixed population of Germans, Poles and other Slavs, was such a free city from 1919 to 1939 when, through the Soviet-Nazi Pact, it was taken into Germany. Tangier had this status from 1923 to its incorporation in Morocco in 1956. Trieste was a 'Free Territory' from 1947 to 1954 when it was divided between Italy and Yugoslavia. In Europe such city states as now survive – Monte Carlo, Liechtenstein, Luxembourg, Vatican City and San Marino – are political oddities, historical survivals that have found a *modus vivendi* with their more powerful neighbours.

Singapore

Today Singapore is a state with four million people packed into a city of 700 square kilometres. Its economy booms with a combination of high-tech manufacturing, financial services and tourism. It has one of the highest per capita GDPs in the world. Its population is predominantly Chinese – many of them third and fourth generation immigrants – with large minorities of Malays and Indians. The city has existed for only two centuries. Founded as a British trading post at the foot of the Malay peninsular in 1819, it developed into an important commercial, military and naval base. Its evolution into a city state is very recent. In 1963 it ceased to be a British colony and joined the new Federation of Malaysia, only to be expelled after two years, following ideological conflicts, and become a sovereign state. Constitutionally, Singapore is a democracy with an elected President. Politically, since independence it has been dominated by the People's Action Party which, critics maintain, has an authoritarian streak. The party promotes 'Asian values' as a counterpoise to Western liberalism and free speech. Censorship, limitations on opposition politicians, tough restrictions on public behaviour (fines or 'corrective work' for gum chewing, littering, spitting), corporal and capital punishment, laws against homosexuality exist; but there is little corruption, much greenery, few billboards and an efficient public transport system. The state plays a major role in the economy, investing in housing, welfare and infrastructure (including a very successful national airline) and promoting the city's economic development. The metro is full of exhortatory government adverts: 'Thinking Hands Create Success in the Global Economy', 'Everyone has a Role to play in Service Excellence', 'Suspect it. Report it' are a few of them.

Today the only city states among the United Nations 193 members are Bahrain, Kuwait, and Qatar in the Persian Gulf and Singapore. All are former colonies or protectorates that, on the dissolution of the British Empire from the mid 20th century, chose to become independent rather than to incorporate in adjoining nations. Other such former imperial cities have become incorporated, though sometimes on terms that – like the earlier city states –

preserved something of the reality and more of the appearance of continuing independence. Such were Goa and Pondicherry in India and Macau and Hong Kong in China. Of these, only Hong Kong – since 1997 a Special Administrative Region of China with its own laws, government and commercial regimes – still seems like a city state. Although these city states are political creations, their survival owes much to their realisation of global commercial success. Singapore is the supreme example.

Cosmopolis

Though it sounds ancient, the word 'cosmopolis' is a mid 19th century creation: a conjunction of 'cosmos' (world) and 'polis' (city) to describe a city inhabited by people from many different countries. Until the last few centuries, the scale of migration that creates a cosmopolis was exceptional. Only traders, the odd divine or scholar, a few potentates with their courtiers and soldiers, and maybe a few settlers took up residence in the cities of other lands, and in small numbers. The big exception was the Jewish diaspora, whereby over many centuries Jewish communities became established in cities across Europe, North Africa and Arabia, sometimes flourishing, sometimes persecuted or even expelled.

Those regions of the world where a succession of mercantile or political regimes held sway provided fertile ground for cosmopolises to flourish. One such was the eastern Mediterranean which from the 16th to the 20th century was variously under Venetian, Ottoman, Greek, French and British rule. It was a frontier zone between the Christian and the Muslim worlds, a marketplace for the goods of East and West – both before and after the construction of the Suez Canal in the 19th century – and an exotic, cultural magnet for orientalist Europeans. In his grand panorama of the Mediterranean in the 16th century, the historian Fernand Braudel comments on 'the extent and immensity of the intermingling of Mediterranean cultures, all the more rich in consequence since in this zone of exchanges cultural groups were so numerous from the start… [and]…the extraordinary charivari suggestive of eastern ports as described by romantic poets: a rendezvous for every race, every religion, every kind of man, for everything in the way of hairstyles, fashions, foods and manners to be found in the Mediterranean.'[4] Here the cities of Salonika, Constantinople, Odessa on the Black Sea, Smyrna, Aleppo, Beirut, Jaffa, Jerusalem and Alexandria became homes to combinations of Greeks, Turks, Italians, Syrians, Armenians, Russians, Jews, Copts, Maronites, British, French, and Palestinians.

Salonika[5]

Salonika started and has ended as a Greek city. But from the 15th to the 20th century it was a true cosmopolis, known variously as Salonicco, Selanik, Solun, Salonika, Salonique or Thessaloniki. Before then, it had for seventeen centuries been a Hellenistic, then a Roman and later a Byzantine city. In 1430 it fell to the Ottomans on their drive westward to capture most of the Balkans. At the end of that century, the city's new rulers invited Sephardic Jews, expelled from Spain with its reconquest from Islam by Catholicism, to settle there. The city's everyday language became Ladino, a Jewish language derived from Castilian Spanish. At the start of the 20th century about half its inhabitants were Jews and Turks, with Greeks, Bulgarians, and Albanians making up the rest. Though different communities had their home neighbourhoods, over time class had become just as important as nationality in the city's social geography. But the Ottoman grip on the Balkans had been weakening through the 19th century, and in the Balkan Wars of 1912-13 Greece captured Salonika. Bulgarians, the wars' losers, were expelled. The Muslim Turks also started leaving, as did Jews who had lost homes and livelihoods in a major fire in 1917. After the First World War, a formal exchange of Greeks and Turks took place. In a final blow to the city's cosmopolitanism, under Nazi occupation from 1941-44 almost the entire remaining Jewish population was deported and exterminated. Rebuilding of the city and its subsequent expansion largely eliminated relics of its non-Greek past – Ottoman palaces, mosques and synagogues disappeared as the city was recreated as Greek in culture and Orthodox in religion. Only lately – partly under the stimulus of Salonika's status as European City of Culture in 1997 – has its cosmopolitan past been acknowledged, recognising it as the birthplace of both Aristotle and Atatürk.

But these cities are no longer cosmopolitan. That character fell victim, one way or another, to the 20th century's rising tide of nationalism and its associated ethnic cleansing. Salonika, once home to a large Jewish community as well as Turks, Greeks, Bulgarians and Albanians, is now the Greek city of Thessaloniki. Smyrna, on the eastern shore of the Aegean, experienced a reverse fortune:

handed to Greece in 1919 after the defeat of the Ottoman empire in World War One it was seized by resurgent Turkish nationalists in 1922 and became the modern day Izmir. Most of Jaffa's Palestinian population fled in 1948 in the face of the city's forced incorporation in the new state of Israel. In Alexandria, it was after the debacle of the Anglo-French-Israeli invasion of Egypt in 1956 that all British and French citizens were expelled, many Jews were driven into exile and other foreign communities dwindled as enterprises were nationalised; only a few Greek traders remained.

Other long cosmopolitan cities have likewise fallen victim to nationalism and racism: the Jewish populations of many European cities were murdered by the Nazis; Germans were expelled from many central and eastern European cities at the end of the 1939-45 war; the partition of India in 1947 led to massive emigrations of Hindu, Sikh and Muslim populations who had formerly cohabited cities in Bengal and the Punjab; Asians were expelled by Idi Amin from Kampala and other Ugandan cities in 1972; and European colonials in Asia and Africa have died off or drifted home. In many cities of the world there are just ghostly reminders, in the form of places of worship and burial, of the foreign communities who once lived there.

Today cosmopolises are mostly to be found among our major world cities. Above all, many of the cities of western Europe, North America and Australasia have acted as magnets for people from many other lands over the last one hundred years. So that today cities like Melbourne, Sydney, Vancouver, Toronto, Los Angeles, San Francisco, Washington, New York, London, Birmingham, Paris, Frankfurt and Amsterdam have populations that are very diverse in terms of nationality, ethnicity, religion, and language – they have been called 'mongrel cities.'[6] This diversity was evident, sadly, in the 2005 terrorist attack on the London public transport system: among the dead were people from Romania, the USA, Montserrat, Nigeria, Italy, France, Ghana, Poland, Mauritius, Turkey, Israel, Sri Lanka, Australia, Iran, Afghanistan and New Zealand; and the suicide bombers' forbears were from Ethiopia, Jamaica, Somalia and Pakistan.

Various migrations have created this diversity. Foreign cities have long served as refuges for people fleeing persecution, seeking there both fellow-nationals and sympathetic hosts. Various European cities received the Jews from Spain in the 1490s and later from Russia, Eastern Europe and then Nazi Germany; the Huguenots from France in the early 18th century; the radicals escaping after Europe's many failed revolutions in the 19th century (in 1880 Samuel Smiles described London as 'the world's asylum'); the émigrés from

Bolshevik Russia in Constantinople, Prague, Paris and Berlin in the 1920s. To that trend was added those fleeing poverty or searching for a better life, always the dominant motive for migration. The geography of such economic migration varies from time to time: in the 19th century it was outwards from Europe to the new worlds of the Americas and Australia; in the last century it was back from their former colonies to the cities of France, Britain and Holland ('We are here because you were there' is a wry immigrants' comment on this

---

Brick Lane, London[7]

Brick Lane is a street in the Spitalfields district immediately east of London's financial centre. It is also nicknamed Banglatown for it is lined by restaurants and shops run by the local Bangladeshi community who settled here in the 1950s in the home country of the erstwhile British Empire. At the heart of Brick Lane, on the corner of Fournier Street (that name is a clue to what follows) stands the Jame-e-mashid mosque. On Fridays, at the end of Muslim devotions, hundreds of men emerge, wearing their prayer caps, reclaiming their shoes, conversing in Bengali. A hundred years ago similar congregations gathered there on Friday evenings and Saturday lunchtimes, except that the men wore yarmulkes and they spoke Yiddish. For between 1898 and 1976 the building was the Spitalfields Great Synagogue when the surrounding area was home to Jewish families who had been arriving in London since the 1880s, many driven out of eastern Europe and Russia by wars, revolutions and pogroms. Before it became a synagogue, the building had briefly been occupied by the Methodists but had then fallen into disuse for some decades. The Methodists had inherited it from the Huguenots – Protestants fleeing persecution in France – who had built it in 1743 as the Neuve Eglise. Their arrival brought a new word to the English language, 'refugee', and a new industry, silk weaving. Settling in Spitalfields, just outside the city boundary, they built themselves terrace houses with broad windowed weaving lofts and in due course the austere but elegant church. At that time the area was known as Petty France. In time the Huguenots and after them the Jews prospered and moved out of the area, yielding space, and their place of worship, to successor immigrant communities. But each community was, in its turn, greeted with hostility from those there before, only to become in time an accepted part of London's mixed population. Now the Bengalis themselves are under pressure as fashionable bars, clubs, boutiques and galleries move in to serve the workers in the neighbouring financial services district.

---

movement), from Latin America and Asia to the USA, from Asia to Australia and from Turkey and North Africa to Europe; and most recently from the former Communist countries of Central and East Europe to West Europe and again North America. As a final modern trend, the globalisation of business and politics and culture has internationalised the labour market for highly skilled people – financiers, consultants, clinicians, scientists, artists, entrepreneurs, international bureaucrats – whose career paths pass through the world's major cities. These successive waves of migration are nicely illustrated in the history of Brick Lane, London.

In these modern cosmopolitan cities, immigration and multiculturalism have become political hot potatoes. Some factions argue for tougher limits on immigration to stem the tide of strangers, even repatriation of those already settled. Others demand that immigrants must assimilate, that is, to be accepted as full citizens they should adopt the indigenous culture and show exclusive loyalty to their new country. Yet others adopt an integrationist position, accepting a two way process in which the indigenes and the immigrants adapt to each other, each retaining partially separate identities and loyalties. Another view is that equal rights and responsibilities should provide basis enough for living together. Whatever form of accommodation is sought, in reality cities are far better than towns or villages at receiving immigrants. Here their differences are only one among many in the existing, diverse population; there will be kinsfolk already settled who are able to provide support and guidance to newcomers in finding their feet; and city economies provide entry routes into employment for people with limited experience, language or recognised qualifications – construction, retailing, catering, taxi driving, cleaning, personal services are where recent immigrants often find work in cosmopolitan cities. Later, through hard work and luck, they – or more probably their children – may move into other better rewarded, higher status occupations and neighbourhoods.

Neighbourhoods

There are not just cities *as* communities but also cities *of* communities. For our cities are typically made up of parts, variously called districts, *quartiers*, *barrios* or neighbourhoods. Sometimes these may be acknowledged, appearing on street signs or on maps of the city; sometimes they will be known only tacitly by city residents and maybe some visitors. The basis for this naming of parts varies greatly. As a start there is always geography: most simply as in Northside or West End and east and south variations; cities divided by rivers may have Left Banks and Right Banks as in Paris; New York has Uptown, Midtown and Downtown and the latter term has since been adopted in other cities. History may also matter – many places have an Old Town and some, like Edinburgh, a New Town as well; there are often socially the wrong and right sides of the (railway) tracks; and frequently the villages outside the city that have been absorbed by its expansion retain their name and identity as city neighbourhoods. There may also be administrative districts with distinct identities, like Paris's *arondissements* or New York's five boroughs. And most cities now have postcodes; in some these have only functional value in getting the mail delivered, in others they also have become signifiers of a district's social character, indeed status. In some cities the 'wrong' postal address can kill a job or loan application stone dead.

There are always powerful social influences at work in defining the parts of the city. Nationality, ethnicity, faith, wealth and class are common distinguishing features of city districts. Sometimes this is a matter of choice as like people congregate together in city neighbourhoods. In particular, new immigrants gain footholds upon arrival that, over time, become consolidated into their dominant neighbourhoods. You find Little Italys, Chinatowns, Greek and Jewish neighbourhoods in many of the cities of north America, Australasia and Europe. Black and Hispanic neighbourhoods exist in many US cities. In West European cities there are districts with communities drawn from their former colonial territories: North Africans and Vietnamese in French cities; Indonesians in Amsterdam and Rotterdam; Afro-Caribbeans, Indians and Bangladeshis in London and other British cities. In some cities racial or religious strife has driven retreats into monocultural communities: Catholics and Protestants in Belfast, Muslims and Hindus in Mumbai, Blacks and Whites in many US cities.

Wealth and class also differentiate parts of the city, chiefly through the workings of the property market. Location is the prime determinant of urban land values. For residential values, location relative to the city centre, to schools and parks, to places of employment matter; but also important is location relative to other like people. So, in cities, the rich live together because only they can afford their neighbourhoods. Building type, density, layout, public and private services and, importantly, maintenance standards adjust to what residents

31

expect and can afford. So that, over time different parts of the city, especially its richer and poorer residential areas, begin to look different, glossy or tatty. Occupational distinctions may also characterise districts, as with the artist's quarters found in many cities, where convertible, spacious property and mutual support bring creative people together; or the universal red light districts of prostitution; or the districts in many cities of South America and Southeast Asia where backpackers find the cheap accommodation, bars, cafes and services they need for their travels; and those neighbourhoods in the cities of the South where Western ex-pats, working on well-paid contracts, rent high security homes with walls, CCTV and security guards.

The concept of the neighbourhood has had a profound influence in city planning. An American Clarence Perry was its theorist with his 1929 report titled *The Neighborhood Unit: A Scheme of Arrangement for the Family-Life Community*. The 'arrangement' was for a neighbourhood defined as the catchment area of the local elementary school. So its key features would be the local school and an associated playground, reachable on foot within half a mile; local shops placed at the corners of several neighbourhoods to be within a quarter of a mile; and a central space where 'on Independence Day, the Flag will be raised, the Declaration of Independence will be recited, and the citizenry urged to patriotic deeds by eloquent orators.'[8] Something orderly like this became a standard component of the new towns and cities subsequently built in Europe and north America and, in a somewhat degraded form, it also appeared in much new suburban development. The neighbourhood concept also carried over into the replanning of cities. A classic example was Patrick Abercrombie's plan for London, prepared in the 1940s for a post-war world. He proposed 'to create a new spatial order for London: in it, fast traffic highways not only solve the traffic congestion problem, but also give definition and shape to the reconstructed communities they separate, by flowing through green strips which additionally bring much-needed open space to London... a solution that imposes order on the world's least orderly great city; but in a way so natural that no one would notice.'[9]

After Abercrombie this redesign of the city as a composite of neighbourhoods was reproduced for many decades in city plans around the world – even in the cities of Africa, the Middle East and Asia, socially far removed from Clarence Perry's USA. Everywhere the concept of a distinctive neighbourhood within the city has been taken up enthusiastically by property professionals who are ever busy branding places as 'villages', 'quarters', 'quaysides', 'parks' (and variants in other languages) – and as 'communities', of course.

Social capital

But the communities within cities are not always coterminous with neighbourhoods. Only some aspects of our modern city lives are rooted exclusively in one particular locality. This is mostly true of domestic life based on the home with its local support in shops and neighbours. These may bind the young, the old, the homeworker, the workless and the infirm most strongly to their neighbourhood. For others our family, friends, employers, providers of goods and services, and people who share our interests are likely to be dispersed across or beyond the city. This is clearly true of the well-to-do who can afford to dash hither and thither in cars and taxis, but it is also the case with some poor people who often have to travel vast distances across the city, by bus or train or foot, especially to work.

Some late 19th century observers of the first industrial cities in Europe regretted that they lacked the intimacy of social contact found in small communities. Close, local, mostly face-to-face interaction, governed by custom, had become replaced in the cities by remoter, more occasional, distant interaction, governed by laws and contracts. The German terms *Gemeinschaft* and *Gesellschaft* were used to express the distinction: the former (translated as 'community') had been replaced by the latter (translated as 'society'). Successive later advances in communications – the railway, the car, the phone, email and the internet – have led to renewals of this argument. For some these mechanical and media technologies have dehumanised social relations and resulted in a regretted 'loss of community' within cities.

Recently the concept of 'social capital' has provided a more sophisticated insight into what is going on. Social capital is defined by its key theorist, the political scientist Robert Putnam, as 'features of social life…that enable participants to act together more effectively to pursue shared objectives.'[10] Use of the term 'capital' seeks to put this on a par with the economist's classical factors of production – land, labour and capital. The argument is that, to achieve anything, these tangible factors must be complemented by intangible social capital. That is, networks of people who know and trust each other, formal and informal rules that guide how people behave with each other, and the sanctions that help to ensure compliance. In cities these processes of socialisation operate in different contexts and at different scales – for example, through family support for children's schooling, through sanctions on dangerous driving, through neighbours looking out for each other's property.

Three forms of social capital are distinguished: bonding, bridging and linking. 'Bonding' within homogeneous groups – like family members, close friends, faith or ethnic communities – creates strong ties. These reinforce identities, sustain solidarity and provide mutual support, but such bonds can be inward-looking and exclusive and even provoke hostility from or towards outsiders. 'Bridging' is characterised by weaker, more impersonal and distant

---

Soap opera

Originating in the USA in the 1930s on radio and in the 1940s on television, soap operas – named as such because the commercials in the early versions were for cleaning products – are now made and shown on TV around the world. Some are distributed beyond their country of production, others are adapted for local audiences, yet others are unique to particular countries. By no means do all tell urban tales, but the requirement that most soaps follow the lives of a large group of characters who live and work in a particular place makes cities an attractive setting for them – evidenced in the titles of the long-running British soaps *Coronation Street* set in Manchester and *Eastenders* in London, the Australian soap *Neighbours* set in Melbourn, and the animated American soap *Sesame Street*. Some tend towards a romantic view of life, others to a more realistic view, often admittedly in overblown and melodramatic terms. Either way, soaps are focused on how their characters get by in their communities, dealing with personal ambitions, struggles, victories and defeats and their interactions with relatives, lovers, neighbours, friends, workmates, police and bureaucrats. Soaps capture many aspects of city life and export them to national, even international, audiences.

---

relationships, as typically with work colleagues, neighbours and acquaintances and club members, often bringing together people from different social groups around a common interest or to achieve a common purpose. Such bridges can promote tolerance and cross-cultural understanding. Finally, 'linking' describes the connections between people of differing power and authority, between customers, clients or citizens and those private or public agents who serve them. Such links are relatively impersonal contacts, often one-offs, but require commitment and mutual respect to work well. All three kinds of relationship – bonding, bridging and linking – are evident, without any grand theorising, in the narratives of soap operas. For, above all, soaps are about the good and bad sides of living together.

The cultural critic Raymond Williams, reviewing the meaning of 'community' as a keyword of modern thinking, observed that 'unlike all other terms of social organisation (state, nation, society etc) it seems never to be used unfavourably.'[11] This is undoubtedly so: just think of such terms as community arts, community associations, community development, community leader, community park, community policing or community spirit – they are all good things. In the metaphor of the city as community there are two implicit senses: actual social groups with a shared identity and/or a particular quality of relationship. Both can be found in the concepts of ideal cities, city states, cosmopolises and neighbourhoods and the social practices associated with them.

3.

Legacy: Venice past and present

Riva degli Schiavoni 2005. *One evening my companions and I set out in search of supper. We decide to look for somewhere in the Castello district so, emerging onto the Riva degli Schiavoni from an alley behind the Doge's Palace, we turn left towards the Public Gardens. We walk eastwards much occupied in conversation. Then slowly, as we mount one of the bridges, we become aware that large numbers of people are standing or sitting on the steps, facing us, clearly preoccupied with something behind us. We turn round. And there is the classic Venetian sunset, the sky glowing golden-red, placing a halo of light round the domes and campaniles, enriching the red-tiled roofs, reflecting in the water of the Basin, giving all our faces an unnatural tan. People take cameras out to try and capture the moment for keeps, but I know they will not succeed. You have to be here to get it.*

No ordinary city

The American writer Truman Capote declared that 'Venice is like eating an entire box of chocolate liqueurs in one go.' There is indeed something excessive about Venice. Its location on islands in a lagoon, intersected by canals and dependent almost entirely on boats for its transport, makes it one of the most extraordinary places to experience. It's history as much as geography that counts. The travel writer James Morris explained that 'As their Republic grew in grandeur and prosperity, and their political arteries hardened, and a flow of dazzling booty enriched their palaces and churches, so Venice became entrammelled in mystery and wonder. She stood, in the imagination of the world, somewhere between a freak and a fairy tale.'[1]

It's not just that the place is so richly full of grand palaces, churches, bridges, halls, monuments and paintings. It is also that the richness has – for Western tastes – a quite exotic flavour since, through Venice's historic trade with the

East, the structures and styles of Islamic architecture became incorporated in its buildings.[2] The Basilica of St Marks and some other churches look like mosques, the Doge's Palace could be in Cairo, the Rialto Market is souk-like, behind studded doors there are cool courtyards, and the ubiquitous screened balconies serve – as in Islamic cities – for the concealed observation of the world outside. From the same easterly connections, the city also acquired a collection of relics unequalled in the Christian world, often stolen, like the body of Saint Mark himself from Alexandria and the four gilded bronze horses on his Basilica from Constantinople.

Venice has also often been the setting for extreme expression in art and life. It was the city in which Casanova indulged his voracious sexual appetite. In fiction Henry James saw Venice as 'the refuge of endless strange secrets, broken fortunes and wounded hearts'.[3] And it has maintained – admittedly with some lapses over the centuries – the ancient celebration of Carnival. Masks, conferring anonymity while behaving badly, are the essential feature of the Venetian Carnival.

Venice in fiction

Shylock's perverse bargain and subsequent humiliation in Shakespeare's *The Merchant of Venice* set the tone for Venetian stories. Henry James used Venice frequently as the setting for his novels. In *The Aspern Papers* it is here that the reclusive American spinster Juliana Bordereau lives in her crumbling palazzo, hoarding the love letters from her youth that the unscrupulous narrator covets. In *The Wings of a Dove* it is again in Venice that the impecunious Kate Croy and Merton Densher lay siege to the young, rich, dying Milly Theale. Venice also hosts the forlorn figure of Aschenbach in the Thomas Mann novel and Luchino Visconti film *Death in Venice*, infatuated with a beautiful boy but dying of the Asiatic cholera overwhelming the city. In Nic Roeg's film *Don't Look Now* (from a Daphne du Maurier story) the English couple, grieving over their drowned child, are beset by fears and fantasies that worsen their sense of dislocation and guilt. And in Donna Leon's modern series of Venetian crime novels the melancholic Commissario Brunetti exposes the corruption and cruelty of the city's elite.

La Serenissima

This exoticism is the product of a long history. In 1797 Napoleon declared war on the Most Serene Republic of Venice. Little resistance was offered and the city fell to the French. The conquerors demolished sundry churches, turned convents into barracks, outlawed long established customs and institutions and made off with works of art. Then the 1815 Treaty of Vienna handed the city to the Austrians, who ruled there – with an insurrectionary interlude in 1848 – until it was incorporated in the new Italian kingdom in 1866. By then Venice had not just fallen politically; the period after 1797 was also the culmination of a commercial decline that had been underway for the previous two centuries. So that, in the early 19th century, Venice was generally regarded as an odd but rather depressing wreck, a city whose time had come and decisively gone.

Then Venice was rediscovered. It was North Europeans, and later North Americans, who brought about this change of fortune. It's a complicated story involving poets, painters, critics, novelists, do-gooders, travellers and foreign residents. Byron and Shelley each spent some of their exile from England in Venice in the 1810s – much of Canto IV of Byron's *Childe Harold's Pilgrimage* is an evocation of Venice. Other writers – Robert and Elizabeth Browning, Goethe, Balzac, Henry James, Proust, Thomas Mann, Hemingway – fixated on Venice in subsequent decades. Likewise did painters: Turner, Bonington, Dufy, Manet, Monet, Whistler. Turner only visited Venice three times, in 1819, 1833 and 1840, staying less than four weeks in all. But he filled his sketchbooks with images used in later paintings that present the city as an enticing, magical illusion, though with darkness lurking behind the brilliant facades. For architects and architectural critics the Venetian legacy was more contested. Its oriental attributes were often thought disturbing; its Renaissance and Baroque buildings were more admired and the palazzo facade was reproduced to front many new iron frame buildings in Europe's growing commercial cities. Ruskin in *The Stones of Venice* (1851) declared that the Doge's Palace was the central building of the world, because of its fusion of East and West, of Gothic, Renaissance and Baroque.

From these intellectual and artistic sources, the idea that Venice was to be treasured grew in conviction through the 19th century. There were also some practical reasons for this change of attitude: easier travel there with the extension of the European railway network, the end of Austrian rule, improvements in water supply reducing the risk of cholera. Increasing numbers of well-heeled foreigners, as visitors or as expatriates, came to Venice. Then, in the mid 1870s an international row blew up about the restoration of the Basilica of San Marco. In his book *Venice Rediscovered,* John Premble reports that 'The force of Anglo-Saxon remonstrance now put Venice high on the agenda of international debate and completed the reversal of its reputation. The monument of human pride, the uncouth provincial city redeemed by nature, disappeared; and in its place emerged a unique and priceless inheritance, universally cherished and adored. Venice, declared *The Times* in 1879, was "the pride and possession of the whole world".'[4] Thereafter, Britain's formidable Society for the Preservation of Ancient Buildings established its St Mark's Committee, the first international group formed to campaign for Venetian conservation. The collapse of the Campanile of St Marks in 1902 gave rise to concerns about the state of other buildings. A major flooding in 1966 further galvanised action. Today there are thirty organisations in eleven countries devoted to 'saving' Venice. Venice became iconic.

This rediscovery of Venice came from a change of perception rather than any change in the city itself. It has been called the 'aestheticisation' of Venice, since it involved a reappraisal of its art, architecture and cityscape. Beyond that, as tourism has exposed millions to the experience of Venice, its image has become part of the language and iconography of advertising, retailing and entertainment. Today it sells ice creams – the praises of the Walls Cornetto sung by a gondolier. It names hundreds of Rialto cafes and restaurants around the world. It lures gamblers –the Venetian casino and hotel in Las Vegas features full scale replicas of the Doge's Palace, the Rialto Bridge, the Ca d'Oro Palace and a segment of the Grand Canal, complete with gondolas; another version has recently opened in Macao.

In all this there was little recognition that the fabric of the city, from which this myth of Venice had been woven, originated with the political and mercantile shrewdness that had characterised the city in its heyday. The independent Republic of Venice was founded in 697 with the election of the first Doge, a non-hereditary but lifelong post. In time, power in the republic became the exclusive preserve of a group of patrician families, from whom the rotating membership of its governing Councils was drawn. These constitutional forms were buttressed by ruthless tyranny. Politically, the Venetian Republic was part democracy, part police state. Its stability was the background to its great commercial success. Throughout the 14th century, following the collapse of the Byzantine Empire, Genoa and Venice competed to control trade with the East.

Venice won and consolidated its imperial grasp, both inland, to include the towns of Padua, Verona, Brescia, Bergamo, and overseas, through a string of trading posts and fortresses in Dalmatia, Corfu, Crete, and Cyprus.

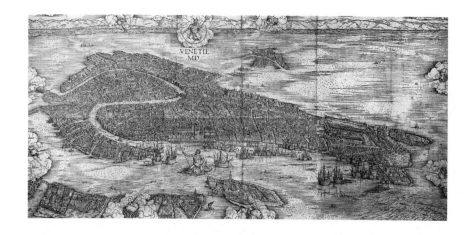

de Barbari's *View of Venice* 1500

Venice was then the centre of the world economy. In de Barbari's famous aerial view of Venice, the Piazza San Marco and the Doge's Palace are in the foreground, the Basin is full of fine ships, the city is surrounded by the protective waters of the lagoon; more than that, Mercury hovers above the city (declaring in Latin 'I, Mercury, shine favourably on this above all emporia') and Neptune rides a dolphin below ('I, Neptune, reside here smoothing the waters of this port'). This map is a symbolic expression of Venice at the height of its power. The state owned a fleet of vessels that it chartered to merchants. It had ambassadors and mercenaries posted abroad to maintain its authority. It regulated foreign traders tightly – the *Fondaco dei Tedeschi* and *Fondaco dei Turci,* where German and Turkish merchants respectively were accommodated, still stand (the former is now the main Post Office). The city controlled all the major commodity trades in the Mediterranen: pepper, spices, cotton, grain, wine, salt. From the northern lands it drew iron, hardware, linen and silver. It became 'a sort of vast warehouse of the world'[5] with its traders, bankers, money changers, insurers, and tax collectors operating in the streets around the Rialto bridge – precisely where Shylock strikes his deal with Antonio in *The Merchant of Venice.* The coming and going of the ships dictated the rhythm of the city's life.

In the heydays of its commercial success Venice's population reached around 150,000. Of these about 10,000 were the privileged elite, members of families directly engaged with the city's commercial or political life; not all were native Venetians for it was a cosmopolitan place with Germans, Jews, Slavs, Turks, Armenians and Greeks. Of the rest, two thirds of the workers were in trades like leatherwork, glass, weaving, often processing the materials passing through the port, or shipbuilding. The remaining one third were unskilled workers, including porters, stevedores, seamen and oarsmen. It was a city where commerce dominated industry. But its commerce was threatened from around 1500 onwards by the advance of the Turks in the East, by the resurgence of some West European states, and by maritime expansion in the rest of the world. The Venetian Republic lost its trade and lost its empire in a long, slow decline culminating in Napoleon's *coup de grâce*.

Earth, water, air and fire

By then, at the end of the 18th century, Venice's layout was already in place, with all four elements present in its townscape. According to legend, Venice was founded in the year 421 by refugees from the mainland, fleeing from barbarian invaders to the mudflats of the lagoon. Its territory took shape through centuries of damming and filling to extend the islands until what was left between them was a network of narrow waterways. In the heart of each island were fields and running away from these to the water's edge were tracks, often terminating in bridges or quays. Thus the present-day Venetian naming of its parts – *Canali, Campi, Campielli, Calli, Ponti, Fondamenti* – expresses its evolution.

Since the 12th century Venice has been divided into six *sestrieri* or wards: to the north and east of the Grand Canal are Cannaregio, San Marco and Castello and to the south and west are San Polo, Santa Croce and Dorsoduro (that includes Giudecca). Today you can best see the city as three zones.[6] First, there is a triangle whose points are the Piazza San Marco, the Rialto bridge and the Accademia: this is the area that contains most of the most popular sights and that is largely given over to tourism, with hotels, designer shops, restaurants, souvenir stalls, fast food sellers, street merchants, artists and pickpockets. This area is crowded all day long through most of the year, the narrow *calli* restricting walking to a crawl, the *campi* – particularly the Piazza San Marco – packed with sightseers, photographing and being photographed, the canals filled with motor launches

41

and gondolas. Tentacles stretch out from this zone along the main routes connecting it to the tourist entry points of the railway station and the Piazzale Roma, where road traffic arrives. A second zone, fronting the Grand Canal and stretching into the districts behind it, has more spacious buildings, some with gardens, and the churches and *campi* at the heart of their neighbourhoods. This is where those 19th century visitors and expatriates settled, often in *palazzi* that could then be picked up cheap, and today their successors and the many service workers who support them also live and stay here. There is a third zone where most native Venetians now live; on Guidecca, beyond the Arsenal in Castello and Sant'Elena where the Public Gardens and the sports stadium can also be found, on the outer fringes of Cannareggio and Dorsoduro. They are often in squalid old buildings or uninspiring new public housing. For the most part these residents are the oldest, least educated and poorest of the Venetians remaining in the city. Recent expansion of the University of Venice in this zone has brought new life but more pressure on housing. Even here attractive properties, like small waterfront *palazzi*, are being converted to hotels and apartments.

To this triple zoning of the land of Venice should be added the Lido, the 12 kilometre long sandspit that separates the lagoon from the Adriatic. It was only developed from the 1870s with beaches, hotels, restaurants and amusements to become the smart bathing place captured in *Death in Venice*. The Hotel des Bains opened in 1900, the Excelsior in 1906, an airport was established in 1926, the Venice Film Festival started in 1932 and the Casino arrived in 1938. The Lido remained fashionable until the 1950s but has now – in true Venetian style – lapsed into faded elegance. For those who wish to combine Venice and the seaside, its role has been largely taken over by newer beach towns to its north and south.

'Streets Full of Water. Please Advise.' the American humorist Robert Benchley reportedly cabled home when he first arrived in Venice. The canals are indeed the streets of Venice, comprising a network that both connects and divides up the city. The sinuous double curve of the Grand Canal – like a watery Los Angeles motorway – joins the city's entrances at the railway station, bus station and car park to its historic heart in Piazza San Marco. A few larger canals lead off from here to the outer edges of the city, where the quaysides offer departure points for other islands in the lagoon. Filling in the network are the myriad small canals, squeezed between or sometimes under buildings that rise straight out of the water. The canals still represent the most direct way to move about Venice and many kinds of boat use them.

The Grand Canal – like a watery motorway

The lagoon is also part of Venice's watery character. It's vast, about 150 kilometres in circumference. In distant vistas from the lagoon the city appears as a cluster of buildings floating on the water – not unlike, though the scale is quite different, Manhattan or Hong Kong. Pottering around the lagoon by boat this image – with the Campanile of St Marks as a key element – appears and disappears in endless variations. Traditionally you approached Venice by boat across the lagoon. The construction of the railway viaduct in 1846 and the parallel road in 1931 substituted more conventional routes into the city. But today, when you arrive at San Marco airport on the mainland, you can take a boat that transports you across the lagoon to the city, just like your 18th and 19th century predecessors.

Dotted about the lagoon are many islands connected by navigation channels marked out by stakes. Historically some of these were settled before Venice itself. Torcello – now little inhabited but increasingly visited for its cathedral mosaics and its restaurants – was home to 20,000 people in the 1500s. Other islands have retained their populations, notably Burano, traditionally a fishing and lace-making settlement, and Murano, once the premier glass manufactory

Venetian boats

The water buses called *vaporetti* (meaning 'little steamers', but now diesel-driven) appeared in the 1880s, a water equivalent of the motorised omnibus introduced in other cities at that time. They are now the workhorses of public transport in Venice, frequent, fast and reasonably comfortable, if noisy.

If you must have private transport, the motor launch *motoscafi* are the boats of choice, either privately owned by firms, the police, rich families or available as taxis and, occasionally and spectacularly, dressed for funerals or weddings.

Larger powerboats, called *mototopi* (because their diesel engines go *mototopo mototopo mototopo*) are also to be seen on the canals, collecting refuse, pumping sewage, moving furniture, fire fighting, delivering goods to shops, hotels and restaurants, supplying construction sites. They are widely held responsible for damage to canalside buildings from their wash, despite the speed limit of 7 kilometres per hour.

The *gondola* is, of course, the traditional and unique Venetian vessel, its design and use exactly adapted to the city's waterways. Once the dominant mode for everyday transport, gondolas are now just there as a tourist experience, more often than not moving in convoys around a fixed, fifty minute route and charging you about $70 for the pleasure. Cheaper are the three *traghetti,* gondola ferries that cross the Grand Canal between the bridges.

Tourism has introduced new specialist boats. There are glass roofed tourist boats, known as *lancioni di granturismo,* carrying one hundred or more passengers around the sights with accompanying commentary. Even more out of scale with the city are the enormous cruise ships that call in at Venice for a day or two on their Mediterranean itinerary, essentially floating hotels up to ten storeys in height which disgorge 2,500 or more passengers at a time.

of the West. There are other islands that are now small fishing settlements, sanatoria and asylums, monasteries or just market gardens. And there is the island cemetery of San Michele, to which Napoleon decreed that all the city's dead should be carried.

Water has a symbolic as well as a functional importance in Venice. Founding its fortune on seaborne trade, its nautical prowess demanded celebration. In the time of the Republic, part of the celebrations at Ascension was the Doge's Marriage to the Sea, when the ruler, with accompanying dignitaries, was rowed out to the open Adriatic where he threw a wedding ring into the water. Still, in the third week of July, for the *Festa del Redentore*, a temporary pontoon bridge is built across the Guidecca Canal to create a processional route to the Redentore church in remembrance of a 16th century plague that carried off nearly a third of the city's population. There is also a modern, annual rowing competition, the *Vogalonga*, with a course starting in the Basin, out across the lagoon to Burano, then back past Murano into the Canareggio canal to finish in the Grand Canal.

But the water is also potentially malign. Occasional flooding from the coincidence of *sirocco* winds and lunar high tides, the so-called *acqua alta*, has been a feature of Venetian life for centuries. It's on the increase and substantial parts of the city, including the low-lying Piazza San Marco, are now flooded up to one hundred days a year. Some tourists like it, as part of the Venetian experience, particularly when the city authorities get out the *passarelle* (wooden planks on metal frames) to create walkways above the water level – and the café orchestra in Piazza San Marco may play the theme from the *Titanic* movie. The city is also slowly sinking from natural subsidence, exacerbated by mainland industries pumping out water from the aquifer. The erosion of salt marshes and the deepening of navigation channels have opened the lagoon to greater incursions of water from the sea. Work is now underway on raising the level of the quays, on restoring the salt marshes and on the construction of flood barriers at the entrance to the lagoon, measures with aesthetic and ecological impacts that are endlessly argued over.

Venice's canals are also its sewers. In theory the daily tidal movements flush them out but in practice this happens sporadically. For some years the smelly process of dredging the canals was abandoned. The large visitor numbers worsen the problem. In response many buildings have installed storage tanks that can be pumped out by tanker boats, whose large hoses snake across the *Fondamenti* and even sometimes through hotel lobbies or restaurant dining rooms. Industrial effluents from the petrochemical plants and pesticide and fertiliser residues, both from the mainland fronting the lagoon, add to the water's pollution.

Sewage and pollution can make Venice's air smelly from time to time. But it's the qualities of sound and light borne on the air that are uniquely Venetian. Even 18th century tourists contrasted Venice's quiet with the street racket in other cities from iron-shod horses and iron-banded carriage wheels. Mechanisation of urban transport has sharpened the contrast with cities where noisy cars, trucks, motorbikes, buses and trams dominate the streets. It's easy to realise how the introduction of the noisy, motorised *vaporetti* to Venice in the 1880s was a momentous change.

Whether Venetian light is objectively different is a moot point. Certainly the interplay of sky and water produces sparkling reflections of sunshine and moonlight, especially in the open water of the basin and the lagoon. The city is also full of *trompe l'oeil* effects – false perspectives, distortions, hallucinations, mirages. James Morris observed that 'If you take a boat into the Basin of St Mark, and sail towards the Grand Canal, it is almost eerie to watch the various layers of the Piazza pass each other in slow movement: all sense of depth is lost, and all the great structures, the pillars and the towers, seem flat and wafer-thin, like the cardboard stage properties that are inserted, one behind the other, through the roofs of toy theatres.'[7] But if blazing sunsets, shimmery moonlight and reflections on water have become essential images of Venice – witness the contents of any postcard stand – it is as much to do with artistic representations of Venice as with reality.

And the last element: fire? In 1996 *La Fenice,* the opera house in Venice, burned down. It had burnt down before in 1836. It was originally built in 1792 on the site of an earlier burnt-out theatre. So its naming as *La Fenice* – 'the phoenix' – was appropriate and prescient. The 1996 fire was the consequence of arson by contractors facing heavy fines for delays in renovation work. Two electricians were jailed; the then Mayor of Venice was prosecuted for negligence but acquitted. Legal wrangles ensued and it was not until 2004 that the opera house re-opened. Venice is no more prone to fire than other cities, but it has phoenix-like qualities of survival and renewal.

Backstage

In this extraordinary stage set of a city, ordinary Venetians have only minor walk-on roles. The indigenous population has fallen from 150,000 in its heyday to 65,000 today. Once Venice produced luxury goods: glass, leatherwork, cloth and spices. Now it is, and has been for a long time, principally a tourist venue, hosting twelve million visitors a year in what is a rather small and compact place. On an average day, there are about ninety visitors in Venice to every one hundred residents, the highest such ratio in Europe. (Three times that in Salzburg, the next highest, and nine times that in Florence.) Most are day visitors, many on bus tours or boat cruises or visiting from the nearby Adriatic beach resorts. Tourism employs 40% of the locals, running hotels and restaurants, guiding visitors, selling souvenirs and street food (including corn for feeding the pigeons), guarding the galleries and museums, offering gondola and water taxi rides. But that leaves 60% of the locals – schoolchildren, pensioners, public service workers, neighbourhood shopkeepers and those in service trades – trying to live their lives among the massive tourist presence; as must the other 40% in their off-duty hours.

So native Venetians must cohabit with visitors to their city. For their own convenience, even survival, they have their own back routes off the main pedestrian thoroughfares, some just short cuts, some quite long alternative routes between the main city destinations, using un-named passages and alleys that visitors hesitate to enter for fear of getting lost. Similarly there are smaller canals that only the locals use, evident from the large number of boats moored along them that visitors may look down on as they pass over a bridge or along a quay. These land or water routes pass through and connect Venice's backstage, largely away from the tourist gaze, where local shops, small churches, street-side shrines, houses and minor palaces stand, often in rather decrepit condition, their walls posted with funeral notices or other neighbourhood announcements. Here too are the public toilets that the locals know about but conceal from the visitors.

This backstage has, however, become increasingly visited in recent years. Travel writers, in search of something new or personal, have encouraged their readers to escape the sightseeing hordes and discover the 'Venice of the Venetians' in Cannaregio or Dorsudoro or Castello. The city authorities have encouraged tourists away from the honeypots of San Marco, the Rialto and the Accademia in order to spread the load. The changes in the Ghetto district illustrate the process. Once just another unvisited neighbourhood, it became discovered for its historical importance as the first Jewish ghetto, located initially by independent travellers, then promoted on tours as a secondary, optional attraction along with the Murano glass works or the Lido. Now, it has become the most restored area of the city after San Marco.

Inevitably, tensions arise with these backstage incursions. The *campi*, in particular, have become contested ground. Traditionally these were the centres of neighbourhood life, where local traders set up their stalls; where children played, teenagers flirted and adults gossiped; commonly flanked by a church, a palace or two, shops and taverns. Many such *campi* now receive wandering tourists, but crucially they have become the sites for an expansion of alfresco drinking and eating

47

The Ghetto

in Venice's traffic-free environment. Restaurants and bars have claimed large parts of the *campi* for themselves and their customers, who often behave without much regard for the people whose space they have invaded. But it is not just Venetian space that has been appropriated by foreigners; the same has happened to some Venetian culture. The Carnival, the *Festa del Redentore* and the *Vogalonga* rowing event are heavily marketed to tourists and have grown in scale and scope, supplementing traditional customs with rock bands, corporate sponsorship, outdoor TV screens, fireworks and, of course, unremitting tourist photography.

Ancient and post-modern

Most large cities across the world now have an 'old town', 'historic centre' or 'native quarter'. That is, some part of the city representing its past history and helping to define its present character. Their authenticity varies greatly. In some cases their location involves some rewriting of history to present them as the site of the original settlement. Otherwise the historic period to which the surviving buildings relate may be a matter of accident – earlier buildings did not survive – or choice – the modern conservation project chose to recreate the 18th or the 19th century city. Commonly the historic buildings and spaces will not be in historic uses: warehouses have become apartments, retailing and catering have taken over meeting halls and even churches, terrace houses have become offices, streets have become pedestrian only. But, however inauthentic, the quality of these places as 'relics' appeals to city residents and attracts city visitors.

Venice is the iconic old town *par excellence*. It has all those qualities of antiquity, atmosphere, beauty and human scale that are the attraction of old places. Beyond that it has the uniqueness of its watery character – its lagoon setting, the canals, boat travel, reflected light – and its pedestrian supremacy. Venice is also an old town writ large. Certainly there are other cities that have extensive historic quarters – in Italy alone Rome, Florence and Naples do. But, unlike them, Venice is only old Venice, there is no complementary new Venice – except away on the mainland in modern Mestre. There is a scale and completeness to old Venice that is unique.

This is not just because there was no space on its islands for the extension of Venice to create a modern city. It is more because the 19th century largely passed Venice by and did not subject it to the reconstruction that transformed so many other old cities, creating new commercial and residential quarters, adding government buildings, inserting roads and railways, redeveloping slum housing. The economic and political decline of Venice and then later the rise of the conservation commitment froze the fabric of the city. Thus the image of Venice was established two centuries ago. Henry James observed that 'Venice has been painted and described many thousands of times, and of all the cities of the world is the easiest to visit without going there…[so]… 'there is nothing left to discover or describe, and originality is completely impossible.'[8]

There is a paradox here. Venice may have survived in its pre-modern state, but the consequence has been that it has become a post-modern city. It produces and exports no significant goods or services. What it sells to the world is itself in its multiple images: its cityscape, its treasures, its buildings, its street life, its boat rides, its festivals, its light and sound, its restaurants, bars and markets. The souvenir – postcard, Murano glass, Carnival mask, or other trinket; quite probably now made in Asia – is the essential product of contemporary Venice. The French writer Régis Debray summed it up in his hostile tirade *Against Venice*: the city 'exists only in and for the gaze of others. The meretricious does not support solitude well. Naples stripped of its visitors would still be itself, loud, fat and self-confident. But deprive Venice of its spectators, its extras, and it would decline and collapse in a week, its text dissolving, lost, haggard, like a great star forced to play nightly to an empty house.'[9]

4.

Conflict: cities as battlegrounds

Madrid 2009. Picasso's painting Guernica is the prize possession of the Museo Reina Sofia here. Picasso was provoked by the bombing in 1937 of the Basque town of Guernica in northern Spain, undertaken by German and Italian warplanes at the behest of Franco's Nationalist forces in the Spanish Civil War. 1600 people were killed and the fire raged for three days. The painting is enormous, 3.5 metres tall and 7.8 metres wide, and is displayed in a room to itself. On the day of our visit there is a group of about thirty Spanish schoolchildren, between five and seven in age, seated on the floor before the picture. Their teachers are talking them through its interpretation: the bull and the horse as symbols of Spanish history, the woman with outstretched arms appealing for help, the flaming buildings and crumbling walls representing the destruction of war, the dominance of black, white and grey colours to set a sombre mood, the newsprint to show how news of the atrocity spread around the world. But do the children also grasp the wider significance of Guernica? For this was the world's first air attack on an urban population and the precursor of the even worse horrors of the 20th century's subsequent wars. Picasso's painting captures the experience of people caught up in cruel events beyond their control.

Cities under threat

The destruction of cities has been the stuff of history for centuries. Indeed some city names are indissolubly linked to such disasters: the burning of Rome 64AD; the Great Fire of London 1666; the major earthquakes in Lisbon 1755, San Francisco 1906, Tokyo 1923, Mexico City 1985, Kobe 1995 and Port au Prince, Haiti 2010; and the flooding of New Orleans in 2005. Prospectively, rises in sea level from global warming threaten coastal cities worldwide: one estimate is that 13% of the world's urban population is at risk, with an even higher percentage in countries like Bangladesh and China where many of their cities are in coastal zones.[1]

Less dramatic but equally damaging are threats to the health of people in cities. People living cheek by jowl, on poor diets, in inadequate shelter with poor sanitation, in polluted environments are vulnerable. Sharp health differences between their poor and rich residents characterise cities around the world. Above all, the urban poor die young. The quality of health care in different parts of the city is part of the explanation, but often more important are variations in morbidity arising from housing, diet and working conditions. Cholera, diarrhoea, typhus, tuberculosis and pneumonia were common in the 19th and early 20th century cities of the North and are now found in the cities of the South, together with newer ailments like HIV/Aids. Mental illness, though it gets less recognition, is extensive. And everywhere the increase of motor vehicles has worsened air pollution and increased injury and death from traffic accidents.

Other threats to cities can be quite intentional. Putting cities under siege has long been a strategy of warfare to bring an enemy, both military and civilian, to surrender. It's a grim tradition that in the last two centuries embraces the sieges of Delhi by the British in 1857, of Khartoum by the Madhi army in 1884, of Leningrad by the Germans in 1941-44 in which a million people died, the siege of Sarajevo by the Serbians in 1992-93 and of Gaza by the Israelis intermittently from 2009 on. Attacking cities from the air was a military tactic in the Second World War by all combatants and reached a climax of death and destruction in 1945 with the fire bombing of Hamburg, Dresden and Tokyo and the atom bombs dropped on Nagasaki and Hiroshima. Throughout the Cold War the nuclear weapons of the protagonists were targeted not simply at each other's countries but specifically at their major cities. In the last two decades there have also been large scale terrorist attacks in cities, destroying buildings and infrastructure and killing people in order to coerce political enemies – as in Mumbai, London, Nairobi, Madrid and, most spectacularly, on the World Trade Centre, New York on 9/11/2001. The term 'urbicide' has been coined for this modern phenomenon of the wilful destruction of people in their cities.[2]

Fiction provides many stories of cities under attack. The concept of an apocalypse, of an event involving destruction or damage on an awesome scale, derives from the Book of Revelations in the New Testament. Here St John describes a series of visions that culminate in the destruction of the wicked of Babylon: 'And he cried out with a strong voice, saying "The great city of Babylon is fallen, is fallen, and is become a dwelling of demons, and a cage of every unclean spirit, and a cage of every unclean and hated bird".'[3] This allegory has been a powerful force in artistic, literary and musical composition through many centuries. It finds particular expression in the modern 'disaster movie'.

Dresden 1945

Conventionally those under threat are unable to escape from a malign force that may be a fire, flood, bomb, tornado, virus or monster. Often they are trapped on a boat, plane, island, or train; but sometimes they are in the city. Some early science fiction explored this scenario, notably H G Wells' novel *The War of the Worlds* published in 1898, filmed twice since, and famously adapted for the radio by Orson Welles in 1938 leading some gullible listeners to flee New York to escape the advancing Martian invaders. The disaster movie genre flourished in Hollywood from the 1950s onwards with a distinct urban sub-genre.

There are also stories where the malignancy is human in origin with sinister forces seeking to control the city in pursuit of power or wealth, but thwarted by a supernatural hero. These are the 'caped crusaders' – Batman, Superman and Spiderman – who are called upon to shed their everyday, usually nerdy, identities when duty calls. They then don fancy, body-hugging outfits and acquire extraordinary strength, skills and intelligence – Batman has batwings, Spiderman can climb vertically up buildings, Superman can fly faster than a

Urban disasters in film

In *King Kong* (1933, remade in 1976 and 2005) a large ape rampages through New York, most memorably climbing the Empire State Building.

In *The War of the Worlds* (1953 and 2005) Martian invaders destroy New York.

In *Godzilla* (1954, 1985 and 1998) the 300 foot tall monster is awakened from prehistory by an H bomb test in the Pacific and terrorises Tokyo or New York.

In *I am Legend* (1964, 1971, 2007) there is a lone survivor of a virus that has killed the population of Los Angeles (in the earlier versions), New York (in the 2007 version).

In *The Towering Inferno* (1974) fire breaks out in the world's tallest skyscraper.

In *Earthquake* (1974) Los Angeles is destroyed (and Sensurround technology enabled filmgoers to feel the tremors – not very successfully).

In *The Swarm* (1978) Houston is threatened by killer bees from South America.

In *Invasion of the Body Snatchers* (1978) residents of San Francisco are infiltrated bodily by aliens. (In an earlier 1956 small town located version it was implied that the aliens were Communists).

In *Independence Day* (1996) aliens rain down beams of fire on New York, Los Angeles and Washington.

In *Volcano* (1997) the eruption occurs in the middle of Los Angeles and spreads lava over the Beverley Centre shopping mall.

In *The Day After Tomorrow* (2004) global warming melts the ice caps and raises sea level to put New York under water and later ice.

In *Flood* (2007) London's Thames flood barrier is overwhelmed by a storm surge.

In *Tower Block* (2012) its high-rise residents are targeted by a rogue sniper.

bullet – and thwart the villain's evil plans. All three originated in US comics, though later book, radio and film versions were spun off. These films are entertainment first and foremost, but usually there is a moral to the story. Sometimes human folly or greed gets punished; in other cases good defeats evil.

So-called 'urban myths' provide a domestic variation. Urban myths are stories of extreme, but credible, experiences, commonly ascribed to 'a friend of a friend' of the narrator. They start with everyday behaviour before an unexpected and gross turn of events occurs: a car is stolen with a deceased relative's body in the boot, a new hairdo contains spiders, waking from sleep on the beach there is a wound where a kidney has been removed. There are innumerable such stories, largely spread by word of mouth or the internet – type 'urban myth' into Google and you retrieve thousands of items. They lie halfway between horror stories and jokes. That they are 'myths' is obvious, but why are they 'urban'? Few such stories have explicitly urban settings, let alone urban subject matter, but maybe they are called urban myths because they express the anxieties of city people feeling under threat from events outside their control.

Walls and ghettos

Historically, defence against external threats has been a major influence on the design of cities. Massive fortifications – citadels, walls, ramparts, moats, towers, gates – were the most obvious manifestation of this, still surviving in some places. Even where walls have been demolished, their line is often traceable in the modern city plan, replaced by parks and boulevards built in more peaceful times to surround the old city. Or the old, abandoned defences are recalled by place or street names – as with Ludgate, Moorgate, Aldgate and Cripplegate in London or Porte de Versailles, Porte de Clignancourt and Port St Denis in Paris.

The Romans were prodigious wall builders throughout their empire in the 1st century AD. In many places their walls collapsed through neglect in the succeeding Dark Ages. Some were rebuilt and extended in medieval times under the threat of Saracen and Viking attack. This later wall building was often accompanied by social reorganisation. For, as the urban historian Mumford claims, 'The walled enclosure not merely gave protection from outside invasion: it had a new political function... There was safety, once the wall was erected, in numbers. Life in the isolated countryside, even under the shadow of a nearby castle, now ceased to be as attractive as life in the populated town. Labour on the wall itself was a cheap price to pay for such security and regularity in trade and work.'[4] From the 15th century onwards, gunpowder increased the range and power of artillery, so that simple walls and towers, defended by a citizen soldiery, provided inadequate defence. Innumerable treatises and designs were produced by military engineers proposing more and more elaborate fortifications, based on trigonometric and logistical calculations. These commonly produced a polygonal plan form, with massive earthworks and projecting bastions which permitted the defenders to rake the attackers with fire in the cleared no-man's-land surrounding the city. In the event only a few such places were built, mostly

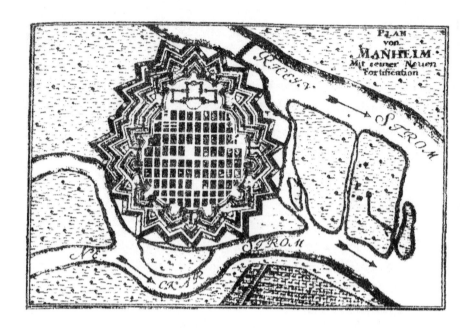

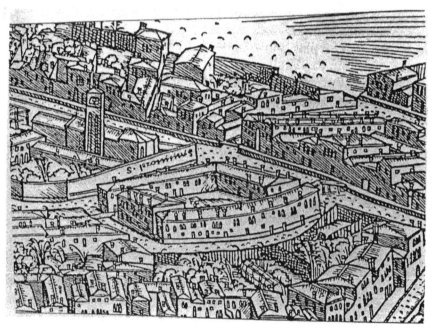

Walls without, walls within the city: Mannheim 1695 and Venice's ghetto 1500

in coastal or frontier regions of France and in the Italian and German states.

It is a historical irony that in the same centuries as these ideas gained currency for restructuring cities to defend them from the enemy without, there was another restructuring underway to meet the perceived threat of enemies within. This was the creation of ghettos for the Jewish populations of European cities, a development that would have more lasting significance than the inventiveness of the 15th century military engineers. This irony is powerfully evident in the story of Theresienstadt. Jewish communities had long been victims of intolerance and persecution. In the 16th century, many cities in Italy, facing an influx of Jews driven out by the Catholic reconquest of Arab lands in Spain, chose to segregate Jews and restrict their activities. In Venice the Jewish quarter was decreed in 1516 and called *Il Ghetto* after the Venetian word *gietto* for foundry, near which it was located. Different trading communities – Albanians, Turks, Greeks, Germans – had always chosen to live in separate parts of Venice. The new Ghetto was different: for Jews it was the only part of the city in which you could live and work. Access to it was restricted to a few bridges

---

Theresienstadt [5]

Theresienstadt (now Terezin), just over 60 kilometres northwest of Prague, was built by the Austrian Hapsburgs in the 1780s as a garrison town to defend their northern border against the Prussians. It could accommodate 14,500 soldiers and their supporters. Its grid street plan covered about 1 square kilometre, enclosed within complex, star-shaped fortifications which border the River Ohre on their west side. But Theresienstadt's walls were never put to test in battle – history had another role in mind for it. In 1941 the Nazi high command decided to turn it into a Jewish ghetto. For them it was an obvious choice: fully fortified, close to the Prague-Dresden railway, with an SS prison already established nearby. The original 3500 inhabitants were moved out, to be replaced by up to 60,000 Jews. In 1942 transfers to Auschwitz started. As in other ghettos, some degree of self-government was required and arranged. In late 1943 a *Verschönerung* (beautification) of the ghetto was put in hand by the Nazis, in readiness for inspection visits by the International Red Cross. A circus tent was erected, opera performances staged, a jazz band performed in the main square. The visitors filed positive reports. By the end of the war 140,000 Jews had been deported to Theresienstadt. Fewer than 17,500 remained on its liberation in May 1945.

across the surrounding canals, which were patrolled at night by boats, so that entry and exit were controlled, but all this without any restriction on the practice of Jewish customs within the ghetto. By and large this became the model for new Jewish ghettos elsewhere: in Prague, Frankfurt, Trieste, Rome and other cities. Here many Jews lived for nearly 300 years until, under the influence of progressive ideals, the ghettos were abolished and their walls demolished in the 19th century.

After 1939, the Nazis created new ghettos for Jewish people in the conquered cities of Eastern Europe. Warsaw was the largest, with 380,000 people – 30% of the city's population – crammed into it, increasing to 480,000 as Jews from Krakow, Lodz, Lvov, Minsk and Riga were moved in. With poor diets, overcrowding, inadequate water supply and little sanitation, hundreds of thousands died of disease and starvation. In 1942 systematic deportations from the ghettos to the extermination camps of Auschwitz, Treblinka and Mauthausen began.

The term 'ghetto' lives on as a generic description of a city district largely occupied by a minority ethnic group. Typically these ghettos originate as ports of entry for immigrants, who seek the material and moral support of their fellows already settled in the city. In many cities these immigrant minorities are generally relatively poor and lack of skills, confidence, language and contacts, as well as prejudice, limit their opportunities. There may be restrictions – legal, economic or social – that stop people moving out of the ghetto as they get on with their lives. Among Western cities today, it is those in the USA that remain most strongly segregated. The 19th century immigrants from Europe and China established themselves in distinct city neigbourhoods and, to some extent, their successors remain there: Chinatowns and Little Italys abound. In the 20th century Latino immigrants from Puerto Rico, Mexico and Central America came and continue to come. But it was an internal migration of African-Americans, moving from the rural southern states in the first half of the 20th century to escape racism, to find work in the cities and to live what they hoped would be a better life, that created the black ghettos of the Midwest and northeastern cities of St Louis, Chicago, Detroit, Washington, Baltimore, New York and Boston. The departure of existing residents – so-called 'white flight' – reinforced the ghettoisation. And discriminatory practices, some legal until outlawed in civil rights legislation in recent decades, kept most black families in the ghettos. In Chicago today two thirds of its black residents still live in neighbourhoods that are at least 80% black.

In South Africa in much of the late 20th century racial segregation was enforced by apartheid laws. These not only defined the areas in which different ethnic groups were allowed to live, but also required the removal of people of the 'wrong' kinds from areas newly reserved for others. The story of one such area, District Six in Cape Town, captures this grim history. Even today, when the legal basis for apartheid has been removed, a clear duality still characterises most South African towns and cities: the leafy, spacious suburbs where richer – mainly white – people live are quite separate from the dense, crowded townships where poorer – mostly black, mixed race or Indian – people live. But the two are umbilically linked, for the work of the maids, builders, security guards and waiters from the townships provides services for the rich and income for the poor.

Walls or fences have continued being erected in some cities to keep hostile, or thought to be hostile, people in or out. Famously a 155 kilometre long wall divided East and West Berlin from 1961 to 1989. Elsewhere barriers have been

---

District Six, Cape Town[6]

As you drive today into Cape Town from the airport, on the left approaching the city centre, is a large vacant area with just a few buildings standing among the grassy plots. This was once District 6, so-called since it became in 1867 the sixth Municipal District of Cape Town. It once housed 60,000 people in narrow streets and crowded houses, with a characteristic inner city mix of communities and activities, closely linked to the city centre and the port, impoverished but lively. Just the sort of place that in many cities around the world became the target for urban renewal in the 1950s and 1960s. But apartheid brought a different dimension to renewal here – renewal became removal. For in 1966 it was declared a White Group Area and a programme of forced dispersal of the black, Indian and mixed race residents commenced. Over fifteeen years, most homes were bulldozed, a few were requisitioned and sold to white owners, just the churches and mosques were left standing. The former residents were resettled in the townships of the Cape Flats, 10 kilometres or more away to the south. Then nothing much happened. A large Technical College was built in the middle of the area, a few luxury townhouses on its fringes, but the rest remained empty. Since the end of apartheid a programme for the restoration of property rights and development of low cost housing has slowly got underway.

put in place in Nicosia since the Turkish invasion of Cyprus in 1974, separating the Greek and Turkish sectors; in Beirut during its civil war in the 1980s in the form of a cleared 'green zone' separating Muslim and Christian districts and their militias; in Belfast separating Protestant and Catholic communities during 'the Troubles' of the 1980s and 1990s; and in some Balkan cities during the civil wars of the 1990s. A new wall, 6 metres high and 51 kilometres long, has been constructed to separate Israelis and Palestinians in and around Jerusalem. And in Baghdad, in response to the civil strife following the overthrow of Saddam Hussein, security barriers were built to separate Sunni and Shia residents. More widely, the increasing creation of 'gated communities' in cities – private enclaves for residence or business with controlled access – is expressive of the continuing urge of some city people to have walls to protect themselves from perceived enemies.

Riots and revolutions

Thus – whether by political edict or by social prejudice – cities can become inescapably divided. Divided communities may mostly live in harmony, mutually tolerant of their differences or even inspired by the novel perspectives and experiences that others offer. But, from time to time or place to place, such differences may be the cause of resentment, conflict, criminal or political action. These are characteristically urban pathologies. At their most extreme, just as there are 'failed states', there are 'failed cities'. That is, cities where the basic necessities for living together – security, health, shelter, neighbourliness – are no longer there.[7] Failed cities in today's world might include Aleppo, Baghdad, Damascus, Gaza City, Harare, Kabul, Kingston in Jamaica, Mogadishu and Port au Prince. At times in the past Algiers, Beirut, Belfast, Bogota, Freetown, Grozny, Kampala, Kinshasa, Nicosia, Palermo and Panama City have had this character, but have happily moved on. Typically in failed cities public services like schools and hospitals, water and energy supply are unreliable, even absent; the city has become segregated on ethnic or religious lines; many buildings are abandoned, others squatted, trees have been felled to provide firewood; feral dogs may roam the streets and vultures hover above them; family lives have fractured and children live on the streets; corruption is endemic in public authorities, kidnapping and racketeering and drug trafficking are prevalent; warlords, gangs and militias, sometimes in cahoots with politicians and the security forces make parts of the city 'no go' areas for anybody without protection; crimes and misdemeanours go unpunished, others are subject to arbitrary punishment by vigilantes. Governments attempt, from time to time, to control insurgency and impose order but often as not – through repressive actions – achieve little but increasing the death toll. These conditions may in some cases last a long time, as in Mogadishu.

Mogadishu

Mogadishu, the capital of Somalia, has been a failed city for nearly two decades. It fell to rebel forces in 1990 and thereafter two factions each claimed the state Presidency. A UN peacekeeping mission in 1992-94 failed to bring peace or stability. The warlord who appeared to secure control of the city in 1996 was killed in a street battle soon thereafter and violence has continued since. Public buildings are in ruins, bombarded, looted, overgrown. Abandoned vehicles fill the streets and wastelands. About a million people live amongst the desolation. Different factions are believed to have their foreign supporters. A transitional President of Somalia was elected in 2004, but the new government never established itself in the capital, basing itself in the small town of Baidoa to the west. In summer 2006 the Islamic Court Union militia gained control of Mogadishu. After a few months they were ousted by government troops, heavily backed by armed forces from neighbouring Ethiopia. Factional fighting resumed with a flimsy African Union peacekeeping force just protecting key infrastructure and the supply of humanitarian aid. In 2010 a newly elected President's forces started to regain control of most of the city. In 2012 new parliamentarians were sworn in – in the car park of Mogadishu airport as the Parliament building was too damaged for safe use.

But it is exceptional for urban disorder to be that anarchic or long running. Short, sharp demonstrations, rampages and riots are more common. This kind of disorder happens more in cities for a number of reasons. The underlying conflicts may be more evident there, the numbers of discontented people greater, radical leaders – students and other dissidents – are more numerous, more people can be mobilised quickly by car, bus, train or tram. Action in the city is nearer to the seats of power and wealth, which *in extremis* may need to be occupied. The weapons for serious, violent disorder can be readily improvised:

paving stones, Molotov cocktails, barricades, car bombs. New forms of media are important; not only can email, texting, Facebook or Twitter recruit and manage street demonstrators covertly and rapidly, but global TV coverage secures widespread attention and has made English – in slogans on posters and banners and in vox pop interviews – the universal language of protest. And it has stimulated the adoption of revolutionary 'street theatre' – witness the jangling of keys by demonstrators in Prague, the partying on the Berlin Wall and the peace sculpture in Tiananmen Square, all in 1989, and the occupation of Tarir Square in Cairo in 2011.

For the most part urban disorder is local in both cause and hoped-for effect, the rectification of some specific wrong. But sometimes it is addressed to wider social, economic or political issues. Occasionally it has been the starting point of political revolution that, in the short or the long term, has successfully overthrown an established regime. Reviewing these events in his history of the 20th century, Eric Hobsbawm observes that in the classic era of revolution, from France in 1789 to Russia in 1917, 'old regimes were overthrown in the great cities, but new ones were made permanent by the inarticulate plebiscites of the countryside.'[9] In contrast, most of the post-1930s revolutions were made in the countryside by activist minorities and, once victorious, imported into the cities – Franco in Spain, Mao in China, Castro in Cuba provided the models for others that followed. Then, in the late 20th century, revolution once more came from the cities: it had to, because by then the majority of a state's inhabitants lived there and they could, not least because of new communication media, give or withhold their loyalty to the regime.

This urbanisation of insurgency is seen by some as a radical shift in the nature of military conflict, for which most security forces are poorly prepared. One US military expert declared that 'The future of warfare lies in the streets, sewers, highrise buildings, and sprawl of houses that form the broken cities of the world…Our recent military history is punctuated with city names – Tuzla, Mogadishu, Los Angeles, Beirut, Panama City, Hue, Saigon, Santa Domingo – but these encounters have been but a prologue, with the real drama still to come.'[10]

The personal and the political

Cities are also the places of more personal tensions. Day by day, you may be irritated, frustrated, often defeated in attempting even the most mundane tasks.

Some seminal urban uprisings

1789   *Paris* – storming of the Bastille prison, the start of the French Revolution

1848   Uprisings *in the cities of France, Italy, Germany, the Hapsburg Empire* and lesser unrest elsewhere in Europe – as historian Eric Hobsbawm said, 'There has never been anything closer to the world-revolution of which the insurrectionaries of the period dreamed than this spontaneous and general conflagration.'[8]

1916   *Dublin* – the Easter Rising, an unsuccessful attempt to secure Irish independence

1917   *St Petersburg* – the start of the Bolshevik Revolution

1944   *Warsaw* – insurgency against the Nazi occupation

1948   *Bogota* – a popular uprising against the ruling oligarchy, that even the police joined

1956-7 *The Battle of Algiers* against French colonial rule

1965   *Los Angeles and other US cities* – riots in the black ghettos

1968   *Paris* and elsewhere – student radicalism takes to the streets

1976   *Soweto* – following the shooting of student anti-apartheid demonstrators

1979   *Teheran* – overthrow of the Shah and instigation of the Islamic Republic

1986   *Manila* – overthrow of the Marcos regime by 'people power'

1987-92 *Palestine* – the first Intifada in Gaza and West Bank cities

1989   *Beijing* – pro-democracy demonstrations in Tiananmen Square

1989   *onwards in Gdansk, Warsaw, Prague, Leipzig, Berlin, Bucharest* – street demonstrations hastening the collapse of the Communist regimes

2000   *onwards Palestine* – the second Intifada

2003   *onwards* – insurrection *in Baghdad and other Iraqui cities* against the US-led occupation

2011   The Arab Spring – street protests in *Tunis, Cairo and Benghazi* that brought down autocratic regimes

There's the rush hour to get to work, but also other rushed hours, for example, getting three children to three different schools or securing a parcel delivery or being delayed in a bus or car while a public demonstration claims the street ahead. There are daily hassles to cope with: the uncertainties of getting somewhere on time and finding what you need when you get there; confronting the aggressive behaviour of others in shops or in the street; competing claims on your personal energy in reconciling work, family life and recreation. No wonder we often say that 'it's a jungle out there', meaning not the flora and fauna but the impenetrability and unreliability of city life, and therefore its danger.

In the cities of the North the majority now lead comfortable and secure lives. Even so there may be disruptions: the unexpected termination of a tenancy or loss of a job, the vile behaviour of neighbours, the child caught up in petty crime. True, these are not exclusively urban misfortunes but there is a greater volatility to urban than to rural life. Some people can struggle for months, years or decades to get their lives onto a more even keel, at last able to withstand life's buffeting. Unemployment, homelessness, school truancy, addiction, crime are still found in even the most averagely prosperous cities. In the cities of the South it is the majority, not the minority, who live this way. In his book about present-day cities in Southeast Asia, Jeremy Seabrook provides accounts of the lives of people in Bangkok, Dhaka, Jakarta, Saigon, Mumbai and Manila. It is very hard for them to escape from such daily struggles. Work and income are slight, unreliable and at times non-existent, so that poverty is the basic constraint on life. Shelter may be inadequate. People cannot stay healthy in these conditions, not just from the threat of infections but also from injuries, mental illness and chronic diseases. They are frequently the victims of violence and crime: extortion, theft, assault, even kidnapping are common risks. In some cities vigilante assassins take it upon themselves to 'clean up the streets' or politicians decide to 'clean up the city'.

The link between personal and political struggles in the city as a metaphorical battleground is skilfully captured by William Blake's poem *London*. It was first published in 1794. The date is important, for in these years the British ruling class was fearful that the revolutionary fervour in Paris would be imported to its capital city. It is an angry poem in which you can sense the despair of city life. Its images are vivid, almost filmic, in the sound and look of the city that they provide: the infant's cry of fear, the hapless soldier's sigh, the blood running down palace walls, the blackened church, the midnight street. But the poem's imagery has deeper meanings, revealing a critical, not just regretful, stance.[13] 'Manacles' and 'chartered' were radical code words of the period directed at the repression of the authorities: Palace, Church and Trade. In Blake's choice of these words are echoes of Tom Paine's *Rights of Man*, a key polemic of the time. Even the River Thames is 'chartered', that is, managed for profit. The Church was not just 'black'ning' because of soot, but also because the Church shrouds

Stories of daily life in Mumbai, Jakarta and Bangkok[11]

Maneka was born in a self-built wood, palm leaf and polythene hut on a strip of wasteland that separated the fishing community from the new apartment blocks in south Mumbai. Her parents had come to the city from their native village. Her father worked pulling a cart of building materials, her mother worked for rich Parsee families. When her father's alcoholism and her mother's tuberculosis prevented them working, Maneka became the family breadwinner, working as a domestic servant. Later their squatter home was demolished by the municipality and her mother died. Her father and brother were relocated 30 kilometres away. By then Maneka was married and had a child, but her husband and his family abused her. She moved back with her father and travels two hours each way to work, while her new stepmother cares for her child. Maneka was then sixteen.

Hira and *Mirim* are female friends who work in a garment factory in Jakarta, owned by a Singaporean company, under contract to Levi-Strauss and others. Working hours are from seven in the morning to three in the afternoon, but with compulsory overtime until nine if there is an urgent order to be met. The management is routinely abusive. The factory is very hot and cramped, with only one toilet for the 200 workers. Home for the two friends is a single room, two by three metres in size, separated from other such rooms by rough plywood partitions, on the upper story of a shack in a slum area. The room is cheap, costing four and a half day's pay per month, but cans of water have to be paid for. Everyone in the building works in factories making roasted peanuts, snacks, biscuits or garments, all for export.

Pong, aged twenty five, works as a bell captain in a serviced apartment block in Bangkok, much used by visiting business people. He had come to Bangkok five years before on leaving the temple school to which his parents had sent him. He earned 4000 baht a month (about $135), of which 1200 baht went on the rent of a shared room and 2000 baht was sent home to his mother. He spoke good English. But he was a troubled young man, uncertain about himself, bored and lonely in the city. One day he gave up his room, abandoned his job and returned to his home province, to look after his ageing mother and seek work in the local Wella shampoo factory at 80 baht a day.

the city in its oppressive doctrines. And the harlot's curse has a double meaning: on one level a shriek of anguish, on another the venereal disease passed to a married man and then to his wife and ultimately the 'Marriage hearse' of death. Thus, for Blake, the daily struggles of Londoners to get by – personified in the chimney sweep, the prostitute, the soldier and the infant – are manifestations of disparities in power and wealth in the city and their attendant injustices. The personal and political battles of city life are conjoined.

William Blake's *London*[12]

'I wander thro' each charter'd street,
Near where the charter'd Thames does flow
And mark in every face I meet
Marks of weakness, marks of woe.

In every cry of every Man,
In every Infants cry of fear,
In every voice; in every ban,
The mind-forg'd manacles I hear.

How the Chimney-sweepers cry
Every black'ning Church appals
And the hapless Soldiers sigh
Runs in blood down Palace walls.

But most thro' midnight streets I hear
How the youthful Harlots curse
Blasts the new-born Infants tear
And blights with plagues the Marriage hearse.'

5.

Transformation: Mumbai's many worlds

North Mumbai 2010. *Coming in to land in the late afternoon at Mumbai's International Airport I look down on a city of white residential towers, their shadows cast across the brown, mostly treeless, spaces between them – seemingly a typical modern cityscape. But as the plane drops lower I realise that the brown spaces are in fact the roofs of one and two storey shanty homes packed tightly together. As the plane approaches the runway, it skims over them and the busy activity in the lanes between the shanties comes into view. A few days later, visiting these districts on foot, I can look up at the neighbouring towers. But the Mumbaikars looking down from the towers and the Mumbaikars looking up from the shanties live in different worlds: cheek by jowl but separated by income, possessions, comfort and prospects.*

Full-on

The modern chronicler of Mumbai life, Suketu Mehta, calls it 'Maximum City'. In explanation of his choice of that term, he describes the city as the biggest, fastest, richest city in India and ruefully observes that 'Bombay is the future of urban civilisation on the planet. God help us.'[1] It's partly the size of the city – now with a population of twenty million in Greater Mumbai – that maximises its impact. But it is also the density of what goes on in the place. Overall there are on average 27,000 people per square kilometre. (In comparison New York has 9,500, Mexico City nearly 6,000.) But in parts of central Mumbai population density approaches 100,000 people per square kilometre. It's not just that buildings, whether low- or high-rise, are packed closely together; also homes are fully occupied with family and relatives and sometimes servants and lodgers; workshops and offices are tightly packed with workers; streets are crowded with vehicles and pedestrians; transport is overloaded with people and goods. So that, beyond the city's size and density, there is an intensity to Mumbai life – the city seems to be bursting at its seams.

You sense this strongly riding the suburban trains. Mumbai has three rail lines, running north-south through the city. They carry over six million passengers every weekday. The carriages are designed for these heavy loads: few seats, many hanging straps, open doorways. But at peak times the press of people – typically about fifteen standing passengers per square metre – also requires some adjustment of behaviour. To get on you must first secure foot and finger hold in the doorway, then push to ease yourself further in. To get off you must start squeezing past others long before your destination to position yourself by the open doorway so you can jump off before the train comes to a halt, because if you wait longer you'll be swept back inside by people getting on. There are separate 'ladies' carriages' but the same rules apply. Fatalities are frequent: about 500 people die annually from falling out of the doors or hitting trackside poles.

Train travel in Mumbai

In the streets there is a similar crush. Pedestrians mix with hawkers, beggars and sleepers. Pedal bikes, motorbikes, auto-rickshaws, taxis, buses, cars are – like the trains – mostly loaded to full capacity. There are few delivery vans, so goods are carried on heads (sometimes while texting with the spare hands), on handcarts (some needing three men to propel them) and piled up high on bicycles. Big, heavily decorated lorries bring supplies into the city. They thunder along the main roads that have been widened, given flyovers and traffic lights at junctions to try and speed traffic along, but still are flanked by homes, workshops, traders and parked vehicles. Congestion is endemic. Only in the outskirts of the city have a few new freeways been constructed.

Almost everyone here lives cheek by jowl with their neighbours. There are some districts with spacious homes, a few of them bungalows left over from the period of British colonial rule, others as houses built more recently in new developments in the outer suburbs. But the tenement, the apartment block, the shanty – or the street – is the typical home for Mumbaikars. So-called 'chawls', a three to five storey tenement block of 3-400 dwellings, each just one room plus kitchen with shared latrines, was the common building type as the city expanded in the 19th and early 20th centuries. Around 1900 of these chawls made up about three quarters of the city's housing stock. Town planner Patrick Geddes said that they were not housing but warehousing for people. Many are still there. More recently apartment blocks, built to ten or more storeys, have become the norm. They often stand jumbled together, for land ownership fragmented into hundreds of parcels has inhibited large scale, more orderly property development. Rent control and shared ownerships mean that maintenance standards are often poor. And, even where the rich live, the spaces outside their apartments – the stairs, the lobbies, the compound – are often unkempt.

Below, around and adjacent to these tenements and apartments for the better off are shanties, the homes of the poor. In the early 19th century a commentator observed that 'the lower classes content themselves with small huts, mostly of clay and roofed with cadjan, a mat made of the leaves of the Palmyra or coconut trees plaited together. Some of the huts are so small that they only admit of a man's sitting upright in them, and barely shelter his feet when he lies down.'2 Today the huts are still there, just as small though now built using timber, tarpaulin, plastic bags, tyres and tin. Some are workshops as well as homes. They fill every nook and cranny in the city, lining the main roads, occupying scraps of spare land, flanking railway lines and sitting on top of water mains, clinging to water edges and on slopes too steep for conventional building. Their occupants rarely have title to their sites, often connect illegally into power supplies, must share water taps and latrines. From time to time the city authorities or land owners evict shanty dwellers, demolishing their homes usually without offering alternative housing. The victims move in with friends or relatives, maybe build shanties elsewhere or go to live on the streets.

Mumbai has over one million street-dwellers, many of them families, some of them single men or women or even single children. Most are in work and compelled by their jobs – in transport, construction, catering, trading – to live in the otherwise unaffordable heart of the city. Arriving at the main railway station in the late evening you find the concourse taken over by families bedding down for the night, containing themselves within areas marked by white lines, leaving spaces between them for travellers to get to and from the platforms. Elsewhere the homeless are asleep on pavements, beneath market stalls, in alleyways and doorways, anywhere. Together the shanty dwellers and the street dwellers in Mumbai are over half of the city's population.

Towering on scaffolds above the shanties, at road intersections or sitting on top of buildings are enormous billboards garishly promoting corporate brands, new movies or consumer products, often in English. The sides of lorries and buses, the roofs of roadside shacks, lampposts, even bicycle baskets carry adverts. The government too has its public messages. To a stranger in the city some are clear: 'Less Noise, Better City!' and 'Please Pay Heed. It's a Desperate Need! CLEAN UP!' and 'Don't Use Plastics!' But others – like 'Nationalists Support Hockey!' – leave you bewildered.

Living and working in Mumbai is tough. It's noisy, the air is polluted, water and energy supplies are uncertain, travel is slow. Streets and open land are rubbish strewn. Taxis and auto-rickshaws are obliged to use natural gas but the smell – like rotten vegetables – is pretty nauseous. It's also hot here: maximum daily temperatures stay above 30C throughout the year. In the monsoon months from June to September up to 900 mm of rain can fall in twenty four hours, soaking people, destroying unsound structures, corroding others, causing landslides, filling streets with water and playing havoc with water supplies and sewage. But people survive. One guidebook warns the visitor not to come armed with checklists of sights. Rather Mumbai 'is the sort of city that is relentlessly fascinating simply for not having imploded; for continuing to function despite the state of anarchy in which it appears to exist. It is in the people of Mumbai, the hectic activity of its streets and railway stations, the chaos of its bazaars, the visible frenzy of commerce, the ridiculous contrasts of appalling poverty and overblown wealth – and the complete indifference with which Mumbaikars deal with them – that the appeal of the city lies.'[3]

India's powerhouse

Mumbai is India's biggest and richest city. Delhi is India's political capital, but Mumbai is undoubtedly the nation's commercial capital. Its economy provides 25% of Indian industrial output and is growing at 6% per annum. Its per capita income is three times the national average and its residents pay about 40% of the nation's taxes – it's where you go to make money. Its literacy rate is higher than the national average.

Right from the colonial incursion of the Portuguese and later the British into India in the 16th century, the city has been commercially important. It was here that the East India Company – leasing the place in 1668 from the British Crown for £10 per annum – set up its headquarters. In the early years trade was with China, Java and other south east Asian islands, the east coast of Africa and Europe. The commodities included tea, coffee, sugar, spices, cotton, silk, porcelain, opium and gems. Imports and exports expanded in the 19th century with the consolidation of British rule in the Indian subcontinent, the progressive removal of the East India Company's trade monopolies, and with transport improvements like the introduction of the steamship (much faster than sail), the opening of the Suez Canal in 1869, and the inland extension of the Indian railway system. The docks were built and the city expanded onto reclaimed land. It was then that cotton – grown in the inland provinces – came to dominate Bombay trade, first as raw cotton, then spun, later as finished goods, thereby providing the basis for manufacturing as well as commerce. At the time it was said that 'Bombay has long been the Liverpool of the East – she is now becoming the Manchester.'[4] As in Lancashire, vast textile mills with tall chimneys were built dominating the cityscape and rural immigrants were drawn into their workforces, such that by the end of the 19th century there were eighty two mills employing 73,000 workers, almost a tenth of the city population. Most mills were Indian-owned.

Then cotton lost its dominance. Among new industries were railway workshops, shipbuilding, steel making, dyes and chemicals, leather, oil and paper mills. Since Indian independence in 1947, Mumbai's economy has diversified further. The port remains important, handling 70% of India's maritime trade, and the international airport is the nation's busiest. Many kinds of engineering have flourished. Services like finance, information technology, media and consultancy too, especially since government liberalisation measures in 1991. Mumbai is today home to the Reserve Bank of India, the Indian Stock Exchange and the corporate HQs of numerous Indian banks and companies. Among them is the Tata Group, the Indian-owned multinational with interests in steel, chemicals, energy, vehicles (they own Jaguar and Land Rover), tea (the Tetley brand), IT, financial services and consultancy, telecommunications and hotels, including the city's famous 5 star Taj Hotel. Today you find Tata's name and T-shaped logo on buildings, vehicles and billboards across Mumbai. The bureaucracies of the city and state governments also employ many. Most of India's major TV and satellite networks, as well as its publishing houses, are headquartered here. Mumbai is also the home of Bollywood, India's Hindi language film industry, which has a global market, even outselling Hollywood

---

Bollywood

The Mumbai film industry has been active since the 1930s. It produces films in a wide range of genres, but it finds its largest audiences – in India and increasingly abroad – for its Hindi language blockbusters. The term Bollywood – acquired in the 1970s – generally refers to them. To appeal to diverse audiences the films follow what is known as a 'masala format' with a little of everything: romance, action, comedy, song and dance, dream sequences, festivities. Some of this is building on the Indian tradition of narrating mythology through song and dance; otherwise the Hollywood musical has been influential and more recently the frenetic style of MTV videos. The plots ramble rather and the films last a long time: as a non-Indian you may think when the story stops after ninety minutes that the film is over, but it's just the intermission and the second half is still to come. In recent years, as Western cultural influence has grown in India and as Bollywood has seen the potential of global markets, the films have changed somewhat. Budgets are bigger, the production values (sets, costumes, special effects and cinematography) aim for world class standards, English phrases creep into the dialogue and overseas locations are woven into the storyline. Increasingly Bollywood presents images of modernity: modern young people, modern relationships, modern families, a modern nation. In all of this some traditional values are getting subverted.

production in ticket numbers. The city also retains long-established craft industries: jewellery, silk weaving, furniture, cosmetics, food, leatherwork.

Mumbai's retail trade is also vibrant, evident in what Mehta in *Maximum City* calls 'the psychedelic chaos of the streetscape. Rows of small shops each dedicated to furnishing the city with a microscopically precise commodity or service: wood furniture polish, typing, hair oil, fireworks, roasted chapatis, coffins, handmade footwear. These shops are now run by the fourth generation of the same family. They live in the building above, paying fifteen rupees, forty-five rupees, as rent. The shops are open from 11am to 9pm, and the owners know where to get the best rose sherbet, the best sabudana khichdi, in that universal intimacy small traders have with street food.'5 As well, Mumbai's wealthier residents require an ever wider range of consumer goods and services; shopping malls to serve them have sprung up in the outer suburbs.

This is the formal sector of Mumbai's modern economy. It also has a flourishing informal sector – work that goes unregulated, untaxed or even hidden to officialdom. Here are street hawkers, taxi and auto-rickshaw drivers, water sellers, cooks, waiters, delivery men, repairers, recyclers and ragpickers, as found in many other cities of the South. But Mumbai has some unique informal entrepreneurs. One group are the dhobis, who run open air laundries near Mahalakshmi suburban railway station. Each morning mountains of washing are brought here from all over the city, soaked in concrete vats of caustic soda and then thumped to squeeze out the water, hung up to dry, pressed with charcoal-heated irons, folded in newspaper and bundled for return to their owners next day. Even more original is Mumbai's lunch delivery service. Every day a few thousand white-capped members of the Nutan Mumbai Tiffin Box Suppliers Association (known colloquially as 'dabawallahs' – the word translates as 'person with a box') deliver freshly cooked food from 160,000 suburban kitchens to offices in downtown Mumbai. The food is prepared by a wife or mother, packed into a tiffin box (a set of stacked cylindrical containers with a handle on top) and colour coded, then passed to collectors who take them to the nearest railway station for transport into the city, where they are taken by others to the sons or husbands at their workplace. Later the empty tiffins are collected with the daily fee and the process reverses. The dabawallahs make around 5,000 rupees (£70) a month – not a bad income by Mumbai standards.

Mumbai's dhobi laundries

Old and New Mumbai

To a visitor the naming of Mumbai's districts is confusing. What is commonly called Central Mumbai is not the city centre, that is South Mumbai. Most of the modern city is in North Mumbai. And then there is New Mumbai, across the water to the east. All this derives from geography and history. Mumbai is contained on a narrow peninsular projecting into the Arabian Sea, about 1 kilometre wide in its southern tip, extending to 5 kilometres as you go north. Originally it was seven coastal islands, inhabited by farmers and fishermen. As the colonial city of Bombay expanded, the creeks between the islands were filled in and the ocean margins reclaimed, often excavating the hills to provide landfill. This process has continued in the city's development right up to the present day.

The initial colonial settlement was on one of the southern islands. Here a walled town grew up with an associated harbour – the district is still called 'Fort' today. Over time the walls were pulled down and adjoining areas built over for commerce, culture, government and housing, leaving a rich legacy of neo-Gothic, Italianate, Indo-Saracen and Art Deco architecture. Here you see the city's signature structure The Gateway of India, a monumental waterside arch intended as a disembarkation point for passengers from P&O steamers, but now remembered more as the site of the Raj rulers' ceremonial departure from India in 1948. The docks were also massively extended. Fine parkland – the Maidans, now largely devoted to cricket games – was created. Other adjoining areas became the Native City, a riotous mix of bazaars, dwellings, mosques and temples. In the last century, South Mumbai expanded further through major reclamations on its eastern waterfront to create upmarket housing along Marine Drive and at Chowpatty and to the south in Colaba and a new commercial quarter at Nariman Point. South Mumbai remains the commercial and government centre of Mumbai into which workers pour everyday – hundreds of thousands of them through Churchgate and CST (Chhatrapati Shivaji Terminus) railway stations.

Further north, Central Mumbai was where the 19th century cotton mills were established. Around them was built a chaotic jumble of chawls and shanties. Disease was widespread, culminating in a major outbreak of plague in 1896 killing, at its height, 1,900 people each week. Urban improvements – new roads, slum removal, new housing colonies, schools and colleges, hospitals, water and drainage systems – have been undertaken over the years, but the chaos persists. Most of the mills have now closed and their sites have been used for a modern mix of residential and commercial developments. But chawls and shanties remain. Today it is in these areas that you most fully experience the commingling of 'the kutcha and pukka city'[6] in Mumbai.

North Mumbai is a product of the 20th century, replacing a landscape of villages, and now many times larger than Central and South Mumbai. It is lightly separated from the older city by still unfilled creeks and marshes. But it is tied in by the Central and Western Railways and the Western and Eastern Express Highways that run spine-like through it. It displays all the contrasts of modern Mumbai: luxury apartments, upmarket shopping and cafe life for the well-to-do; new business centre of glass and steel high-rises to rival South Mumbai; low- and high-rise housing for the commuting middle class; and also vast shantytowns. North Mumbai's sprawl is punctuated by both the international airport and the Sanjay Gandhi National Park.

Mumbai's political and business elites have long had modernising ambitions, to make it a 'world-class city.' Shanghai in China, with its gleaming skyscrapers and efficient transport and communications networks, is the model and rival. There have been many plans, but relatively little achievement – not least because of the confusing and rivalrous relations between the bureaucracies of the Municipal Corporation of Greater Mumbai, the Mumbai Metropolitan Region Development Authority and other agencies separately responsible for housing, building repair, slum rehabilitation, roads and railways. One ambitious project was the creation of 'New Bombay' (now renamed 'Navi Mumbai') across Thane Creek to the east, intended as a twin city offering both homes and jobs in order to decongest Mumbai. First promoted in the 1970s by government, it languished until the 1990s when better road and rail connections were built and private developers were invited to participate. Today nearly three million people live in Navi Mumbai. They are predominantly young, middle income, home-owning families with many breadwinners commuting to work in Old Mumbai – not dissimilar to the demographics of North Mumbai's other new dormitory suburbs. New Mumbai's objective of decongesting Old Mumbai has failed.

The social mosaic

Mumbai people have many different faiths, ethnicities, castes, languages and classes. To an outsider they are bewildering. For a local they still matter greatly in your daily life, in many cases influencing your education, what work you do, where you live, how you worship, who you marry, your friendships, how you dress (varieties of headgear can be a giveaway), what you eat, even which cricket club you join. And, importantly, they underpin the social connections that people need to exert influence on the bureaucracies that control much of Mumbai life. There are long histories for each of these identities. They have not been supplanted by people's sense of themselves as Mumbaikars.

Religion pervades Mumbai. The city is stuffed with temples, mosques, and churches. Mobile shrines travel the streets and smaller versions sit in homes, workplaces, buses, taxis, cars and shops. The calendar is full of religious festivals devoted to deities and myths when the streets are taken over for celebrations. Three fifths of the people are Hindus, another fifth Muslims, the remaining fifth other faiths. The Hindu and Muslim communities co-exist uncomfortably. There have been outbreaks of violence between them in 1947 during the partition of British India on independence, in 1992-3 in the wake of the

Festivals in Mumbai

Makar Sankranti (January) – a celebration of the transition of the sun from Sagittarius to Capricorn according to Hindu astrology: sesame sweets, flowers and fruit are exchanged and kites flown in the parks and on beaches.

Holi (March) – marking the beginning of Spring when you can expect to be bombarded with coloured water.

*Easter (*March/April) – running from Lent to Easter Sunday.

Ramnavami (March/April) – Hindus celebrate the birthday of Lord Rama with processions of floats of Rama, his consort Sita, his brother Lakshmana and the devotee monkey-general Hanuman.

Mahavir Jayanti (April/May) – the birthday of Mahavira, founder of Jainism.

Buddha Jayanti (April/May) – Buddha's birthday.

Gokhulashtami (August) – the joyful Hindu celebration of Lord Krishna's birthday, when terracotta pots (filled with curd, sweets and cash) are hung from balconies for human pyramids of small boys to grab.

Pateti (August) – the Parsi New Year: time to dwell on past sins and wrongs and atone for them, thus closing the account on the previous year.

Raksha Bandham (August) – the name suggests a 'bond of protection': brothers and sisters exchange tokens and presents with great fervour, the brothers promising to protect their sisters from all harms and troubles, the sisters praying to God to protect their brother from all evil.

Ganesha Chaturthi (August/September) – a ten day Hindu celebration of Lord Ganesha's birthday culminating with the immersion in the sea at Chowpatty Beach of huge effigies of the elephant-headed god Ganesh.

Narial Purnima (September) – Koli fisherman launch decorated boats to mark the end of the monsoon.

Navratri (September/October) – Gujarati festival featuring the traditional dandiya dance.

Ramadan (September – October) – Muslim month of daytime fasting, with an all night food market in the lanes around the Minara Masjid mosque.

Diwali (October/November) – the Hindu festival of lights, signifying the triumph of good over evil, celebrated with great pomp.

Christmas (December) – largely secularised.

destruction of a mosque in Uttar Pradesh far away from Mumbai (by far the worst case: more than 1000 people were killed in the city), in 2006 when terrorists bombed commuter trains and again in 2008 when the Taj Hotel and other buildings were targeted. With each outrage, Hindu-Muslim resentment ratchets up and the two communities have ended up living more and more in separate neighbourhoods.

There are also many small minority faiths: Buddhists, Jains, Christians, Sikhs, Jews and Parsis. The Christians are mostly Catholics originating from conversions by the Portuguese in the 16th century. Most of Mumbai's once thriving Jewish community left for Israel after 1948; but the lovely, blue Kenneseth Eliyahoo synagogue, its erection funded by the Sassoon family in 1884, remains. The Parsis have had a particular role in Mumbai history: originating from Persia centuries back, driven out as religious followers of Zarathustra by the conquering Arabs, they thrived under British rule as traders, brokers, landowners and philantropists – a tradition that continues with the modern Tata business dynasty. The total number of Parsis in the city has dwindled to about 90,000. Today they feature in the city guidebooks principally for the seven Towers of Silence on Malabar Hill where traditionally the Parsi dead are laid for their bones to be cleaned by vultures, to avoid pollution of the sacred elements of air, water, earth and fire. (Recent practice has shifted to electric crematoria and concrete coffins.) Another wave of Persian immigrants about a century ago established the city's charming, old fashioned Irani cafes (their classic mutton pulao with tart red berries is especially delicious), but these too are in decline and only about thirty remain.

Separate provision for religious groups has been part of the city's history. Some housing schemes – both the 19th century chawls and the later colonies – were built for Parsis or Muslims or others. In the 19th century separate gymkhanas – the word for a sporting club – for well-off Catholics, Parsis, Hindus and Muslims were built near each other on the eastern sea front; along with the Ladies Gymkhana, initially for European women only but later – after a 1905 visit by the Princess of Wales – opened to women of all communities.

In recent years ethnic and linguistic differences among the Mumbai population have, as much as religion, caused aggravation. About 60% of the population are Maharashtrians, that is, born in the state of Maharashtra of which Mumbai is the capital. Its official language is Marathi, Hinduism is their dominant religion. There are, though, sizeable groups originating from other Indian states, notably a fifth of the population from Gujerat. Sixteen major languages are spoken in the city: apart from Marathi, the most common are Hindi, Gujerati and English, this last common in business. Since the mid 1980s Mumbai politics has been dominated by Maharashtrian interests, in the form of the right wing, nativist Shiv Shena party, which alone or with coalition partners has ruled the city. It was they who in 1996 renamed the city from Bombay to Mumbai along with renaming many roads and places in the city to remove associations with the British Raj and, in cases, with Islam. At this time the Victoria Terminus, the main railway station built by the British in 1887, became Chhatrapati Shivaji Terminus (CST for short) in honour of a historic Marathi warlord. Marathi language teaching also became compulsory in schools. Language emerged again as a hot political issue in 2010 when some local politicians floated proposals for language tests in Marathi for taxi drivers in the city. The barely hidden agenda here was a further clampdown on immigrants.

In Mumbai's modern economy class is the growing social distinction. Everywhere you see evidence of India's expanding middle class:– in the high-rise apartment blocks with quarters for maids and cooks, the new suburban housing further north or across the bay in Navi Mumbai, the rising vehicle ownership, the fashionable young people in clubs and cafes, the multiplex cinemas, mobile phones, the new shopping centres replete with global consumer brands. This expansion is a product of the high rate of economic growth in the last two decades, offering well-paid work – as managers, entrepreneurs, movie people, professionals – to well-educated Indians. But Mumbai's middle class is at most a quarter of its population. Above them, at the tip of the class pyramid, is a smaller number of the super-rich closely connected to global society and the global economy – equally at home in, some even with homes in, Paris, London, Cape Town, New York or Los Angeles. Malabar Hill, overlooking the Arabian Sea on the east side of the city, has been the favoured neighbourhood for Mumbai's rich almost since the city was founded. Its Raj bungalows have now been largely replaced by apartment blocks. One recent addition is a new home for India's richest man Mukesh Ambani plus his wife and three children: an astonishing twenty seven storey tower with domestic and guest suites, a swimming pool, health club, ballroom, hanging gardens, nine lifts, three helicopter pads, and parking for 160 vehicles – estimated cost £630 million, number of staff 600.[7]

But the vast majority of Mumbaikars are at the bottom of the class pyramid. Many are ill-educated, underemployed or unemployed, living in tiny spaces (often no bigger than a rich man's SUV, to make a telling comparison) in shanties or on the streets, often far from workplaces, prone to illnesses like typhoid, malaria and jaundice. And, above all, poor. Dharavi is the best known of the shantytowns, in part from being featured in the Oscar-winning movie *Slumdog Millionaire* (2009).

Dharavi

Dharavi, in the middle of Mumbai, is home to one million people, spread over 175 hectares, flanked by railway lines. It is a maze of narrow alleyways, running between one and two storey shanties, with electricity cables overhead, water pipes below. A typical family home might be 4 square metres in which people cook, work and sleep, maybe paying 200 rupees (£2.50) rent a month. Many single men and women live in dormitories over their workplaces. Toilets are communal and flow into open sewers. There are shops and some services, including a school (with children in their neat uniforms) and two banks. Everywhere there are posters for local politicians claiming the support of residents. But the surprise of Dharavi is its economy. Traditional skills were brought by immigrants establishing workshops for bricks, pots, leather goods, vehicle repair, toys, tailoring, cloth dyeing, baking, and soap making. But the big local business is recycling. Here are workshops that crunch plastic, cutting it into postage stamp-sized pieces, washing and drying it before compressing it into pellets for reuse; others taking used oil drums, cleaning them, knocking out the dents, burning off old labels and selling them back to manufacturers; yet others destapling cardboard boxes, turning them inside out to conceal the printing and reselling them as new packaging. Altogether there are 15,000 workshops in Dharavi, some owned by entrepreneurs living elsewhere (you can see their BMWs parked, and guarded, on the outskirts), employing a quarter million people at wages mostly above the national average, and turning over an estimated £700 million annually. The Mumbai municipality has a redevelopment scheme for Dharavi providing housing in apartment blocks, parks, schools and roads, but offering resettlement only to those living here from before 2000, eliminating polluting industries and releasing some of the site for private residential and commercial development. The residents are opposed.

There are, within the classes, many fine occupational distinctions. Caste, a social attribute inherited at birth among Hindus, still underlies some of them. Traditionally the distinction has been between *Brahmins* (priests and teachers),

Kshatryas (rulers and warriors), *Vaishyas* (merchants and cultivators) and *Shudras* (menials); below these four are *Dalits* (whose jobs involve contact with dirt or death such as undertakers, leather workers or cleaners). In *Maximum City* Suketa Mehta, returning to the city from living in New York, observes 'the caste system of the servants: the live-in maid won't clean the floors; that is for the "free servant" to do. Neither of them will do the bathrooms, which are the exclusive domain of the *bhangi*, who does nothing else. The driver won't wash the car; that is the monopoly of the building watchman. The flat ends up swarming with servants.'[8]

Whatever their religion, ethnicity, language, class, caste or occupation, one thing many Mumbaikars have in common is that they are immigrants from outside the city. Mumbai's population grew by about fifteen million over the last half century. Some of these new people were the children of Mumbai families, but most were new arrivals in the city. Many are single men, come to work and often leaving families behind, giving the city a high male to female ratio. Talk to most Mumbaikars – both rich and poor – and they will soon tell you their roots are elsewhere. Pandit Nehru, India's first post-independence leader, had a vision of India as a nation of villages, but it has turned into a nation of cities – though with strong links back to the villages where city people return to visit relatives and attend celebrations. Mumbai is also a city from which people emigrate: richer people to work in business and the professions (notably as software engineers in the USA), poorer people to work in construction or domestic service (especially in the Gulf states). These are the NRIs (Non-Resident Indians) – India has the second largest diaspora in the world after China. So Mumbai's social mosaic has links back to the Indian countryside and out to the world overseas.

Underworld and overworld

In recent years the 'Mumbai novel' has flourished. The critic Soutik Biswas comments: 'Bangalore may be a kinetic technology hub teeming with expatriates and bright young Indians, Calcutta a decaying dowager brimming with a million stories, and Delhi the capital where power meets noir. But cosmopolitan, energetic and chaotic Mumbai, where the rich live cheek-by-jowl with the poor, is the city where the story-tellers… are turning for inspiration and fodder.'[9]

This is not an entirely new trend. Since 1964 H R F Keating (though an Englishman) has written a series of detective novels set in Bombay, now Mumbai, where Inspector Ganesh Ghote must struggle against bureaucracy, the indifference of his colleagues and the protective self-interest of rich and powerful people in order to solve the crimes. And Salman Rushdie's famous *Midnight's Children* (1981) and *The Moor's Last Sigh* (1995), both international best sellers, were in part set in Mumbai. More recently Vikram Chandra's *Sacred Games* (2006) – a mix of social reportage, crime fiction and Bollywood movie plotline – dissected the nexus in Mumbai between wealth, power and crime with corruption as the adhesive.

Vikram Chandra's *Sacred Games*

The book tells of a cat and mouse game between gang boss Ganesh Gaitonde and Detective Sartoj Singh, who is determined to bring him to justice. Both are singular Mumbai characters. Gaitonde is the boss of G Company, one of the city's leading gangs, involved in many crimes and rackets, protected by tough bodyguards, his affairs managed by crooked accountants and lawyers, with the assistance of compliant politicians and bureaucrats and a favoured guru. He mostly stays abroad, moving around the world– from Moscow to Dubai, from LA to Frankfurt, and offshore on his luxury yacht – using false identities in pursuit of criminal endeavours, but also to keep prosecutors and, more importantly, murderous rivals at bay. Singh is the only Sikh inspector in the Mumbai police, recognisable by his turban, beard and the sharp cut of his trousers, his marriage over, past forty years old and with his career on the slide. His pursuit of Gaitonde is unsuccessful, frustrated by his superiors and their political bosses. But finally an anonymous tip-off leads him to an underground bunker in north Mumbai where Gaitonde is, on his return to the city, holed up with the Bollywood star Jojo with whom he has become infatuated. His crazed suicide robs Singh of his prize.

Mumbai has a big underworld of organised crime. Its revenues come from protection rackets, extortion, kidnapping and ransom, counterfeiting, currency deals, gambling, bootlegging, prostitution and drugs. To secure and safeguard this income there are gangs ready to inflict damage and death on any who get in the way, including rival gangs. You get regular reports of their exploits in the press and on radio and TV. Behind the gangs is a support system of doctors, lawyers, arms dealers, scouts, money launderers and people running safe houses. This underworld is controlled by an overworld, that is, by bosses mostly located outside Mumbai, even outside India, often in Dubai or Karachi. These criminal organisations call themselves 'companies', which is appropriate to their sophisticated nature. Occasionally gang members are brought to justice, very rarely are their bosses.

Such crime flourishes in Mumbai for a number of reasons. The police are underpaid and undermanned, sometimes corrupt or brutal, often prepared to turn a blind eye. The judicial process is bureaucratic and slow, so the criminals can provide an alternative justice system to which people turn, resolving in weeks – through violence or the threat of it – disputes that would take years in the courts. And politicians, who in a democracy like India need votes, will sometimes strike covert deals with criminal elements in their constituencies. In this context it is unsurprising that some gangs are expanding into more legitimate business like property development and entertainment. Most Bollywood productions don't get bank loans, they are financed privately. Here is an opportunity for the underworld to convert black money into white – and the crime stories that are one of the staples of movie plots flatter the bosses too.

In transition

Every day on the Maidans, the strip of parkland that runs through South Mumbai, you can see serious cricket matches underway. The pitches are well-maintained, the players wear immaculate whites, they change and wait in timber or tented pavilions. The teams have a mix of names, all in English. Some seemingly reference hangovers from the British Raj (for example, Lord Northbank Cricket Club, Fort Vijay), others are seemingly vernacular (Prabhu Joly Yarn Cricketers, Muslim United, Shree Lads), yet others sound as if invented by a modern PR consultant (Young Achievers, Parsee Cyclists). This variety of names illustrates Mumbai's complex relationship with the English language: as the language of its former colonial rulers (still evident in the nomenclature of the city despite the political enthusiasm for renaming), as the present-day lingua franca in a city of diverse ethnicities (Mumbai has four English newspapers), and as the essential language – Globish, some call it – of global business, politics, media and consumerism.

This linguistic connection to both tradition and modernity is mirrored in other ways. Take forms of greeting: *namaste* with modest bows among adults but high fives among their kids. Take clothing: in Mumbai you will observe people wearing traditional *dhotis* or loose tunics and trousers for the men, saris or *hajibs* for the women, but also T shirts and jeans on both sexes, backpacks and baseball caps, schoolchildren in neat uniforms, business men in suits or well-groomed women in designer dresses and well-cut trousers from the pages of Indian *Vogue*. Or take food: the city's eating places – from its street stalls to its high-class restaurants – are mostly serving traditional Indian food, itself very varied, but increasingly you'll find the new global imports like burgers, pizzas, pastries, cappuccinos and cocktails. And take personal transport: here the city offers the full gamut of old and new public transport with auto-rickshaws, taxis, the trains, buses (including some London style double-deckers) and the start of a Metro system to serve the airport, and for private transport there are bicycles and motorbikes and growing numbers of cars, and some SUVs for the super rich.

Mumbai is a city in transition from a colonial past to a global future. The elements of its past, present and future are all there, juxtaposed. Just as other contrasted elements – its various faiths and ethnicities, its formal and informal economy, its rich and poor people, its decent homes and its slums, its comforts and its chaos – coexist within the city. Mumbai's continued growth is expected: by 2025 it may be the world's second most populous city (after Tokyo) and the eleventh largest urban economy (measured by Gross Domestic Product).[10] As it rises up the rank of world cities, all its characteristic divergences will adjust, hopefully to become a more equal, more tolerant, and more orderly city.

6.

Images and narratives: artists' cities

Marrakesh 2004. We have come here in pursuit of Islamic culture, after previous encounters in Andalucia and Sicily which had both been, in the Middle Ages, under Arab rule. So we visit the Koutoubia Mosque, the Ben Youssef Mosque, the Saadian Tombs, the remains of the El Badi Palace and the Menara Garden, the ramparts and the gates. But it is something else that really bowls me over – the look, the sound, the smell of the place. To start with there is that bright, clear African light and with it the awareness that just beyond the Atlas Mountains, visible to the south of the city, lies the Sahara Desert. And that light illuminates the glorious colours of the buildings, their tiling, the carpets and clothing – no wishy washy pastels or lurid technicolour here, just strong but muted ochres with occasional flashes of emerald green or cobalt blue. Many artists – Matisse, Klee, Macke – have captured these colours in their paintings of the cities of North Africa. But the smells and sounds escaped them. The smells are mainly of food, most especially from the stalls in the great square of Djemma El Fna and from the spices on sale in the souk, but also the smell of leather and cedar from workshops. The sounds are of animated conversations, water sellers' bells, braying animals and the muezzin's calls from the mosque. All these – the colours, the smells, the sounds – are not contrived for the visitor, rather they are just part of daily life. They make Marrakesh the most sensuous city I know.

Subjects and settings

In presenting the Turkish writer Orhan Pamuk with the 2006 Nobel Prize for Literature, the Swedish Academy declared that in his writing he had made his native city of Istanbul 'an indispensable literary territory, equal to Dostoevsky's St Petersburg, Joyce's Dublin or Proust's Paris – a place where readers from all corners of the world can live another life, just as credible as their own, filled by an alien feeling that they immediately recognise as their own.'[1] Other authors and cities might have been named: Dickens' London, Kafka's Prague, Lawrence Durrell's Alexandria, Salman Rushdie's Mumbai. What these writers provide in their books is not just a narrative and characters situated within a city, but that and more in creating a strong, believable sense of city life in that place and time. For them the city is not just the setting but is, in part, the subject of the novel.

Novels use various literary devices to create these portraits of a city. Most common is a diverse set of characters whose lives interweave. Often these characters' fortunes are contrasted in terms of success, wealth and status. Some rise, some fall and their social journeys may be mirrored in their relocation from one part of the city to another, so that districts of different social character take on a symbolic importance. This is very true of Dickens' London novels like *Bleak House* and *Our Mutual Friend*, and of Balzac's Paris novels in his *Comédie Humaine* series. Sometimes the social observation of city life is made through a protagonist who is an outsider, new to the city or socially marginal, like the social climbing Becky Sharpe in Thackeray's *Vanity Fair* or the student Raskolnikov in Dostoevsky's *Crime and Punishment*. Another device is the chronicle of events focused on a central character over a short period of time – a day, a week, a month, a year. James Joyce's *Ulysses* is the epitome: it reports, through 250,000 words in what was then a groundbreaking stream of consciousness technique full of puns, parodies and allusions, the passage through Dublin of Leopold Bloom on June 16th 1904 encountering, in his wandering, musing, boozing and whoring, Stephen Daedulus, Molly Bloom and a cast of other characters.

There are also painters and photographers who have captured the essential character of particular cities at particular times. We have a strong sense of the look of the Dutch cities in their 17th century Golden Age, especially Amsterdam, Delft and Haarlem, from paintings of cityscapes and domestic interiors which portray emblematic versions of everyday life there. Canaletto's topographical paintings of 18th century Venice show a cityscape that we can still recognise today. Hogarth's 18th century paintings of London life ranged from characterful portraits of the rich and famous in elegant interiors to riff-raff in bawdy brothels and riotous street scenes. In some cases he combined such scenes in a series of moralising paintings telling ironically of *Marriage a la Mode* or *A Rake's Progress*.

In the modern period a succession of artistic movements drew inspiration from city life. In the late 19th century the French Impressionists created a lasting image of Paris. For the later Cubists – breaking up, analysing and reassembling subjects in abstracted forms, and often depicting them from a multitude of viewpoints – the geometry and perspective of the cityscape offered attractive subjects. In the 1920s the Russian Constructivists and the Italian Futurists, in their different ways, celebrated industry and the city as the apogees of modernity. But among these avant-gardes of the early 20th century, it was the Expressionists – creating an art of subjective feeling – who engaged most fully with city life. These artists worked particularly in Berlin. Here Ernst Ludwig Kirchner, Georg Grosz and Emil Nolde created intensely emotional portraits

Ernst Ludwig Kirchner's *Potsdamer Platz* 1914

of the city and its people, focusing especially on workers, street vendors, prostitutes and the capitalists, profiteers, spivs and soldiers who exploited them – like Hogarth, their work was political. In Kirchner's *Potsdamer Platz*, 'in the foreground stand two streetwalkers of different ages, both 'ladylike' as police regulations demanded; behind them hover black-suited men, anonymous, faceless. The triangle of the pavement, its shape echoed by the striding legs of the male figures, is thrust like a lance between the converging streets towards the round traffic island, where the female figures present themselves as if on a revolving stage. The combination of forms, round and pointed, has clear sexual connotations.'[2]

In the mid 20th century street photography began to complement painting as a visual medium for compelling city portraits. The introduction of smaller, handheld cameras and cartridge film spools brought a new mobility to photography, for which the street scene provided an appealing subject. Some early photographers produced photo-books which connected images of the city into a narrative, much like a documentary film. But, for the most part, it was the new, popular, illustrated magazines like *Picture Post*, *Life* and *Paris-Match* that provided their outlets. Paris and New York were the cities where such photography first flourished; today it is universal. Street photography celebrates the interest and beauty of everyday city life. A key tenet is to capture the spontaneity of the 'decisive moment' – a stolen kiss, a passer-by's critical glance, children at play, a meditative solo drinker, even a murdered corpse. Some deception to hide the photographer's intention from the subject may be needed to achieve this. The telephoto lens is an obvious aid, but there are others: Paul Brand had a trick camera that shot to the side; Paul Martin disguised his camera in a satchel; Henri Cartier-Bresson would wrap a large handkerchief around his camera and pretend to be blowing his nose while he took the picture. Today some street photographers eschew such deceptions, believing that an interaction, even confrontation, between them and their subjects adds veracity to the image – an attitude taken to its extreme by paparazzi photographers, snapping celebrities on the town.

Film fuses the novelistic and photographic traditions to tell stories with both words and images. In doing so it can readily capture the complexity and dynamism of the modern city, through combining sound and vision, shooting on location, enhancing natural light, adding soundtracks, by editing and montage. The culture critic Walter Benjamin observed effusively that, before the advent of film, 'Our taverns and our metropolitan streets, our offices and furnished rooms, our railroad stations and our factories appeared to have us locked up hopelessly. Then came the film and burst this prison-world asunder by the dynamite of the tenth of a second, so that now, in the midst of its far flung ruins and debris, we calmly and adventurously go travelling.'[3] Many of the most admired and remembered films have been firmly rooted in particular cities, reinforcing their iconic quality. *The Worldwide Guide to Movie Locations*[4] gives Los Angeles as the most common movie locale with over 300 entries, London and New York equal second, followed by Paris. Some cities have, for a time, become associated with particular distinct genres, such as the London-based Ealing Comedies of the late 1940s and early 1950s; Rome, Milan and Naples and the neo-realism of the 1950s; the Paris of the *Nouvelle Vague* in the 1960s; or John Woo's Hong Kong action films of the 1980s and 90s. Other cities have been filmed in very contrasting ways, even in the same period: take New York in the 1970s and compare Martin Scorsese's rough and tough *Mean Streets* (1973) and *Taxi Driver* (1976) with Woody Allen's celebratory *Manhattan* (1979) – hard to believe it's the same city.

Decades, or even centuries later, these powerful painted, literary, photographic or film portraits persist in shaping present day images of their cities. The French critic Baudrillard wrote of the 'feeling you get when you step out of an Italian or Dutch gallery into the city that seems the very reflection of the paintings you have just seen, as if the city had come out of the paintings and not the other way round...[likewise] the American city seems to have stepped right out of the movies.'[5] More prosaically, American Airlines has used an advertising pitch: 'You've seen the movie, now visit the sets.' James Joyce claimed that *Ulysses* gave a picture of Dublin so complete that if the city suddenly one day disappeared from the earth it could be reconstructed from his book. That book has also become a tourist resource for the city – June 16th is celebrated annually as Bloomsday and a map and guide for explorers of Bloom's 29 kilometre odyssey are available. You can similarly take tours of Kafka's Prague and Dickens' London.

Low life

Like film, crime fiction is a modern genre. In its initial form – as pioneered by Edgar Allan Poe in the USA and developed in Britain by Wilkie Collins, Arthur Conan Doyle, Agatha Christie and Dorothy Sayers – it presented an orderly society in which crime was an aberration. The crime might be a murder in the vicarage or on a country estate, likely the act of a single deranged or avaricious person, and the detective solves the crime using powers of observation and deduction beyond the reader's ability. The popular board game Cluedo captures this well. Later, crime fiction took a new turn. For writers like Dashiell Hammett and Raymond Chandler, crime was not just an aberrant act but a pervasive feature of life, more particularly life in the city. The city's politicians, landowners, police and capitalists were all corrupt, in cahoots with the criminal class. The modern detective is then not just engaged mentally in puzzle solving; he or she must mix it with people of all classes, be traduced, get beaten up,

---

Some detective's cities (and their creators)

Baltimore – Detective Jimmy McNulty in the TV series The Wire (David Simon)

Boston – Detective Jerry Kennedy (George V Higgins)

Chicago – Detective V.I.Warshawski, prototype of the tough woman cop (Sara Paretsky)

Edinburgh – Detective Sergeant John Rebus (Ian Rankin)

Istanbul – Inspector Ikmen (Barbara Nadel)

Italian cities – Dottore Aurelio Zen, each book in a different city (Michael Dibdin)

Los Angeles – Private eyes Philip Marlowe (Raymond Chandler) and Lew Archer (Ross MacDonald) and many others, including the African-American Detective Jerry Rawlins (Walter Mosley) and Sergeant Jo Friday in Dragnet on radio and TV (Jack Webb)

Moscow – Chief Investigator Arkady Renko in novels based in the Soviet era (Martin Cruz Smith)

Mumbai – Inspector Ghote (H R F Keating)

New York – Detective Steve Corella of the 87th precinct (Ed McBain) and Detective Sergeant Andy Sipowitz and colleagues in TV's NYPD Blue (Steve Bochco and David Milch)

Oxford – Inspector Morse (Colin Dexter)

Paris – Commissaire Maigret in over 100 novels and many film and TV adaptations (Georges Simenon)

Shanghai – Chief Inspector Chen investigating political scandals in contemporary China (Qiu Xiaolong)

Venice – Commissario Brunetti (Donna Leon)

drugged and shot at – in Raymond Chandler's much-quoted phrase 'Down these mean streets a man must go who is not himself mean, who is neither tarnished nor afraid.'[6] And he or she may come away without solving anything very much. But along the way the city's landscape and life gets described and dissected, often very laconically. Originating in the USA, this urban version of detective fiction is now dominant across the world – in writing, film and on TV – and many cities have their local detective, often appearing in a succession of stories.

Some of this crime fiction has provided source material for *film noir*, a descriptive term for a large number of films made over the last sixty and more years, from the *Maltese Falcon* of 1941 – for some the original exemplar – to more recent films like *LA Confidential* in 1997 and *Hidden* in 2005. The definition of *film noir* is contested among cinéastes: is it a distinct genre? Is it exclusively a Hollywood form? Was true *noir* no longer made after the late 1950s? What is less in doubt are the common characteristics of visual style, narrative and theme in these films. Visually, they owe a lot to German Expressionism, imported into Hollywood by emigré directors of the 1930s and 40s – chiaroscuro lighting with deep shadows, oblique camera angles and unbalanced compositions, a fascination with reflections and shadows. The narrative is frequently subjective, first person, with voiceovers and flashbacks. Their themes often involve a male investigator, a *femme fatale* or two, corrupt politicians or profiteers, maybe some foreign or racial outsiders, all tied together in a labyrinthine plot. Anyone familiar with *The Third Man,* the much-loved 1949 film written by Graham Greene and directed by Carol Reed, will recognise many of these qualities. It also exemplifies the essentially urban scenario of most *film noir*, in this case a stunning realisation of the sleazy world of post-World War Two Vienna, wonderfully captured in the opening scene with the voiceover, images of the war-torn city and the famous, unsettling zither music.

At the heart of most *film noir*, as in *The Third Man*, is a struggle between good and evil. The city is more than an incidental setting for these moral dramas. Urban life with its complexities, randomness, disorder and menace is presented as a net in which the story's characters are trapped, sometimes struggling to break free and do right, more often passively accepting their fate or seeking to exploit their circumstances. And the filmed cityscape – hard-edged, often seen at night or in fog or rain, maze-like, in turns concealing and revealing the action – provides stunning complementary images that express the pessimistic moral ambiguity of the storyline.

Soundtracks

Along with film, pop music is the other form of modern entertainment loved around the world. Its expansion was eased by a range of technological innovations in music reproduction, from the initial vinyl records played on a gramophone, to the extended play of the LP, then the substitution of the cassette tape, followed by the CD, with the concomitant mobility of the Walkman, and latterly the further miniaturisation and portability of the iPod downloads. The last half century has seen the explosive growth of pop into a global business, fragmented into myriad genres – rhythm and blues (R & B), rock 'n' roll, country music, dance, reggae, soul, samba, calypso, hip-hop, rap and more. Musically they share a strong rhythmic base derived from African roots.

All these forms were intimately tied to cities where they grew and flourished. They are part of a universal, mass culture and it is among the urban population round the world that their big markets are to be found. Cities are also where the creative and entrepreneurial performers, producers, clubs and dance halls, DJs and radio stations are based. Beyond that, the content of the music frequently takes its inspiration from the highs and lows of city life, especially among the young. For confirmation, look at some pop music videos and see how often city life features in them: skyscrapers, traffic, crowds, city lights, and usually some dancing in the streets thrown in. Indeed 'urban music' is now a term for an eclectic mix of soul, hip-hop, R & B, dance and reggae, appealing particularly to black audiences.

Samba, the dominant dance music of Brazil, originated among the descendants of African slaves in Bahia, northeast Brazil, then developed strongly in Rio de Janeiro in the early 20th century and has evolved many sub-forms since, including jazz-influenced bossa nova – of which 1963's *The Girl from Ipanema* captured a worldwide audience. Samba schools were established and still feature strongly in Rio's annual Carnival parades. Highlife music, characterised by jazzy horns and multiple guitars, started in Accra in Ghana, spread to Sierra Leone and Nigeria in the 1920s and since to other West African countries. Reggae originated in Kingston, Jamaica in the 1960s, popularised for a world audience by Bob Marley and the Wailers. Hip-hop was developed in New York in the 1970s predominantly by African-Americans and Latinos. It's not just a music genre – of which record scratching and rapping are part – but also a wider culture involving graffiti, breakdancing and videos. In apartheid era South Africa, the black townships had lively music scenes, developing a wide range of genres, of which the choral singing of Ladysmith Black Mambazo gained international attention from the 1980s onwards.

The origins of rock 'n' roll, today's most universal form of pop, can be traced to Memphis, Tennessee. Here in the 1950s two strains of folk music – the Afro-American blues of the Mississippi Delta and the white country music of the Appalachians – were fused by local musicians. The product was taken up by independent record labels and radio DJs and Bill Haley, Buddy Holly, Little Richard, Chuck Berry and, above all, Elvis Presley burst upon the world. Peter Hall, in his book *Cities in Civilisation*, ranks Memphis with Hollywood and Silicon Valley as key sites in which cultural creativity and technological innovation were joined to create the 20th century's media revolutions.[7] In the subsequent history of rock, other cities have become dominant at different times: Detroit for the Motown label that successfully steered black artists into the mainstream, Liverpool for The Beatles and the Mersey Sound, Seattle for hard rock 'grunge'. Local versions of rock music exist around the world, wherever its influence has crept into youth culture – Japanese rock, French rock, Russian rock, mostly considered risible outside their home countries. Pop music, born in the cities, now provides the soundtrack for city life – in homes and clubs, of course, but also piped into stores, cafes and foyers, spilling out of doorways and car windows, and played in the streets on Walkmans, iPods, smartphones and ghetto blasters.

Fantastical cities

The city is a perfect subject for artistic fantasy. It brings together diverse characters, situations and actions that can be given extreme expression. And the media of novels, film, cartoon and computer graphics serve it well. The fantasy may be a distorted version of present reality, an imagined future or an excavation of the past in the present. All three are ways of providing commentary on the contemporary city.

Distortions of reality are most powerfully achieved graphically. It may be as a printed cartoon strip, or the extended version in a graphic novel, or as the animated cartoon in film, video or computer games. In the last two decades Frank Miller's series of cartoons (some later filmed) has presented *Sin City* as a distinctive urban terrain of The Projects, The Docks, the Old Town, and the Sacred Oaks suburb, where several organisations, including the paramilitary City Police Department, struggle for control of the various criminal enterprises in the city. And the *Grand Theft Auto* video games offer players themselves the chance to be criminals in three different fictional places: (a loose parody of New York), (a composite of San Francisco, Los Angeles and Las Vegas), and (Miami). Both works have all the bleakness of *film noir*, but with more overt violence.

Imagining the future has long been the exclusive domain of science fiction – apart, that is, from utopian writing. Traditionally the 'fiction' lay in dreaming up strange and surprising scenarios for a distant future, and the 'science' lay in the invented technologies that enable and shape those futures: time travel, interplanetary exploration, smart weaponry, robotics and cloning, body implants, cryonics, teleporting and more. Some of which technologies have only come real since they first appeared in fiction. Among writers, Jules Verne and H G Wells were pioneers, later Isaac Asimov and Arthur C Clarke were the most well-known exponents of these so-called 'space operas.' In film, George

Lucas's later *Star Wars* series (1977-) is the prime examples. Sci-fi in this tradition created future communities on other planets or on space stations, which were housed in megastructures, very high-tech in their specification, connected by monorails or guided vehicles, all operating with rational efficiency and orderliness. Implicit was an optimistic view of the contribution of science to progress and of the city as its ultimate expression.

There is another kind of science fiction that is more down to earth: literally so, with stories that, while still strange and surprising, are recognisably about life in our world in the present or near future. They are exploring inner space rather than outer space. From the 1950s to the 1970s, Philip K Dick wrote

Sci-fi city of the future

novels and short stories in which the main characters often discover that their everyday world is actually an illusion constructed by powerful forces of business or government. It was his story *Do Androids Dream of Electric Sheep?* (1968) that was the source for the 1982 film *Blade Runner*. Also filmed was his *Minority Report* (1956), in which dehumanised 'precogs' are used to predict crimes not yet committed. In William Gibson's later *Neuromancer* (1984), brain-damaged, drug-addicted Henry Case is recruited to hack into computer systems at the corporate headquarters of a media conglomerate Sense/Net and the plot develops from there. More recently, in Jeff Vandermeer's *Veniss Underground* (2003) the protagonist embarks on an epic journey through the city's many underground levels in search of a stolen lover. In various ways these writers were exploring social issues arising from electronic communication, virtual reality, environmental degradation, genetic engineering, ever-present surveillance, media saturation, failing governance and the power of global corporations, often long before these had entered popular consciousness or arrived on political agendas. Their mood is pessimistic, in contrast to the optimism of the space operas, and the setting for their stories is urban – indeed the term 'urban fantasy' is sometimes applied to their work. The action in *Neuromancer* takes place in the Sprawl, an urbanised world that seemingly spreads all over the globe. *Veniss Underground* sets the scene with 'Back a decade when the social planners ruled, we called it Dayton Central. Then, when the central government choked flat and the police all went freelance, we started calling it *Veniss* – like an adder's hiss, deadly and unpredictable.'[8]

In contrast to science fiction, psychogeography sees the past, not the future, in the present city. Its precise definition as a genre is elusive but, as its name suggests, it is an attempt to capture the otherworldly spirit of place in the city.[9] Its development is largely a tale of two cities: London and Paris. In London the early tradition includes Defoe's fictional reconstruction of the city in his *Journal of the Plague Year* (1722), De Quincey's drug-fuelled wanderings in *Confessions of an English Opium Eater* (1821) and Stevenson's parable of the city's double life in *The Strange Case of Dr Jekyll and Mr Hyde* (1886). In Paris it is the poets Baudelaire and Rimbaud and the surrealists Breton and Aragon that the tradition embraces. Today, psychogeography is principally a London genre again. Peter Ackroyd has written a series of novels, biographies (including those of Londoners Blake, Dickens and T S Eliot) and portraits of the city in which the past is always evident in the present, affecting the lives, the behaviour, the speech, even the gestures of the people living there. Iain Sinclair has also written of London in poems and novels, as well as documentary studies and films, which mix observation, occult imagination and local London history with a dash of paranoia that matches the spirit of both the earlier London visionaries and the Parisian surrealists.

The most original voice among modern urban fantasists is that of the novelist J G Ballard. His work might be regarded as psychogeography or science fiction or surrealism. He often focuses on cities but not on their traditional cores, rather on the suburban hinterlands of motorways, superstores, airports, industrial parks, multiplex cinemas, reservoirs, high-rise blocks and gated housing. Here he sets tales of unexpected, bizarre and frequently violent behaviour, punctuating the prevailing boredom and seemingly provoked by these cityscapes. In his most notorious novel *Crash* (1972), the protagonist Vaughan cruises the freeways around Heathrow Airport calculatedly causing accidents, in order to scar his body and engage in perverted sex with crash victims, obsessionally hoping for a head-on collision with the film star Elizabeth Taylor.

Cities of memory

Artistic portraits of cities combine reportage and invention. This is as evident in Hogarth's London paintings as in Raymond Chandler's Los Angeles detective fiction or Woody Allen's Manhattan movies. In *Soft City*, his 1974 book of essays on London life, Jonathan Raban argues that writing about cities should combine observation and imagination, arguing that 'cities, unlike villages and small towns, are plastic by nature. We mould them in our images: they, in their turn, shape us by the resistance they offer when we try to impose our own personal form on them. The city as we imagine it, the soft city of illusion, myth, aspiration, nightmare, is as real, maybe more real, than the hard city one can locate on maps, in statistics, in monographs on urban sociology and demography and architecture.'[10] For this reason memory is often a potent force shaping artists' responses to cities. It may be the personal memory of the writer, painter, musician or filmmaker or it may be that artist's take on a collective memory shared by a community.

Alexandria in Egypt has been called 'the city of memory'[11] – or rather 'city of memories' since writers have offered us different portraits of the city. It sprung to prominence in the 1950s when Lawrence Durrell, an emigré

English writer, wrote a series of novels known as *The Alexandria Quartet* that were critically acclaimed bestsellers. In them he told the stories of the complex lives and loves of a cast of characters living in Alexandria before and during World War Two. The books' stylistic novelty was to present the same events again and again from the perspectives of different protagonists – Justine, Balthazar, Mountolive and Clea – whose names each provide the title of one of the books. Durrell claimed to be playing here with Einsteinian concepts of space and time and with Freudian concepts of personality, so as to reveal the layers in the narrative and the city setting in which his characters were trapped.

Alexandria was an appropriate choice for such an account. For unlike Athens or Rome with their monuments, little physical remains in Alexandria as evidence of its past, as created by the Greeks, the Romans (including Mark Anthony, infamous for his love affair with Cleopatra), the Byzantines, the Arabs and the modern European exiles who were drawn to it in the 19th and 20th century. Rather, in the absence of artefacts, it is all intimation – as Balthazar in Durrell's book says, 'The city, half-imagined (but wholly real), begins and ends in us, roots lodged in our memory.'[12] This mood of dreamy recollection is also found in the poetry of Constantine Cavafy, a Greek civil servant who spent much of his life in Alexandria early in the 20th century. The city, its past and present, is a recurrent theme in his work. For him Alexandria also serves as a metaphor for a mood of sadness, failure and regret, from which there is no escape, most evident in his poem *The City*.

Both Durrell and Cavafy had a modern European take on the city, occasionally recognising its Hellenistic origins, but with a colonialist disregard of its Arab history or indeed its predominantly Arab population. Other modern Egyptian writers have brought a different perspective on Alexandria as a city of memory. Naguib Mahfouz, winner of the 1988 Nobel Prize for Literature, used techniques similar to those of Durrell to portray the city in the 1960s in his 1978 novel *Miramar*. Later, Edward el-Kharrat offered in his two novels *City of Saffron* (1989) and *Girls of Alexandria* (1993) a fictionalised memoir of his early life as Mikha'il, a Coptic Christian, in the 1930s and 40s. Each of his chapters starts with an image of some place or event from the past, rather as if it has been rummaged from a box of old photos. This image, and the memories it provokes, serves as a point of departure for stories of his life in the city: as a schoolboy, his family life and neighbourhood mates, his sexual yearnings and encounters, the films and books he enjoys, news stories, his political activism that leads to

Constantine Cavafy's *The City*[13]

You tell yourself: I'll be gone
To some other land, some other sea,
To a city lovelier far than this
Could even have been or hoped to be –
Where every step now tightens the noose:
A heart in a body buried and out of use
How long, how long must I be here
Confined among these dreary purlieus
Of the common mind? Wherever now I look
Black ruins of my life rise into view.
So many years have I been here
Spending and squandering, and nothing gained.
There's no new land, my friend, no
New sea; for the city will follow you,
In the same streets you'll wander endlessly,
The same mental suburbs slip from youth to age,
In the same house go white at last –
The city is a cage.
No other places, always this
Your earthly landfall, and no ship exists
To take you from yourself. Ah! Don't you see
Just as you've ruined your life in this
One plot of ground you've ruined its worth
Everywhere now – over the whole earth?

a period in jail, his struggle to find rewarding work. Through all this he cannot stop talking about Alexandria as 'a blue-white marble city woven and rewoven by my heart upon whose frothing incandescent countenance my heart is ever floating.'[14]

From this tradition, one literary historian claims that 'the mystery of modern Alexandria seems to be not in what it actually is or was at any given moment but in its power to stimulate – as perhaps no other city in this [20th] century – the creation of poetic cities cast in its image, cities that imitate it as it can be, or even ought to be, in its essence.'[15] This may be so. But modern writers, painters, photographers, filmmakers and other artists have found inspiration in many other cities. In truth, every city in the world is a memorial, the repository of stories and myths, recollections and dreams, in the images and narratives fashioned for us by artists.

7.

Energy: novelty and excess in New York

Seventh Avenue 1998. Standing outside my midtown hotel, looking up the street at the southbound vehicles for sight of my airport bus, I notice a ball arcing through the air above the six lanes of traffic. Where it comes from and where it lands are a mystery. It zigzags back and forth, getting closer and closer until I see what is going on. Two kids are walking down the sidewalks, one each side of the street. As one lobs the ball into the air over the traffic, the other must run to catch it before it lands – or strikes a passerby. They never fail. They are clearly practised and confident in this strange game. Seemingly nobody in the street – except myself – finds it a foolish prank. They just pass by. New Yorkers seem immune to all kinds of strange behaviour.

We love New York

New York is rich in signifiers – images, sounds, words that uniquely express aspects of the city. Many are recognisable around the world, like the yellow taxicabs, ticket tape parades, the Statue of Liberty, the Guggenheim Museum and, of course, the skyscrapers in Manhattan. There are also parts of the city that serve as metonyms: Wall Street for finance, Broadway for theatre, Madison Avenue for advertising, Fifth Avenue for high-end shopping, Coney Island for seaside fun. Once there was so-called Tin Pan Alley for popular music, being the name given to West 28th Street between Fifth and Sixth Avenues. The geography of New York has also given the word 'downtown' to the language.

But it is not just buildings and places that signify New York to the world. Many songs also celebrate the city. Wikipedia lists over 500 of them, most memorably *Take the A Train* (Duke Ellington's signature tune), *New York, New York* (a Frank Sinatra classic, always played after the New York Yankee's home baseball games), *Stayin' Alive* (by the Bee Gees, a hit from the 1977 movie *Saturday Night Fever*). On TV the series *Friends* and *Sex and the City,* showing

101

youngish New Yorkers with hedonistic lifestyles, have large audiences around the world. There is the *New Yorker* magazine, offering a characteristic mix of fiction, journalism, poetry, reviews and cartoons for a readership that extends far beyond the city. And there are photos of New York scenes that are widely reproduced, like that of the construction workers sitting nonchalantly eating their lunch on a girder high above the ground, Marilyn Monroe with her skirts flying up from the draught through a subway grating (actually a still from the 1955 movie *The Seven Year Itch*), or the Manhattan skyline seen from the riverside Brooklyn Promenade. Then there is the Edward Hopper painting, titled *Nighthawks*, of sad people in an all-night diner.

Marilyn in New York – in neon

Food too. There is the moniker The Big Apple, originated in horse racing circles but revived by tourism promoters in the 1970s. More precisely there are New York bagels, New York cheesecake, New York pastrami on rye sandwiches. The concept of the delicatessen – a mix of grocery and food 'to go' – probably originated here. And there is the wit and wisdom of New York taxi drivers[1] – some examples: 'There is no chivalry. For that you have to go upstate.' 'Time goes. That's it.' 'If a man keeps telling you he loves you, over and over, then something is wrong.' Above all as a signifier of the city is the 'I♥NY' logo, originally devised in 1977 for a marketing campaign for New York State but since appropriated by New York City.

Outwards and upwards

Where the Dutch established their trading post in the 1620s at the southern tip of Manhattan is now New York's financial district. Evidence of the city's origins remains in the uncharacteristic higgledy-piggledy street pattern and street names like Water Street, Exchange Place, and Pearl Street. Wall Street is on the line of the first wooden palisade built by the Dutch to defend themselves from pro-British settlers to the north. In the subsequent three and a half centuries the city spread outwards, initially northwards up Manhattan island, then across the rivers into the Bronx to the north, Queens and Brooklyn to the east, Staten Island to the south and New Jersey to the west, and later beyond the city boundaries to outlying suburbs. But New York also grew upwards, constructing higher and higher buildings at its core. So the city has grown by processes of both extension and intensification, thereby creating, in geographer Peter Hall's words, 'a new kind of city, the quintessence of the early twentieth-century metropolis, based on massive economies of central agglomeration and equally massive potential for suburban deconcentration.'[2] These processes were made possible by amazing feats of engineering and entrepreneurship.

Through the 17th and 18th centuries, New York grew slowly. British colonial rule supplanted Dutch in 1664. In 1783, when the British left after their defeat in the War of Independence, the city's population was 12,000. Thereafter, the city grew rapidly so that by the end of that 18th century its northern limit was on the line of the present Houston Street, 4 kilometres from Manhattan's tip. In 1807 a Commission for Laying out Streets and Roads in the City of New York decreed that henceforth there would be a grid of streets imposed upon the city, regardless of existing rights of way, property or topography. Its reasoning was very practical: they considered 'whether they should confine themselves to rectilinear streets, or whether they should adopt some of those supposed improvements by circles, ovals and stars, which certainly embellish a plan, whatever may be their effect as to convenience and utility... they could not but bear in mind that a city is to be composed principally of the habitations of men, and that straight-sided and right-angled houses are the most cheap to build and the most convenient to live in. The effect of these plain and simple reflections was decisive.'[3] North-south avenues were to be 30 metres wide, more closely spaced east-west streets 18 metres wide – this at a time when buildings were not expected to rise above two or three storeys. Avenues and streets were both named by number. There were a few divergences from this strict ruling: Broadway was left to wander diagonally across the grid, a few small parks crept in, Park Avenue was substituted for Fourth Avenue and Lexington and Madison Avenues were squeezed in alongside. Other boroughs later adopted a similar grid. Thus New York, at least in its most central parts, acquired not just a characteristic look but a convenient system of direction – 'Ukrainian Museum? Corner of 2nd Avenue and 12th Street.' 'Madison Square Gardens? Take the Line 6 subway to East 33rd Street, then a cross-town bus.' 'Bloomingdale's? Just two blocks south from here and then three blocks east on 60th Street. You can't miss it.'

More east-west streets were planned because it was believed they would carry the heaviest traffic between the two riverfronts. This proved a miscalculation; it was the north-south avenues that became most crowded as the city spread up Manhattan island. It was on these that public transport was introduced. Horse-drawn buses came first, followed by horse-drawn street trams on tracks down the middle of the streets. Then new kinds of transport were built over, and later under, the avenues. From the 1870s privately owned elevated railroads – known as the 'els' – were built along Second, Third, Sixth and Ninth Avenues, connecting with the new railway termini like Grand Central and Penn Stations and extending north beyond Central Park into Harlem and the Bronx. By 1890 New York had 150 kilometres of elevated railways, 420 kilometres of horse-drawn trams and 220 kilometres of horse-drawn bus lines – more public transport than London that then had three times as many residents.

It was not enough: transport was overcrowded, the streets congested and polluted by horse shit, dirt and noise from the elevated railroads. So the street railways were electrified. It was time for the city's transport to go underground. The first subway line opened in 1904, running north from City Hall to the Bronx, headlined as 'The Greatest Engineering Feat of Modern Times.' Over subsequent decades the system was extended, amalgamated with those in Brooklyn and other boroughs and brought into public ownership. Today the New York subway has nearly 400 kilometres of routes, about 450 stations, open for twenty-four hours every day of the year: it's the most extensive metro system in the world. Despite recent improvements to safety and reliability, it remains – in the words of the *Time Out* guide book – 'dirty, noisy, intimidating and initially incomprehensible.'[4] As a visitor you find the mix of local and express trains on the same lines especially confusing.

The subway was not the earliest transport to connect Manhattan Island to the other boroughs across the water. At first there were ferries, steam-driven from 1814, connecting Brooklyn across the East River, New Jersey across the Hudson River, and the Staten Island ferry, which still operates today and stars in many New York films and TV. But there were soon demands for bridges to connect the islands. Both the East and Hudson Rivers were wide and deep and their bedrock required strong foundations. Innnovative design was needed. The Brooklyn Bridge came first, opened in 1883, with its two tall towers and what was then the longest span in the world, carrying road, rail and pedestrian traffic. Numerous other bridges followed, some with taller towers and longer spans. Tunnels were the other cross-river solution. The engineering challenge was to bore them through riverbed mud and silt and to ventilate the traffic smoke and fumes. Railway and subway tunnels were built from 1900 onwards. The first tunnel for motor vehicles was the Holland Tunnel connecting lower Manhattan and New Jersey, which opened in 1927. Other tunnels followed, under both the Hudson and the East Rivers, but are not as numerous as the bridges. In time freeways were built, extending right across the city from the bridges and tunnels. This interconnection of the islands – by ferry, bridge and later tunnel – and the travel patterns they enabled led to the 1898 incorporation of the five boroughs into the City of New York; though Jersey City across the Hudson River to the west, being in another State, has remained outside. Manhattanites still speak disparagingly of their fellow citizens as 'bridge and tunnel people'.

While the spreading city was getting interconnected in these ways, in its Manhattan core it was becoming denser. Tenements (meaning tenant houses) raised residential densities to new heights. The practice of converting existing single family houses into use by two families per floor, often with additional building on the backlot, was well advanced by 1850. Thereafter developers started putting up purpose-built tenements which provided homes for poorer residents, many of them the immigrants flooding into the city. Typically tenements would be five or six storeys high, covering most of the plot, with up to eighteen rooms per floor, most getting light and ventilation from narrow airshafts in the centre of the building. They were variously called 'dumbbells', because of the floor plan shape, or 'railway flats', because the rooms were arranged linearly like carriages on a train. Most families in three or four room flats would sublet to afford the rent. By 1900 there were more than 80,000 tenements in New York City, housing more than two thirds of the total 3.4 million population. Today, you can still see them in lower Manhattan – the iron fire escapes added later to their facades are the giveaway.

It was the advent of the skyscraper from the 1870s onwards that decisively created New York's iconic cityscape. Two inventions were essential for skyscrapers: the elevator that could carry occupants above five floors and metal frame construction to replace load-bearing masonry walls. It probably also helped that New York, like most US cities, had rectangular street blocks to provide useable sites and that, uniquely, Manhattan's island character restricted its outward expansion and pushed up land values. To accommodate its booming commerce, the city grew upwards to the 'frontier in the sky.' The fourteen storey New York Tribune Building of 1875 was the first totally dependent on elevators. But it was the later use of frame structures that literally raised the roof: thirty-two storeys at the 1899 Park Row Building, forty-seven storeys at the 1907 Singer Tower, fifty-seven storeys at the 1913 Woolworth Building, called New York's 'Cathedral of Commerce.' As their names indicate many of these early skyscrapers were built as corporate headquarters. The most frenetic burst of construction was around the time of the Wall Street Crash of 1929 when the Chrysler Building and the Empire State Building, both in midtown, competed to claim the world height record. Later additions to the portfolio were the 1940 Rockefeller Centre (its cluster of towers around a plaza and its underground arcades an inspiration to later sci-fi artists), the 1952 Lever Building (the first to rise straight-sided without setbacks that zoning ordinances had hitherto required), the 1953 HQ for the United Nations, the modernist 1958 Seagram Building, the 1971 World Trade Centre's twin towers, the Citicorp Centre of 1978 and, most recently, architect Frank Gehry's sculpted steel-clad tower at 8 Spruce Street and the so-called Freedom Tower, rising where the World Trade Centre stood. Today the tallest skyscrapers are in the

Middle East and Asia, but Manhattan still has the biggest grouping of skyscrapers in the world.

Today, you do not have to wander far in the city to find strange juxtapositions of glitz and grot, old and new, large and small structures, vacant sites, elegant forecourts and rundown sidewalks, and maybe steam rising from below the street. Travel writer Jan Morris captured this character well: 'Tempered though it has been from time to time by zoning law and social

Third Avenue, Manhattan – glitz and grot

trend, Manhattan remains a mammoth mess, a stupendous clashing of light and dark and illusory perspective, splotched here and there by wastelands of slum or demolition, wanly patterned by the grid of its street system, but essentially, whatever the improvers do to it, whatever economy decrees or architectural fashion advises, the supreme monument to that elemental human instinct, Free-For-All.'[5]

New people

The 'York' in the New York City's name was acquired when the British captured it from the Dutch in 1664 and King Charles II assigned its ownership to his brother the Duke of York. The 'New' in the name was carried over from its former identity as 'New Amsterdam.' It was appropriate to cling to the adjective, for novelty has always been apparent in New York. As travellers we can divide places into two categories: those where a single visit satisfies our curiosity and no return is desired and those where that first visit just whets our appetite for another visit and then another. New York belongs decisively to this second category. For there is always a new New York – new people, new enterprises, new places to visit.

New York was created, and is constantly recreated, by new people: 'refugees, adventurers, idealists and crooks from every land' – Jan Morris again.[6] Today over half of New Yorkers are foreign-born residents and, in cases, their children. This is a return to the proportion in 1910 at the culmination of the big late 19th century immigration. But the sources of the immigrants then and now are quite different. Around 1900 they were mostly from Europe, initially northern and western Europe, later from southern and eastern Europe. The Statue of Liberty expressed their welcome to the city. New York came to have 'half as many Italians as Naples, as many Germans as Hamburg, as many Irish as Dublin, and two and a half as many Jews as Warsaw.'[7] Many immigrants were poor, unskilled and illiterate. They gravitated to densely packed parts of Manhattan where their fellow nationals lived. Even then there were fine distinctions: among the Italians the Neapolitans, Calabrese and Apulians had separate communities; similarly among the Jews the Hungarians, Galicians, Poles, Rumanians and Russians kept apart.

The Statue of Liberty[8]

The famous statue of a woman holding a torch aloft is located on an island off the southern tip of Manhattan, near Ellis Island where immigrants were once processed. To its plinth is attached the poem by Emma Lazarus titled *The New Colossus* that is taken to express the spirit of the statue. Its famous second verse reads –

'Keep ancient lands, your storied pomp!" cries she
With silent lips. "Give me your tired, your poor,
Your huddled masses yearning to breathe free,
The wretched refuse of your teeming shore.
Send these, the homeless, tempest-tost to me,
I lift my lamp beside the golden door.'

But the story of how the statue and the poem came to be associated is not straightforward. The statue was designed in the 1870s by the French sculptor Frédéric-August Bartholdi and intended as a gift from the people of France to the Americans, in celebration of their achievement of independence a century before. So it was intended to symbolise republicanism and liberalism. Fundraising continued for over a decade. Congress refused to support it and only a successful campaign for public donations, spearheaded by newspaper owner Joseph Pulitzer, raised the cash. In 1886 the statue was completed, at 90 metres then the tallest structure in New York. Lazarus's poem had already been written in 1883 for a charity auction to raise funds for the statue. Her inspiration was the recent pogroms in Russia, triggered by the assassination of Tsar Alexander II, which had impelled thousands of Russian Jews towards the United States. The poem was published and then largely forgotten. Then in 1903 it was quietly attached to the statue's pedestal. In 1936, at the statue's fiftieth birthday celebrations, President Franklin Roosevelt articulated the connection between the statue and the poem, declaring that the Statue of Liberty had become the symbol of American freedoms and the beacon of welcome. Ironically, by then further immigration had been restricted.

While restrictions limited foreign immigration through the mid 20th century, New York still attracted internal migrants. The city had African-American residents from the start, initially as slaves. At the time of the mass European immigration around 1900 they were less than 2% of the population. Later expansion was fuelled by mass migration from the American South in the early decades of the 20th century. From 1900-1940 their numbers grew from 60,000 to 400,000; from 1940-1960 they doubled again. Now African-Americans comprise about 25% of the population. Also an internal migration, though from overseas, were the arrivals from Puerto Rica, a US Caribbean colony whose inhabitants had been made US citizens in 1917. By 1970 they formed 10% of the city's population.

In 1965 new US immigration laws ended discrimination based on national origin. The effect on New York was dramatic. Immigration surged upwards again. Now the immigrants came mostly from outside Europe. As before, they were either drawn by the prospect of a better life or driven by violence and turmoil in their home countries; and as before many were poor and uneducated. By 2000, Dominicans were the largest group of immigrants, followed by Chinese, Jamaicans, Guyanese, Mexicans, Ecuadorians Haitians, Trinidadians and people from the former Soviet Union.[9] These were the legal immigrants; also there were the undocumented illegal immigrants, among whom are growing numbers from Mexico and other countries with long waiting lists for visas.

Today immigrants from more than a hundred nations and faiths live in New York. You can run through the alphabet of countries and religions of the world and find people from them in New York – Afghans, Albanians, Barbadians, Belarusans, through Jews, Koreans, and Latvians to the Welsh, Yemenis and Zoroastrians.[10] Some of these groups acquired big roles in the city's life: notably the Irish in politcs through the Tammany Hall organisation, the Italians in the Mafia. In the last few decades Koreans have taken over many of the city's corner stores, especially for grocery and dry cleaning. At times their presence has brought tension – boycotts, pickets, even attacks – in some black communities. Also, typically, Indians run newsstands, Jamaicans work in nursing, Dominicans own bodegas and the Chinese do homeworking in the garment trade. And New York taxi drivers famously come from all over the world. In addition the city continues to attract cosmopolitan people in the arts, the media, the professions and business, and the United Nations, with delegations from 193 member states, has its HQ here. 'Melting pot' is the term commonly applied to what happens in New York with this ethnic, religious and national mix. But it is an inappropriate metaphor. There is no urge here to formally and forcefully Americanise the Bulgarians or Bangladeshis, the Moroccans or Mexicans; rather the diverse communities retain their identity, while informally adjusting themselves to indigenous customs and values – more griddling than melting.

It is not just human immigrants that get to be in New York. As in other cities, there are rats and mice, cockroaches and pigeons. In Flatbush, Brooklyn, there has been a large colony of feral parakeets since the 1970s.[11] Nobody seems to know how they arrived. Like most immigrants, despite attempts to restrict or eliminate them, they survive.

New enterprises

Over the last four centuries, New York, like other cities of the North, has undergone a transformation of its economy, from the dominance of trade to manufacture and then to services. First it was a port, its riverbanks lined with wharves and warehouses for the seaborne import and export trade, extending across the Atlantic and down the east coast to the Caribbean. Flour from inland farms was shipped through the port to the West Indies, there traded for sugar to be carried to Europe and sold to pay for manufactured goods, which were imported into the colony. The port expanded enormously after the opening of the Erie Canal in 1825, and other later canals, all joining New York to a bigger and bigger North American hinterland. Then railroad connections arrived. From 1900 to 1950, New York had the busiest port in the world. From early days manufacturing complemented trade. Initially this was processing imports or exports, but through the 19th century production of both capital and consumer goods expanded: machinery, vehicles, printing, furniture, textiles and clothing – this latter in the infamous sweatshops of the Lower East Side, so-named because, whatever the weather, a stove had to be kept alight to heat the irons for pressing the garments. Both trade and manufacture have now declined in comparison with services.

But services are not just a modern activity in New York. The Bank of New York opened in 1784 on Pearl Street and a Stock Exchange in 1792 at 22 Wall Street. Today New York is, with London and Tokyo, in the trio of centres for global finance. When things go well, its well-paid workers can see themselves as 'Masters of the Universe'.[12] But twice in the last one hundred years, in 1929 and 2008, the collapse of confidence in Wall Street has brought the whole world's financial system crashing down.

High-end retailing is also long established in New York. By the 1820s Broadway was the fashionable street for the well-to-do to shop for what were called 'dry goods', that is, fabrics, clothing and toiletries. As wealthy New

Yorkers moved uptown, the shops to serve them and also restaurants, hotels, theatres and clubs moved with them. Initially they created what was known as 'Ladies Mile' on Broadway and Sixth Avenue, between 9th and 23rd Streets. Here Macy's and Tiffany's first located. By the early 20th century, these and other of New York's renowned department stores – including Lord and Taylor, Bloomingdales, Brooks Brothers – were in midtown. Other parts of the city also gained new local fashion stores. Today, the reputation of New York as a shopping destination belongs more to the designer outlets, like Ralph Lauren, Donna Karan and Marc Jacobs, and to a vast range of specialist stores.

Quite as much as high finance and high-end retailing, present-day New York does culture and media. Here are the country's major TV news organisations, its main book and magazine publishers, major charitable foundations, two national newspapers (the *New York Times* and *Wall Street Journal*), the main US fine arts market, leading opera and dance and theatre companies, and internationally important galleries and museums like the Museum of Modern Art and the Metropolitan Museum. Only filmmaking is missing, lost to Los Angeles almost a century ago. Though New York scenarios have continued to attract directors like Martin Scorsese (*Mean Streets* 1973, *Taxi Driver* 1976, *The Age of Innocence* 1993, *Gangs of New York* 2002), Woody Allen (*Annie Hall* 1977, *Manhattan* 1979 with Gershwin's *Rhapsody in Blue* on its soundtrack, often seen as a homage to the city) and Spike Lee (*Do the Right Thing* 1989, *Summer of Sam* 1999, *Inside Man* 2006).

American theatre is synonymous with Broadway, shorthand for the Theatre District around Times Square, where most large commercial theatres are located. In recent decades musicals have been the dominant offer and New York has been celebrated in many classic musicals: *On the Town* (with sailors on shore leave in Manhattan), *Guys and Dolls* (with gamblers and Salvation Army evangelists drawn from Damon Runyon stories of Broadway) and *West Side Story* (reprising *Romeo and Juliet* among rivalrous Italians and Puerto Ricans) to name just three. But there is also Off Broadway and Off Off Broadway, signifying smaller venues of 200-500 seats and less than 100 seats respectively and located all over the city; increasingly it is here that the most innovative theatre is to be found.

After World War Two, New York supplanted Paris as the cultural and commercial centre for modern art. It now houses the world's greatest public collection of 20th century art in the Museum of Modern Art (MOMA) on West 53rd Street in Manhattan. In the 1940s and 1950s two prototypically American, but very different, movements were strongly associated with New York:

112

Abstract Expressionism and Pop Art. The Abstract Expressionists eschewed any material subject matter, covering vast canvases with just gesture, pattern and colour without explicit representation. Some critics see in them a response to New York.[13] For them Jackson Pollock's splash paintings provide images of frenzied action, expressing a state of mutual tension between the artist and his environment and Mark Rothko's spectacular blocks of solid colour capture moments of transcendence – maybe ecstasy, maybe alienation – in the experience of the city. Pop Art could not have been more different. It adopted the material ephemera of commerce, news reporting and popular culture as its subject matter producing what, at first glance, seem just impersonal reproductions of cartoon strips, movie stills, adverts, press photos or products. Some of its exponents explicitly acknowledged New York as an inspiration – Robert Rauschenberg maintained that 'Times Square is America's greatest work of art' and Claes Oldenburg likened Manhattan streets to desolate plains or torrential rivers and saw the shops and adverts as tangled, teeming forests.[14] Andy Warhol, probably the most well-known pop artist, worked across a wide range of media – painting, photography, drawing, sculpture and film – as well as being a leading celebrity in New York's social life in the 1960s and 70s, renowned for his much-quoted observation that 'In the future, everyone will be world-famous for fifteen minutes.'

Recently, New York has also created a modern culture of dining. As a port city it receives the best foodstuffs from around the globe; as an immigrant city it attracts chefs who can cook all the world's cuisines superbly; and its foreign populations know the real thing. That has long been so. What is new are the 'foodies', people who just love food: to shop for, to cook, to read and talk about as well as to eat. New York is full of them and full of the food retailers, cafes and restaurants, magazines, cookbooks, TV programmes and websites that serve their needs. *The Rough Guide to New York* declares that 'restaurant hopping' is now one of the city's most popular pastimes.

New places

New enterprises and new people create new places within the city. There is a dynamic permanently at work in New York, captured by John F Kennedy's reported observation that 'Most cities are nouns, but New York is a verb.' The city's neighbourhoods seem in a constant process of change, as they become colonised by new kinds of enterprise and inhabitants. The famous examples in the last decades have been part of the re-emergence of downtown Manhattan as a favoured place to live. Initially Greenwich Village gained a new reputation in the 1950s and 1960s as the home of Beat poets, folk music and radical politics – Bob Dylan's early career was here. Then successively a series of neighbouring areas became fashionable, were upgraded and often given new names – SoHo, TriBeCa, the East Village, NoHo, Nolita and Alphabet City. Artists, gays, bohemians or ethnic minorities are often the vanguards of such migrations that later bring in more mainstream households.

Smart downtown neighbourhoods

SoHo (South of Houston Street) – an area of 19th century cast iron frame industrial buildings, established as the centre of the city's art scene in the 1980s but latterly become an area of upmarket boutiques and bars.

TriBeCa (Triangle Below Canal Street) – once the food wholesaling and textile district, where the concept of loft living in its former industrial and warehouse buildings originated, now with some of the city's smartest restaurants.

East Village (that is, east of Greenwich Village, itself now renamed *West Village*) – extends east from Broadway and north of Houston, historically strongly working class though with a sprinkling of radical politicos, artists and writers, but in the last two decades invaded by the intelligentsia who can no longer afford Greenwich Village rents. One corner of the East Village is known as *NoHo* (north of Houston Street).

NoLita (North of Little Italy) – christened as such in the 1990s and home to many small vintage or custom-made clothing shops.

Alphabet City (named from its grid of avenues labelled A,B,C and D) – once a notoriously dangerous neighbourhood run by drug pushers and gangsters, now police crackdowns and new young immigrants have turned it into an attractive area famous for its public art and over one hundred community gardens.

The *Meatpacking district* where slaughterhouses have been converted into bars, upmarket boutiques and galleries.

Such changes are not just a novelty of late 20th century downtown Manhattan, they have occurred throughout the city's history and across its territory. Take

Harlem, north of Central Park on Manhattan Island, now the most famous African-American community in the US and, arguably, the birthplace of modern black culture. In the late 19th century its country mansions and fine estates for the city's wealthy gave way to terraced housing, connected by the new elevated railways to downtown. It was here that large numbers of German and Russian Jews relocated from the Lower East Side. But in the early decades of the 20th century the arrival of African-American families induced a panicky 'white flight' and Harlem became, and has remained, New York's pre-eminent black neighbourhood. Most of the city's black churches moved here, followed by fraternal organisations, political clubs, theatres and night clubs. The so-called Harlem Renaissance of the 1920s was born: 'less a place than a spirit.'[15] Writers and artists travelled here from all over the United States. Its culture – theatre, jazz, writing, dance, painting – became a New York, indeed American, fashion. Duke Ellington, Billie Holiday, Ella Fitzgerald all launched their careers in Harlem. But the political aspects of the Renaissance, the growing self-awareness and confidence of African-Americans and their sometimes extreme expression, were less readily handled by fellow New Yorkers. Fear of the Negro became common. Then the Depression years of the 1930s sent Harlem into a decline, characterised by overcrowding, unemployment, drugs and crime, from which it has only slowly recovered.

Many other New York neighbourhoods have been in flux in recent times. The South Bronx, which experienced in the 1970s and 1980s decay, widespread arson and abandonment, has been renewed and repopulated through new housing, though it still remains one of the city's poorest areas. In Brooklyn the stately 19th century brownstone terraces of Park Slope have attracted, since the 1970s, a large number of lesbian couples. Further out, at Brooklyn's southernmost end, Brighton Beach, once an affluent seaside resort, is now known as Little Odessa, for it is here that immigrants from Russia, Ukraine, Georgia and Armenia have settled: Russian souvenir shops, food emporia (shop here for pickles, smoked fish and vodka) and supper clubs abound. Still in Brooklyn, to the north is Williamsburg, initially settled by Irish and Germans, then by Jewish families leaving the Lower East Side; latterly it is where New York's art scene has blossomed with more than 100,000 resident artists. Astoria in Queens has the largest community of Greeks outside Greece. Also in Queens, Flushing is known as New York's second Chinatown, though Koreans, Malaysians and Vietnamese add to the mix. Similarly Belmont is now home to more Italians than Manhattan's Little Italy.

Governability

In 1987 Tom Wolfe published *The Bonfire of the Vanities*, a novel which offered a portrait of New York City at that time. It was not a pretty picture. The narrative revolves around a hit-and-run accident in the Bronx when a rich Wall Street banker and his mistress in their Mercedes kill a black youth. Everyone involved behaves badly: the banker denies responsibility, the mistress commits perjury, the District Attorney exploits the case to secure his re-election, a detective has an affair with a juror, a tub-thumping black preacher takes up the case for political reasons, an evangelical charity naively bankrolls him, an alcoholic journalist sees a muck-raking opportunity to rescue his faltering career. The novel was a bestseller, for its drama about ambition, racism, social class and greed captured the essence of New York at that time. While Wall Street was booming, its excesses were apparent. Real life financiers like Michael Milken and Ivan Boesky made fortunes for themselves and others by means that ultimately landed them in jail. The phrase 'Greed is good' was expressive of the times, spoken by the fictional Gordon Gecko, played by Michael Douglas, in the 1987 film *Wall Street*. The city was also a hotbed of racial and cultural tensions. One in four of New York's population was officially classed as poor. Homelessness and crime were growing. Some public schools needed armed police at the gates. The municipality's finances were in meltdown with a budget deficit of $1.5 billion by the end of 1990. Part of the cause was the loss of revenue from the flight from the city of businesses and the white middle class. All this attracted more than local interest. Many commentators argued that New York's malaise was where, at that time, many of the world's major cities were headed – abandoned by all but the poor, slipping into dereliction, riven by strife, the city coffers empty – in short, ungovernable. Cities like New York had become a major political headache.

But New York turned itself round. Strong mayoral leadership was crucial. New York has had directly elected mayors since 1834 and their power has been progressively extended since then. But few mayors have acquired national or lasting reputations. From the mid-late 20th century only the names of Fiorello La Guardia 1934-45, John V Lindsey 1966-73 and David Dinkins 1990-93 (the first black mayor) now ring any bells. As well, if not better, known is Robert Moses, who masterminded, from a string of administrative posts he held from the 1920s to the 1950s, the rebuilding and re-engineeering of the city with freeways, parks, housing projects, tunnels and bridges. But in 1993 Rudolph

Giuliani defeated David Dinkins and became the city's first Republican mayor for twenty-eight years. It was on his watch, from 1994-2001, that the city's recovery began.

Giuliani described himself as 'a Republican pretending to be a Democrat pretending to be a Republican', which captured his rather maverick politics. He took a tough stance on crime, not just breaking criminal control of wholesale markets and solid waste disposal but crackdowns on minor misdemeanours like graffiti, turnstile jumping in the subway and aggressive street trading: the so-called zero tolerance policy seeking to restore popular faith in city living. Homeless people were moved from the streets and into shelters. Hardworking immigrants, even illegals, were encouraged to move to New York. Campaigns were started to get low income people into public health entitlement programmes. But Giuliani was a contentious figure: there were numerous allegations of trigger-happy conduct and civil rights abuses by the New York police; he never got to grips with the problems of New York's public schools; some accused him of racism in his dealings with African-American and Hispanic communities. But the city's economy looked up, in particular tourists flooded in, and the municipal finances moved into surplus. Some of Giuliani's policies were copied in other cities in the USA and elsewhere. There was a renewed sense of optimism about the future of cities. But, for New York, the worst was yet to come.

9/11

On 11th September 2001, quite out of the blue on a warm, sunny morning, Islamic terrorists flew two hijacked passenger planes into the twin towers of the World Trade Centre in downtown Manhattan. In the TV images that went instantly round the world, the planes just seemed to be swallowed by the buildings, before all burst into flames. Within an hour or so the two 110 storey towers, New York's highest skyscrapers, collapsed into ruins. The prominence of the towers and the sightlines along the streetgrid gave the city a live view of the evolving spectacle. South of Houston Street became a war zone of dust, fire, smoke, stench, police, firefighters and medics. Buried in the rubble were the body parts of nearly 3000 people. 2000 vehicles were destroyed. Just outside that zone, walls were quickly plastered with homemade posters of smiling faces with text below, searching for the missing. Further afield, once over the shock people began to shop, perhaps not so much from fear of shortages as from a desire to maintain normality. Within 24 hours there were comments and condolences from all round the world, messages from politicians, and funds opened for the bereaved. Commemorative T shirts went on sale. The Governor of New York State declared: 'On that terrible day, a nation became a neighbourhood, all Americans became New Yorkers.'

The immediate comment was that this was an unprecedented act of destruction, at least in the USA. But it was not. Washington was burned by the British army in 1814, Atlanta was razed in 1864 in the final stages of the Civil War, in Chicago the Great Fire of 1871 and in San Francisco the earthquake of 1906 created scenes of vast devastation. Much of New York itself had been burned down in the fires of 1835 and 1845. Moreover, in modern times, the destruction of New York – by fire, flood, monsters, creatures from outer space or human evildoers – has been a recurrent storyline in written and film fiction. Of course Manhattan provides a cityscape – with its big buildings, bright lights, busyness – that offers dramatic, visual opportunities for fictional mayhem. But there may be more to its role as victim.

New York has been more successful than probably any other city in projecting its energy to the world. Some of this is positive, some negative, displaying both the upside and downside of capitalist metropolitanism: wealth and poverty, enthusiasm and lassitude, excess and deprivation, glitz and decay. For many people New York expresses an aspiration. As the protagonist of *The Bonfire of the Vanities* remarks: 'Just think of the millions, from all over the globe, who yearned to be on that island, in those towers, in those narrow streets! There it was, the Rome, the Paris, the London of the twentieth century, the city of ambition, the dense magnetic rock, the irresistible destination of all those who insist on being where things are happening.'[16] But for others the city is a warning: cruel, heartless, corrupt. Either way, iconic New York is the potent symbol of US power and influence. In choosing the city as his target Osama Bin Laden knew what he was doing.

8.

Transactions: cities as marketplaces

Lima 1995 Taxis are cheap here – at least to a visitor. But travelling in them is not without hazard, given their clapped out condition, the traffic congestion and the crazy style of driving. Nor is one insulated from the clamour of the streets, for at traffic lights, while waiting on red, someone bangs on the passenger window, pitching for sale a wide range of goods. Over a few days in the city, passing through the same road junction, the same young man offers us matches, disposable razors, bananas, condoms, a paper skeleton (it is near the medical school), bottled water, Inca Cola (the local competitor to Coke and Pepsi), perfume (clearly fake) and sunglasses. Upon inquiry, his opening price falls quickly as the traffic lights change to green. We never see him make a sale. But he is there day after day, presumably earning some sort of living from even a low turnover and low margins.

Markets and malls

In the remote past people's goods were mostly inherited, made or grown by themselves, or bartered and exchanged with others. As societies urbanised, industrialised and capitalism grew, a cash economy developed and within it a distinct retail sector. Retailing is now big within cities, in terms of both the number and the variety of goods and services their populations demand. Street hawking – as in Lima – is the simplest form of retailing. Alongside it, in most cities, are the more complex practices of markets, shops and modern malls.

Markets are one of the oldest and most universal features of cities. They existed in ancient China, in Babylon, in classical Greece and in the Roman Empire, evident at Pompeii, for example. Today, there can hardly be a city in the world without at least one market, a place where temporary stalls are set up to sell goods in the open air. German has a phrase that captures the essence of market trading: *Hand in Hand, Auge in Auge Handel,* meaning 'selling hand to hand, eyeball to eyeball'. Most likely a market will be on a street or in a square

119

or on some open land; exceptionally it may be on water, as with the famous floating markets of Bangkok, or on a frozen river, as was once common in winter on the Moskva in Moscow. Markets may be held daily, weekly or seasonally, sometimes associated with fairs or festivals like the Christmas markets common in German cities. Some traders may be producers of the goods on sale, an old tradition reinvented with the farmers' markets and craft markets that have now become common in North American and European cities. More often they are selling goods that they've bought from wholesalers or importers. These lines of supply are sometimes evident in the names of markets: Istanbul has an Egyptian Market, Phnom Penh has a Russian Market, Cork in Ireland has an English Market, Berlin has a Turkish Market. Some markets offer a wide range of goods, others specialise in antiques, books, plants, pets, horses, flowers, or second hand goods in the so-called flea markets. La Paz in Bolivia even has a witchcraft market, the *Mercado de Hechicheria*, selling potions and charms. Then, in most cities, there will also be black markets, places – probably known only by word of mouth – where illegal transactions of currency, narcotics, stolen goods or anything scarce can be made.

In some cities the local ruler, a landowner or a group of traders, built market halls or bazaars to complement or replace open-air markets. Many such buildings survive in the cities of Europe and the Levant, though are not always still in market use. In the European cities these covered markets were often specialist – a corn market, a cloth market, a butchers' market, a fish market – and some were and are more for wholesale than retail trade. General markets were also built, sometimes in the middle of open-air markets that continued around them. *Les Halles*, that came to be known as 'the belly of Paris', acquired its first buildings in the 12th century, though the famous glass and steel halls dated from the 1850s; they were demolished in 1971. Many other cities built such general market halls, mostly selling food, in the 19th and early 20th century: fine surviving examples are *La Boqueria* in Barcelona, the *Saluhall* in Stockholm, the *Mercato Centrale* in Florence. The Oriental equivalent of the European market hall is the bazaar, likewise an enclosed building with gates controlling access, but typically vaster and more maze-like. The core of the Grand Bazaar in Istanbul was constructed in the 15th century after the Ottoman conquest of the city; it has fifty-eight narrow streets and 4000 shops and today still attracts hundreds of thousands of customers daily in search of jewellery, leather goods, antiques, fabrics and clothes, carpets and ceramics; the surrounding streets cater to more everyday shopping needs. The Grand Bazaar in Teheran is equally vast, having grown incrementally over the last four centuries. Iran is rich in such bazaars; there are others in the cities of Isfahan, Shiraz and Tabriz.

Istanbul's Grand Bazaar

In all cities shops complement and now outnumber market stalls. Probably the first shops in most cities were the workshops of artisans – bakers, tailors, blacksmiths and others – who sold to customers direct, instead of, or as well as, in the market. In time, their windows to the street became used for display. Today shops in cities are amazingly diverse – some just selling basic convenience goods from the front room of a dwelling in a shanty town; others, neighbourhood stores in a residential area; or more specialist services for shoe repair, furniture, stationery or a hundred other urban necessities and upscale boutiques for fashionable clothing and accessories. These may be single, independent enterprises or chain stores found in most cities of any country. In cities across the world, some have now become global brands, especially in clothing – like Levi-Strauss, Gap, Nike, Prada – and food – like McDonalds and Starbucks, the latter with 20,000 outlets in sixty countries.

When cities were smaller and personal contact was achieved on foot, trades that served the same customers or were interdependent located themselves together. This traditional street by street specialisation has been long established in many old cities. Newer specialisations are found in contemporary cities: streets where you can go comparison shopping for furniture, jewellery, computers, phones and cameras, books, cars, art and antiques, perhaps different streets in different parts of the city for upmarket and downmarket options. And there may be districts where certain services congregate, such as lawyers, accountants, doctors – and also prostitutes, in the red-light district.

Hanoi's Old Quarter[1]

Hanoi's merchant quarter, covering a square kilometre, was closed behind walls and gates until the 19th century. Both have now gone, but the rest is fairly intact – a maze of narrow streets fronted by low, deep buildings that serve as display space, workshops, store rooms and living quarters, all dense enough without the modern addition of motorbikes parked on the pavements and filling the roads. The street names date back five centuries to when thirty-six artisans' guilds dominated business, each with premises clustering around a temple and meeting house dedicated to their patron saint. Thus *Hang Thiec* means 'the street for tin goods', *Hang Ma* 'the street for paper goods'. In these two cases these are still the street's specialities. But in other cases the street's trade has transmuted over time. *Hang Hom* (meaning 'wooden chests') now sells glue, paint and varnish; *Hang Dau* ('oil') now sells shoes; *Hang Bo* ('bamboo baskets') now specialises in haberdashery. These are still vibrant parts of the city's retail economy.

Shops have got bigger and taken on different forms: as department stores, supermarkets or shopping malls. The department store was a great innovation of the 19th century in most Western cities, serving for the first time as a general retailer or emporium. Many European cities claim to have hosted the first department store: by the 1850s Delany's in Dublin, *Bon Marché* in Paris and Bainbridge's in Newcastle were already trading and the last two are still in business today. This new kind of shop spread rapidly and they were initially resented (like supermarkets today) by small traders. Some department stores have become indelibly associated with their host cities, not just for their retail offers but often also for their distinctive architecture, like the GUM store in Moscow, *Galeries Lafayette* in Paris, Liberty in London, and Macy's in New York. In contrast to department stores, supermarkets were a US invention. The self-service concept originated in the Piggly Wiggly store in Memphis in 1916. But it took the addition of other features like high volume, low margins, pre-packaging, car transport, and cash-only purchasing (that is, no customer accounts) to develop the supermarket business model from the late 1930s onwards in North America and later in the rest of the world. Now the even bigger hypermarket, usually out on the city fringe, combines the features of the supermarket and the department store.

The shopping mall with many shops, massive car parking and usually at an out-of-town location is another US invention. In its form, though, there are historically clear connections to the older market halls and bazaars as well as to the pedestrian shopping arcades built in some 19th century cities. The first shopping mall in the USA was the Country Club Plaza, opened in Kansas City in 1924. But malls only really took off in the USA in the 1950s and since then have spread to cities around the world, with the rise of consumerism and car ownership. Now the most ambitious mall developments are in Asian cities, like Beijing's Golden Resources Mall (2004), the SM City North in Manila (2006), and Central World Plaza in Bangkok (also 2006). All these and other shopping malls in the world will, though, be dwarfed in size by The Dubai Mall of Arabia (started 2008) which, when completed, promises over 350,000 square metres of retail space and parking for 15,000 cars.

Retailing in all these forms is now pervasive in cities. It's found not just in markets, stores and malls but also as an adjunct to the prime function of railway stations, airports, museums and galleries, sports stadia, even churches. In many cities shopping and eating out in restaurants has become a major leisure activity for well-off people, not just city residents but also visitors – many cities, like Tokyo, Dubai, New York, Hong Kong and Singapore, promote their varied retailing and cuisine as principal tourist attractions. Cities have become sites of consumption, window shopping an important way of passing the time. Strangely, many of the goods purchased in rich cities, especially clothing, once discarded find their way into the supply chains that sustain the open-air markets of the cities of the South – sometimes not too distant from the manufactories where they originated.

City economies

Cities are not just for shopping. To see the sheer variety of city businesses, take a current *Yellow Pages* from any city in the world, turn to a letter of the alphabet at random, and see what it lists. Here is something of what is currently on offer under P in Baltimore, USA, in the capital of Bahrain, and in Brisbane, Australia.

Some kinds of business in Baltimore, Bahrain and Brisbane [2]

Baltimore	Bahrain	Brisbane
Packaging	Packaging material	PA systems
Paging systems	Paint – auto	Packaging products
Painting	Paint – decorative	Padlocks
Panelling	Palm and herbal water	Paediatricians
Paper products	Paper distributors	Painting
Parenting services	Parking meters	Palmistry
Party planning	Pastries	Panel beaters
Pasta products	Pearls	Paper merchants
Patent agents	Perfumes	Parachute equipment
Paternity testing	Pest control	Parent education
Paving	Pet shops	Pastry cook supplies
Pawnbrokers	Petrol filling stations	Patio builders
Peanut products	Petroleum products	Patrolmen
Performing arts groups	Pharmacies	Paving
Personnel	Photocopying	Payroll services
Pest control services	Photographers	Pens and pencils
Petroleum products	Physiotherapists	Perfumes
Pets	Pianos	Pest control
Pharmacies	Picture frames	Pet cemeteries
Photographers	Piling contractors	Petroleum products

Some are businesses with which as a resident you have regular transactions. They will be well-known to you, maybe long-established, heavily advertised or with many branches across the city. Others may not be known to you until you need them, very specialist, maybe with just a few outlets in the city, tracked down by an internet search or recommended by word of mouth. Again, there are trades found in most cities, as shown by some of those listed for more than one of the three cities: for example, packaging, paint, pharmacies. People in all cities around the world need certain goods and services to keep them going, most obviously food, premises, healthcare, education, entertainment, transport and finance. Other trades will be unique to particular places – like the palm and herbal water available in Bahrain and the patio builders of Brisbane.

Most cities have economic specialisms that differentiate and characterise them. Some of these are well-known, almost brands, such as Paris fashion, Antwerp for diamonds (half the world's trade is done there), Guinness from Dublin and Nashville country music. In many cases the monopoly that a product's city association once expressed has been lost, so that today linen does not come just from Belfast or damask from Damascus. In broad terms, the city specialism may be as makers, thinkers or traders.[3] Makers manufacture goods and provide services. Thinkers produce knowledge in its various forms through research and development, the media, design, education and training, culture and entertainment, tourism, consultancy. Traders handle transactions which range from the tangibility of transport and communications, through wholesaling and retailing, export and import, to the intangibility of finance. Most cities have one, usually more than one, kind of these specialist functions. They will not necessarily be dominant in terms of the total employment or output of the city, but through exporting goods or services they provide a base on which other businesses can build.

Specialisation arises from economies of agglomeration, that is, the benefits of close, localised connections and interdependencies between businesses in the same trade. Almost a century ago the economist Alfred Marshall noted the urban specialisms of early 20th century British cities: cutlery in Sheffield, printing in Watford, shipbuilding in Glasgow, lace in Nottingham, cotton in Manchester, wool in Bradford. He argued that three connections sustained these specialisms: connections between the businesses and workers with relevant labour skills; between the businesses and their suppliers of raw material, machinery, finance and other services; and, last but not least, between the businesses themselves who – though they may be competitors – nevertheless exchange ideas and information and thus propel innovation. Thereby, as Marshall put it, 'the mysteries of the trade become no mysteries; but are as it were in the air and children learn many of them unconsciously.'[4] Today analysts talk less of 'economies of agglomeration' and more of 'information richness', 'business clusters', 'support services' and 'critical mass'; there is also recognition of the importance for cities of good connections to other cities. The continuing importance of all these factors can be seen in contemporary city specialisms. The global financial centres of London, New York and Tokyo are obvious examples, but – even in this trade – other cities in those countries have developed sub-specialisms: Chicago for derivatives trading, Boston for fund management, Edinburgh for personal savings, insurance and pensions. In some places the cluster may spread outside or between cities – as with the IT specialism of Silicon Valley in California or the fashion industry of the Po Valley cities in Italy. Specialisation is also apparent in the developing cities of the global South: for example, in India there is IT and software in Bangalore, in China the eastern city of Yimu produces more than half of North America's and Europe's Christmas decorations.

The origin of these city specialisms is often in the exploitation of a local resource: a unique raw material, a strong trading location, an individual entrepreneur. But this only happens because the nascent city provides an innovative milieu open to new ideas and practices, not bound by conventions, not too dominated by existing interests. Often the innovators are themselves outsiders in the city. Lewis Mumford observed that 'the stranger, the outsider, the traveller, the trader, the refugee, the slave, yes even the invading enemy, have had a special part in urban development at every stage.'[5] History has many famous examples: the German Rothschilds who developed finance businesses in London and other European cities in the early 19th century; the British taipans, like Jardine and Matheson, who developed Hong Kong's trading role; Henry Ford, from a farming background and an electrical engineer by training, who experimented with gasoline engines for self-propelled vehicles before establishing the Ford Motor Company in Detroit in 1903. For innovation to succeed, the person, the time and the place need to come together.

The innovation process must be maintained if cities are to thrive economically. The urbanist Jane Jacobs declared that 'Cities that do not add new kinds of goods and services, but continue to repeat old work, do not expand much nor do they, by definition, develop.'[6] She went on to argue that such new work commonly grows out of the old, arising from new applications for either the materials or the skills used or the markets served in the old work; or sometimes as a response to a problem faced in the old work. Cities are places where this innovation process proceeds vigorously. It's simpler to start new enterprises in cities, for so much of what you need is already there: local markets for new niche products or services, premises in which space can be rented, a large and diversely skilled labour force, established businesses to act as suppliers, partners or agents, sources of capital and professional advice. Clearly the scope of such support systems varies from city to city and time to time; some new enterprises will fail. But cities mostly provide a fertile soil for business growth. The quote from Alfred Marshall above continues: 'Good work is rightly appreciated, inventions and improvements in machinery, in processes and the general organisation of the business have their merits promptly discussed: if one man starts a new idea, it is taken up by others and combined with suggestions of their own; and thus it becomes the source of further ideas. And presently subsidiary trades grow up in the neighbourhood, supplying it with implements and materials, organising its traffic, and in many ways conducing to the economy of its material.'[7]

This synergy is recognised in published rankings of the 'business climate' in cities around the world. The concept of the 'business climate' embraces factors like access to customers and clients; staff costs, availability and qualifications including languages spoken; tax and regulatory regimes; quality of premises, transport and the city environment. A 2010 survey of European cities, in terms of employers' views on such matters, ranked the following as the top ten for business: London, Paris, Frankfurt, Brussels, Barcelona, Amsterdam, Berlin, Madrid, Munich and Düsseldorf. The first four had been in that position in a comparable 1990 survey; but in the intervening twenty years Barcelona had risen from eleventh rank to fifth, Madrid from seventeenth to eighth and Berlin from fifteenth to seventh.[8]

Boom towns

Some cities do not just prosper, they boom, expanding at breakneck speed. Their economies and populations double, treble, quadruple in size in a short space of time, sucking in migrants, attracting entrepreneurs, creating new businesses, building outwards and upwards. They are also often places where conmen flourish, moral standards slip, community tensions are near the surface, labour exploitation is rife and violence is common. Life there can be rough and tough.

The classic boom town is associated with the discovery of natural resources. Western colonialism, exploiting new resources for the benefit of home industries and markets, provided the impetus for many 19th century booms. Oil, timber and precious metals were common attractions in the Americas, in Africa and in Asia. Modern Baku overlooking the Caspian Sea is the capital of Azerbaijan. The discovery of oil in the 1870s was the basis of its boom and for a few decades it dominated world oil production. Swiss, Belgian, English, French, German and Swedish companies arrived to run the oil business, skilled workers and specialists flooded in. A new town was built outside the old city with Beaux Arts architecture for the mansions of new millionaires, their business premises, new museums and theatres. In Soviet times its economy became sluggish, but it is now resurgent. Something similar happened with Manaus, deep in the Brazilian interior near the confluence of the Negro and Amazon Rivers. Founded as a Portuguese fort in the 17th century, it boomed from 1890 onward from rubber production. Immigrant workers poured in, the plantation owners and traders became very wealthy. An opera house (featured in the 1982 film *Fitzcarraldo*), a market hall (based on Les Halles in Paris), a Palace of Justice and a university were built and survive. But its rubber boom ended in 1920 when the invention of synthetic rubber and the growth of Southeast Asia plantations caused a drastic plunge in the price of rubber. Manaus is still a large city, accessible mostly by air or river, but its economy is now heavily state-subsidised. Even in modern times new resources bring booms. Aberdeen on the east coast of Scotland, with a declining economy based on fishing, textiles, shipbuilding and paper, revived in the 1970s with the discovery and exploitation of offshore oil in the North Sea, to become known as the Oil Capital of Europe. And Gaborone, the capital of Botswana since independence in 1966, has become the fastest growing city in Africa fuelled by wealth from diamond mining.

But the resource that feeds the boom can be of other kinds. Avignon is today a modest city of 100,000 people, best known for its grand Palace of the Popes. In 1309 it was chosen as the seat of the Papacy after its eviction from Rome. The Pope brought 4,000 others with him: cardinals, chaplains, knights, squires, grooms, bodyguards, clerks. The city boomed as financiers, traders, artists, craftsmen and shopkeepers found new business; a university was founded; palaces, churches and fortifications were built – all fuelled by papal riches and greased by corruption. But boom times lasted only a few decades until 1377 when the Papacy returned to Rome. Relocations of political as well as religious power can bring booms. There was a wave of these in the 1940s – Bonn as the new capital of the postwar West German Federal Republic, Karachi as the initial capital of independent Pakistan, Taipei as the capital of Formosa when the Chinese Nationalists retreated there after their expulsion from mainland China by the Communists.

In the 20th century, human talents have underpinned some booms. As recently as the 1970s Bangalore was a quiet hillside city in southern India. In the next decade it emerged as a world centre for software development and IT services, driven by entrepreneurs grasping the global advantage of the local young, well-educated, English speaking workforce. It now has over 500 high-tech companies, many with European and North American business partners. Different, but equally astonishing, is the rise of Las Vegas, the product of a decision in the 1930s to legalise casinos for the amusement of local construction workers and air base personnel. It is still the fastest growing city in the USA with a population approaching two million and another thirty million visitors a year. Today, the Gulf cities of Dubai, Bahrain and Oman seem set on a similar trajectory as global centres of shopping and entertainment.

Booms may be followed by busts, as the resource is exhausted, or changes in markets, technology or politics remove the city's advantages. Avignon, Manaus and Bonn all suffered this fate, though none became ghost towns. But in some countries whole regions have seen their once prosperous cities fall into decline. These mostly contain cities that boomed in the 19th and early 20th century as places where machines, textiles, clothing, steel or chemicals were produced, like the Ruhr cities in Germany, the northern cities in Britain and the Midwest and Northeast USA, nicknamed the 'rustbelt.' Typically their economies focused on large scale factory production using low-skilled workers to produce a limited range of goods. When trading conditions changed – such as falling demand, automation, competition from locations with lower labour costs – they failed to innovate and adapt. Detroit is a prime example.

In other cases, the early boost from the boom has been successfully consolidated into a modern, diverse urban economy. San Francisco boomed initially with the Californian Gold Rush of the 1840s and 1850s, for which it provided a point of embarkation and a supply depot (Wells Fargo started here in 1852 and Levi Strauss in 1853), but it continued to prosper when the gold ran out. Johannesburg's gold rush boom came later, in the 1880s, and there is still gold and diamond mining there, but it too has diversified its economy to become South Africa's largest city. Hong Kong is similarly a survivor: seized in

The rise and fall of Detroit[9]

From 1900 onwards Detroit was the home of US vehicle manufacturing – that's why it was called Motown. It originated as a trans-shipment point for food brought by road, rail and river from the Midwest farmlands to transport across Lake Erie, into the Erie Canal at Buffalo and on to New York and overseas. Shipbuilding followed and later vehicle manufacture. Henry Ford launched his first car here in 1899; Olds, Buick, Chrysler and Dodge followed. In the early years of the 20th century Detroit was like Silicon Valley in the 1960s and 1970s, a hotbed of entepreneurs as product developers, suppliers and financiers. But mass production took over and all were absorbed into integrated car companies with supersize factories employing low-skilled, unionised workers in suburban locations. Motown became synonymous with Ford, Chrysler and General Motors – the Big Three. But by the 1980s these companies had lost their competitive edge to European and Asian producers.

Today Detroit is just a ghost of this former self. Between 1950 and 2010 it lost over a million people, 60% of its population. One third of its citizens now live in poverty. Its median family income of $33,000 is about half the US average. Its unemployment rate is more than 2.5 times the national average. House prices have dropped severely. Detroit has one of the highest murder rates among US cities, more than ten times higher than New York's. Vast areas of the city are vacant or derelict. The city has lost its tax base and public services are minimal. Politically-driven attempts to build its way out of decline – new stadiums for the local hockey and baseball teams to keep them in the city, extra office space in the high-rise Renaissance Centre, resort hotels and casinos, a three mile long People Mover monorail, most of them requiring public subsidy – have had little effect. It is human capital – educated, energetic, entrepreneurial people – that Detroit as a city now lacks.

1841 by the British to provide a defensible base for the import of opium to China, it languished somewhat thereafter until an influx of refugee industrialists and workers from China in the wake of the 1949 Communist Revolution created a new manufacturing and finance economy, in which the original merchant houses like Jardine, Matheson and the Hong Kong and Shanghai Bank remained, and remain, powerful.

Abandoned car factory, Detroit

Livelihoods

For individuals and families, the city economy is the source of work and income: they are in a labour market. It also offers livelihoods, that broader experience embracing the subjective as well as the material rewards of work, recognising its capacity for building self-confidence, increasing skills and knowledge, getting their children educated, fostering adaptability and thereby helping people to gain more control over their lives. Potentially, city economies provide good livelihoods through the range of opportunities they offer to match work to skills, to provide the chance of advancement, to challenge people to stretch themselves. But there is also a downside to city work: labour exploitation, dangerous workplaces, long journeys to work, low wages, insecurity of employment. All these were characteristic of work in the 19th century cities of the North and to some degree are still found there today, but they are now more extensive in the 21st century cities of the South.

Women and children, as well as men, commonly get drawn into the labour markets of cities in most parts of the world. In Asian cities, in particular, women now outnumber men in manufacturing and services. Everywhere, as a woman you will tend to be in less skilled, poorly paid jobs, sometimes enduring harsh working conditions, notably in the workshops and factories where Western business corporations outsource production of clothing, toys and electronic goods. In the cities of the South children too are subject to exploitation, working as unpaid family labour, in factories, as scavengers and beggars, even as prostitutes in some tourist destinations. One third of domestic servants in Indonesia are aged fifteen or under; in Thailand half a million children work in urban factories for up to fifteen hour days, earning half of the adult minimum wage.[10] However harsh, the work of both women and children can make essential contributions to family incomes.

As city economies expand they attract migrants, either from rural areas or from other countries. Immigrant labour is now characteristic of cities around the world – sometimes legal, with passports, visas and work permits, but often illegal; sometimes temporary, leaving the family at home, sending them money and returning there from time to time, sometimes permanent. Typically the immigrants take work where there is a shortage of local labour or where they are willing to work for lower wages or in worse conditions. In some cases, migrant workers have valued skills or aptitudes that make them attractive as workers to new city employers: for example, Philippino women provide domestic service in much of southeast Asia, Hispanic women likewise in North America, construction workers from South Asia are found throughout the Middle East, Indian doctors and dentists are common in British and North American cities, Africans as security guards in many parts of the world. The logistics of migration often depends on family or community connections between points of origin and arrival, now made easier by mobile phones, the internet and electronic money transfer. There are also agents operating in both the homelands and in the cities who manage migrants' introduction into the urban labour market – sometimes honest brokers, sometimes dishonest human traffickers charging extortionate fees for minimal or no service.

Even so, unemployment, underemployment and accompanying poverty are the lot of many people in cities, particularly those trapped in slum areas. Welfare payments to the poor are available in only a few, mostly European, cities. In the cities of Asia, Africa and Latin America, over 30% of the population is estimated to be living below locally defined poverty levels[11]; in the cities of the North there is poverty too though the percentage is much smaller. In both cases, given the number and size of the cities the numbers in poverty are large. But then poverty is usually more prevalent and inescapable in the rural areas from which the city immigrants come. Cities still offer the best hope for poor people of creating a livelihood, of acquiring the education and skills that will enable them and their children to better themselves, and of accruing the money that will make them into consumers in the city economy, thereby stimulating its further growth.

Only households with regular, reasonably paid work and not subject to extortionate expenses are likely to generate surpluses for savings and investment. For the rest friends, neighbours or relations may help. Otherwise, where finance is needed there are money markets. The range is immense. At the smallest scale of borrowing there is the local money lender, who may be an individual profiteer or may be a respectable micro-credit organisation, in either case lending to people who are not judged credit-worthy by conventional banks. Then there are the saving and loan businesses, their premises to be found among the shops in the main streets of all cities. Beyond them is the world of high finance which invests in major city projects like business enterprises, new commercial property, transport infrastructure, cultural venues, hospitals and universities. In the past, there were clear distinctions between public and private investment in such projects. Now – in both the cities of the North and South, whether in capitalist, socialist or post-communist economies – there are often complex partnerships between state finance and private finance and both may originate either nationally or internationally; the latter, for example, from multi-national corporations, from rich countries' aid programmes or from the World Bank.

Shelter

For city people seeking to secure a livelihood, a home is a vital starting point. It provides not just a roof over their head, but also access to electricity and water, security for their belongings, privacy and safety for their family, neighbourly relationships, perhaps a workplace for self-employment and a fixed address for dealing with officialdom. It is an essential step to a better life, including entry into the world of work and the income it can provide.

A mixed property market characterises most cities, providing people with different ways of meeting their needs for shelter – buying or renting – always within the limits of what they can afford. Buying and owning urban property is an option mostly just for middle and high income families who can raise the capital and pay the prices, and who often get a return on their investment as property values rise. In some cities, though, lower income households can build for themselves on sites purchased from landowners and with electricity, water and drainage provided by public agencies. Renting is usually possible at all price levels and in all qualities, from luxury apartments to cardboard shacks. There is always a high-end luxury market for the business and government elite; in some cities renting is also the main choice for middle-income households; and there is always a rental market for people with low incomes. This last can take many forms: it may be social housing, provided by state agencies, churches or charitable organisations, which is common in Europe, Hong Kong, Singapore, China and formerly in other Communist cities, but rare elsewhere; it may be houses, flats, hostels or dormitories provided by employers for their workers; or it may be property let by commercial landlords. Letting property to the poor is often exploitative: vast, dense areas of shacks in some African cities have been described as 'rent plantations', owned by politicians and other rich people as highly profitable investments.[12]

Whether for ownership or renting, these are far from perfect property markets, failing to meet the needs of many city people. Homelessness is the most severe failure. Few large cities in the world have no homeless people living in them. Even Los Angeles is estimated to have 100,000 people camped on downtown streets, living furtively in parks or amongst freeway landscaping. Mumbai has what is probably the biggest population of street dwellers in any city, reaching more than one million people. Not all homeless people in cities fit the stereotype of destitute beggars; many have had and lost homes through eviction by landlords or destruction by natural disaster or government bulldozing. Most will be in work and the street may provide the only possible habitation near their work as rickshaw men, cleaners, construction labourers, street sellers or market porters.

Squatting is another option. All over the world, desperate, poor people in cities take possession of empty properties, backyards, rooftops, riverbanks, vacant lots, corners in railway and bus stations and even parts of the street. In many Latin American and Asian cities, the flight of upper and middle income residents from inner districts has left their once elegant mansions and villas to be squatted by multiple families. In Caracas the Torre de David, an empty, incomplete forty-five storey office building is squatted by 2,500 people who not only live there but also run shops, cafes and other businesses on the lower floors. In Cairo 800,000 people live in the City of the Dead necropolis, using its tombs as ready-made housing. More common are the newly built squatter settlements on the fringes of the cities of the South, usually on low value land, often in hazardous locations like hillsides, floodplains, swamps or on toxic land. It is to these places that both new immigrants to the city and city residents displaced by development come, building themselves shelter from whatever material is at hand. Some of these settlements are immense, covering square miles with up to a million residents. Squatting is not always free, often bribes or protection money have to be paid. A variant on such settlements is the temporary camp established for people displaced by floods, famine or civil war – currently Khartoum, Kabul, Beirut, Gaza and Luanda in Angola all host such settlements. Dadaab in Kenya, near the Somalia border, is not just the world's largest refugee camp with a population of over 400,000; it is, in effect, Kenya's third biggest city. These settlements are supposedly temporary so little beyond basic shelter gets provided; in reality, however, they often last for decades.

For many, home is a slum. The massive growth of cities in recent decades, especially in Asia, Africa and Latin America, has been predominantly a growth of slums. The phenomenon of the slum originated in 19th century Europe and North America, as the urban working class crowded into districts near their workplaces. In Manchester in the 1840s Friedrich Engels described how 'Everywhere one sees heaps of refuse, garbage and filth… One walks along a very rough path on the riverbank, in between clothes-posts and washing lines to reach a chaotic group of little, one storied cabins. Most of them have earthen floors and working, living and sleeping all take place in one room.'[13] His description would still fit the slums that spread through the 20th century across

Hillside favela in Rio de Janeiro

the newly urbanising global South. Today a third of the world's urban population lives in slums, commonly lacking clean water and sanitation, overcrowded, in non-durable structures, often at risk of fire, flooding or pollution, and with insecurity of tenure. Mumbai with ten to twelve million slum dwellers heads the league table, followed by Mexico City and Dhaka with nine to ten million, then with six to eight million each come Lagos, Cairo, Kinshasa-Brazzaville, Sao Paulo, Shanghai and Delhi. Slum housing ranges from crowded tenement buildings in Hong Kong to densely packed former palazzos in Havana to mud and tin shacks in Cape Town. The physical inadequacies of slums are remediable; upgrading – through improving local infrastructure, reducing densities, improving building structures – is a process underway, with or without government support and funding, in some cities. But secure tenure is often the most elusive need. Sometimes governments just send in the bulldozers to 'cleanse' the slums. Otherwise, they succumb to property development for more upmarket uses. Either way, the occupants may not be helped with rehousing or, where helped, may be relocated far away.

The (i)n(f)ormal city

In his book *African Cities*, Garth Myers coins this neologism.[14] He does so to challenge the idea that there are distinct 'formal' and 'informal' sectors in the city economy. In characterising the daily transactions of city life, we mostly think of what goes on in the offices, factories, shops, laboratories, government buildings, studios, hospitals and colleges of the city. It is a world of lawful contracts, secure tenancies, defined working conditions, reliable wages and salaries, health and safety regulation, declared and taxed income. This is what gets reported in the business pages of the newspapers, what statisticians count for the Gross Domestic Product, what politicians seek to manage. Economists call this the 'formal economy'.

In every city there is also an 'informal economy'. Here transactions are mostly unregulated, relationships between buyers and sellers are insecure, income is probably untaxed and some activities probably illegal. This informal economy largely goes unrecognised by politicians, uncounted by statisticians and unreported by journalists. Yet in many cities whole sectors of employment are informal: taxis and minivans, delivery, cleaning, street hawking, small scale production of clothing, food and household goods, recycling and repair, catering, food and lodging, construction, domestic service and childcare are all common examples. Some such work is ingeniously entrepreneurial. As well there is all the work that city households do for themselves or for friends and neighbours: shopping, cooking, cleaning, washing clothes, caring for relatives, repairing homes or fixing cars. Well-off families hire others to do some of this domestic work, but poorer families must do it for themselves. For some of them, especially in the cities of the South, this self-help extends to building themselves the homes that provide shelter for their work or their families.

In the past it was widely assumed by economists and politicians that modernisation would lead to the disappearance of such informal activity, as the formal city economy expanded to offer regular work, premises and services to all and drove out inefficient, informal production and trading. In pursuit of this

Informal entrepreneurship

The entrepreneurialism of city people knows no bounds. The sheer diversity of people and activity in cities combined with shifts in the economy, regulation or technology endlessly create new opportunities to turn a penny, honestly or dishonestly. Here are some examples from different places:

In *Monrovia's* Red Light Market, women sell small bags of soap powder drawn from a manufacturer's box that they have purchased with a loan from a local NGO.

In *Delhi* 100,000 or more wastepickers scavenge rubbish dumps for items to resell, together recycling about 12% of the city's solid waste.

In *Lagos,* tailors walk the streets, with a small cushion on their head with an old Singer sewing machine on top, ready to do any quick sewing job they can find.

In *Jakarta,* young boys wait at the entrance to the city centre zone, where traffic regulations insist that cars carry at least three passengers, to serve as 'jockeys', making up the number of passengers, collecting their fee of 500 rupiah (about 3p) when they are dropped off.

Between *Kinshasa* and *Brazzaville*, either side of the Congo River and in different countries, cross-border trade in scarcities is handled by paraplegics on specially designed hand-pedalled tricycles, taking advantage of special low fares for them on the ferries.

belief, governments often took action, and many still do, to eliminate such activities: either directly by closing them down on health and safety, tax evasion or illegal occupation grounds, or indirectly by making the areas in which they operate the targets for new construction projects. But the permanent passing of the informal sector was not to be. Its transactions persist in all cities around the world, both as an important source of livelihood in itself and as a complement to the formal economy, for example, through subcontracting production or providing essential support services like transport and domestic service. In many of the cities of the South half of all employment may be in the informal economy; in cities of the North the proportion is much less, though still important. Above all, in all cities new kinds of informal activity constantly spring into life. In cities as marketplaces, informal is normal.

9.

Space and time: analysts' cities

St Petersburg 2008. In our household division of labour, finding places and how to get there is a role I arrogate to myself. It is partly that I love poring over maps, a residue from school and university geography studies. It is partly that I enjoy planning a trip, however minor. It is also that I do not trust others' analytical skills. There are claims that men are better equipped than women with spatial awareness and that too is probably in the back of my mind. Setting out from our hotel behind the Kazan Cathedral to walk to the Winter Palace, my companion and I disagree on which direction to take along the Nevsky Prospekt. I decide not to argue and we turn right. After almost a kilometre she concedes that we should have reached the palace by now but it is still not in sight. We consult the street plan again and I offer my interpretation of where we went wrong – we should have turned left – and how we must retrace our steps. We agree to do so. 'Trust me, I'm a geographer' I say, and under my breath 'I'm a man.'

Mapping the city

Analysts from many disciplines have studied the city. Centuries ago philosophers and religious thinkers – like Plato and St Augustine – ruminated on what brought people together in cities. In more modern times, economists, sociologists, geographers, historians, psychologists, political scientists and others have sought to understand the patterns and processes that characterise cities. Some would argrue that urbanism has become a distinct discipline.

But mapmakers can claim to be the longest established analysts of cities. For mapping the city is an act not just of representation but of interpretation. How the map is oriented, determining what takes centre stage, may be revealing. As will be the choice of what urban features to highlight and also the sizes of symbols and words used to label them. Colour choices may be significant: green for parks seems obvious, but what gets to be powerfully red: the sites of politics or commerce? The word for place names is often a tricky issue: in colonised cities there may be a choice between native and conqueror's names, and in post-revolutionary cities regime change may get expressed in changes of place names.

Above all, there is an editorial choice of what to include, what to exclude overtly or covertly from the map. John Snow's famous medical map of London's Soho district in 1855 displayed the location and number of cholera cases there and revealed an intensity nearest to the water pump in Broad Street: it was key evidence in his argument that cholera was carried by contaminated water. In contrast, a plan of Jerusalem from 1320 showed the homes of King Solomon, Pontius Pilate, St Anne and the locations of the Holy Sepulchre and the Temple. What it did not acknowledge was that the city had passed from the control of crusading Christians 125 years before and what it concealed were the non-Christian places of worship that now occupied those sites. Even today, in Rio de Janeiro the shanty towns that house a third of the city's population appear as green spaces on the official city plan: officially they are temporary dwellings that pay no property tax, so they do not exist. Throughout history 'Much of the power of the map, as a representation of social geography, is that it operates behind a mask of seemingly neutral science.'[1]

The earliest surviving city maps are incised on clay tablets from Mesopotamia around the 4th century BC. No town plans are known from ancient Greece, but Roman surveyors produced marble tablets bearing a large map of Rome. Chinese stone tablets with town plans survive from the 13th century. Subsequently, city mapping developed through changes in surveying techniques and in printing technology: from woodcuts to copperplate to lithography to digital. But, as cities grew in size and complexity, new cartographic ways of showing them were devised.

One is the bird's eye view, developed in Italy from the Renaissance invention of perspective drawing, representing a city from above, from what was – at that time, before powered flight – an unattainable viewpoint. Bird's eye views of cities are of limited value in finding your way around, for the scale is small so as to embrace all the city, streets are concealed by three dimensional buildings and the perspective shrinks the detail in the furthermost districts. What they provide, though, is an inspirational and memorable image of a city. As such they were often commissioned by real estate developers and chambers of commerce to boost growing 19th century North American cities. The bird's eye view was an expression of a political or commercial perspective on the city, though modern-day versions may serve more as decorative art.

Production of accurate and comprehensive town plans became widespread for European and North American cities in the early 19th century. Later, as a tool for city living, more was needed – street names, transport connections, one way traffic flows, house numbers, postcodes, a street index and, above all, clarity. It was Phyllis Pearsall in 1930s London who conceived the A-Z map that has all these qualities.[2] She created the first edition by walking the streets and visiting public agencies to record the information on an existing topographical map. It took her many years and much persistence for the new map to find its market. Today, the company she founded, Geographer's A-Z Map Company, still produces maps for British cities. Other publishers have adopted the format in cities around the world. CD-ROM and online versions, including routefinders, are now common.

The modern tourist map has an even older history. In the 1830s Karl Baedeker, a Heidelberg bookseller, published a travel guide to the Rhine Valley; others on Belgium, Holland, Switzerland and Austria followed in quick succession. His star system for ranking sights and his maps for locating them became standard. Baedeker's accuracy became renowned – 'Kings and governments may err, but never Mr Baedeker' was a line in Offenbach's 1866 operetta *La Vie Parisienne*. Since then travel guides have become universal; there cannot be a city in the world for which there is not at least one published. And, as tourist tastes have changed, the accompanying tourist maps have come to accommodate not just cultural sights like museums, palaces and parks, but also consumption sites like shops, restaurants, clubs, theatres and cinemas.

The schematised map of a city metro network is also now universal. The first version appeared in London in 1933. Prior to that date, there had been maps of the evolving Underground railway network that showed the routes more or less on their surface alignments. It was the genius of Harry Beck to turn the map into a diagram. In its subsequent eighty year history, it has run through many editions, expanding to accommodate new lines and stations, experimenting with new graphical devices to represent connections and relationships, published in poster and pocket sizes. Over this time, 'many newcomers to London, whether as visitors or residents, have pounced on the Diagram as on a magic guide to a hitherto bewildering city… Above any consideration of the Diagram as a navigation aid was the optimistic vision it offered of a city that was not chaotic, in spite of appearances to the contrary, that knew what it was about and wanted its visitors to know it, too.' Now virtually every metro system in the world has realised that the distortion of the

Harry Beck's London Underground Diagram[4]

The Diagram's strength is its clarity and adaptability. Its originality is in the principle that the internal connections of the lines and interchanges are more important – both for practical use and as a mental map of the city – than any reflection of the city's surface geography. So it distorts reality quite severely: the actual distances in the outer reaches of the network are shrunk; stations that are near to each other on the surface sometimes appear distant on the Diagram; the line of the Thames – the only geographical feature included – is very stylised. But it works. No cartographer would have designed such a map. In fact, Harry Beck, its originator, had worked as a signals engineering draughtsman and so was familiar with electrical circuitry diagrams – surely the inspiration for the concept. He remained associated with new editions of the Diagram over the years. Then his rights over it were disputed and after 1959 he parted company with London Underground. His original contribution has been recently acknowledged in the bottom right hand corner of the current edition of the Diagram.

diagram is of more practical use in getting around than the truthfulness of the map.[3]

Maps have thus become powerful tools for our understanding of the city. Their modern forms – transport diagrams, tourist maps, A-Z gazetteers – are essentially responses to the needs of increasingly literate, busy and mobile city people. As the clock helps us to manage our time, so the map helps us to find our direction: for attending meetings, locating premises, making collections and deliveries, visiting people and places outside our home neighbourhood.

Urban geometry

In the last century geographers, sociologists and economists have joined the cartographers in creating abstract views of the city. They have done so by modelling it spatially in terms of flows, networks, nodes, hierarchies and surfaces.[5]

Trade, exchange and transport have been intrinsic to city life for centuries. Analysts have explored the regularities in their flows and networks: people,

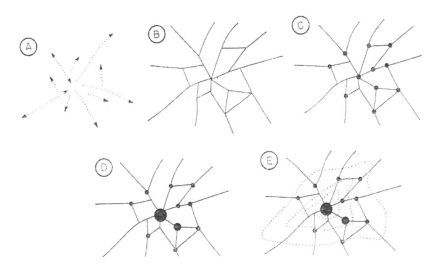

Flows (A), networks (B), nodes (C), hierarchies (D) and surfaces (E)

goods, services, energy, money, information and ideas transported on paths, roads, railtracks and through phone lines, power cables, water pipes, and radio waves. Sometimes this has been tackled theoretically. Newton's law of gravity – that two bodies in the universe attract each other in proportion to the product of their masses and inversely with the square of their distance – has been used to analyse migration or transport flows. In its application to cities the mass will be some measure of population or activity at locations, distance will depend on the modes and networks connecting them. The physicist's concept of entropy in thermodynamics – a measure of the amount of energy in a system – has also been borrowed to understand individual behaviour that results in spatial regularities. And the characteristics of city networks have been analysed using ideas from topology, the branch of geometry concerned with connectivity. An early application of these ideas, by the 18th century Swiss mathematician Euler, was to the real puzzle of whether it was possible for the citizens of Königsberg to visit the four parts into which rivers divided their city by a route that crossed all seven bridges once only. It was impossible.

Nodes and hierarchies have been explored in the broader settlement pattern of which individual cities are a part. One concept here is the rank-size rule that postulates regularity in the relative sizes of cities from the largest to the smallest in a country. Its earliest and simplest version, by the German geographer Auerbach in 1913, stated that the population of the nth ranked city in a nation would be 1/n of the largest city, so that, for example, the fourth largest city in a country would be a quarter the size of the largest. Since then endless variations of the rule have been explored in different countries. It doesn't always apply: for example, in Australia the cities of Sydney and Melbourne, of similar size, cluster together at the top of the rank; in Russia the opposite applies and Moscow is dominant with a big drop in size to the next largest cities. History sometimes offers explanations. Former imperial powers, like Austria, Portugal, Great Britain or Russia, though shorn of their territories often retain large first cities. In some countries accelerated economic growth has boosted the size of one city way above others: this is found with Bangkok in Thailand, Lima in Peru and other capital cities of the South.

There are also nodes and hierarchies identifiable within cities. The traditional concept of a city is monocentric, that is, there is one city centre with major activities there – like shopping, government, business services, religious observance, cultural institutions – serving the city as a whole. Subcentres exist in outer areas, some just providing more local services, others maybe with a specialist function as, for example, a university or a centre for media work or a major retail market. Thus a hierarchy of nodes may be identifiable in the city. But as cities grow larger still, as their populations and activities became more diverse, and as faster transport and communication modes are installed, then the monocentric model is often transmuted into a polycentric model.

Surfaces of land use, density, accessibility and land value are the expression of locational theory that offers explanations of why people and businesses choose to be where they are in the city. Land use is the most apparent pattern. At the broadest level there are residential areas, business centres, industrial zones, shopping and entertainment areas; at a more detailed level there are finer distinctions recognisable between districts of different age, rich and poor neighbourhoods, low and high-rise development, up and downmarket shopping, new forms like office parks, suburban or out of town shopping centres, golf courses or government districts. Underpinning these land use patterns are the related surfaces of variable density, accessibility and land value.

In many cities residential density declines on a negative exponential curve away from the city centre – that is, falling steeply at first and then flattening out. This is often reflected in a familiar sequence of housing types: near the centre are high-rise blocks of flats, then terrace housing, then further out detached houses on larger plots. Over time, through outward population movement and through rebuilding of inner areas, the densities towards the centre may fall, producing a flatter gradient. Accessibility measures how easily a part of the city can be reached from all other parts. The pattern will depend on transport systems: the existence of available and affordable modes of transport, their route networks, usage and congestion, average speeds and frequencies. Traditionally, the city centre was the peak of accessibility, but in many cities the dispersal of activities outwards, the construction of new transport routes and congestion in inner areas have altered this pattern and some outer zones may now have higher accessibility. In land value terms, the most expensive urban land may be anything up to a hundred times the market price of the cheapest and will be where uses offering the greatest return in investment choose to locate.

The nexus between use, density, location, accessibility and land value was extensively studied in the first half of the last century by Chicago sociologists and geographers. From their analyses emerged concepts of city structure that have provided an analytical lens through which many other cities have since been viewed. For the Chicago School this ordering of city space was the consequence of successive processes of competition, dominance, invasion and succession of activities in cities across the United States.

Chicago

Chicago is probably the most thoroughly dissected city in urban geography. It stands, the USA's third largest city, on the western shore of Lake Michigan. The many studies of it suggest the factors that have been at play in shaping it. First, the city surrounds the Central Business District – called The Loop after the elevated railway that encircles it – with its great daytime office population, its high buildings and high land values. Then, secondly, radiating out from the centre are wedge-shaped housing areas, differentiated by income so that, for example, the richer households live alongside the lake, poorer households out to the northwest and southwest. Thirdly, household type refines this pattern through generational differences (distinguishing inner zones with apartment-dwelling people in their twenties or fifties from families with young children further out) and racial segregation (with two distinct black districts in the inner zone). Fourthly, history has also had a hand, influencing the speed of development of different areas at different times and inserting new workplaces into the city structure at various stages, such as the heavy industry at Gary to the south or the employment at and around the O'Hare airport to the west.

These geometric analyses have been predominantly of cities of the North. Analysis of cities elsewhere reveals some major differences. For example, in many cities of the South that have grown explosively over the last century there is no marked density gradient out from the centre, especially where the city fringes are developed as squatter settlements. Even in cities of the North today these classic geometries are less apparent.

Traveller's tales

At the other extreme to these detached abstractions are the engaged accounts of travel writers. Encounters with new places have long inspired Western writers; their expeditions have had different motives, among them pilgrimages, crusades, trade (as with Marco Polo in the 13th century), explorations and voyages of discovery, conquests and colonisations; and some artists and writers have left home to settle as *émigrés* in new places. To our minds today many of these travellers' tales seem condescending, about funny foreign people and their habits. But, as Robert Louis Stevenson remarked 'There is no foreign land; it is only the traveller that is foreign.' Much travel writing is about journeys, often in exotic locations, the author moving on from place to place. But some travel writers have been inclined to stay put, to pause, observe and reflect, in order to engage more fully with one place, cities among them.

In this spirit, in the 19th century a number of writers turned their analytical gaze to the newly industrialised Western cities. They presented them to their readers – in pamphlets, journalism and reports – as equally astonishing as the 'dark continent' of Africa that explorers like Livingstone were revealing at the same time. Friedrich Engels was in Manchester for twenty months in the 1840s to complete a business apprenticeship to his father, who was the German partner in some cotton mills. He was a young man with aspirations to be a writer and was already radical in his politics. He was thus well able to contextualise and interpret his personal observations, which were published in *The Condition of the Working Class in England* (1845). In chapter three of the book, titled 'The Great Towns', he reports his observations of London, Dublin, Edinburgh and the industrial towns of the Midlands, Yorkshire and Lancashire before homing in on Manchester, which he describes in detail. He immersed himself in published records and reports on the city, but supplemented these by direct observation, using his eyes, ears, nose and feet in getting to know its residents. In his words, he sought 'more than a mere abstract knowledge of my subject.'[6] What was powerful in Engel's work was the connection he drew between the decrepitude of the city and the alienation and despair of so many of its people, both rooted in a persistent conflict between rich and poor. Engels went on to co-author *The Communist Manifesto* with Karl Marx.

Engels' book was published in German in 1845, but not translated into English until the 1880s. By then other similar works had appeared. Charles Booth's *Life and Labour of the People* (1889) reported the results of his survey of the life of the poor in London's East End. In New York Jacob Riis documented *How the Other Half Lives* (1890). Later writers maintained this tradition; George Orwell wrote compellingly about being *Down and Out in Paris and London* (1933) and of *The Road to Wigan Pier* (1937) in the 1930s. Much more recently and on a broader canvas Jeremy Seabrook has chronicled the tribulations of daily life *In the Cities of the South* (1996). A recent discovery has been the writings of Walter Benjamin, who died in 1940. In the 1920s and 1930s he had written vast numbers of essays on many subjects, much of it reportage and reflections on life in the cities of Berlin, Moscow, Naples, Marseille and especially Paris. Some was unpublished, most was only available in German and all was largely unknown until the last decade. He is not an easy read (the critic Susan Sontag described his thinking and writing as 'freeze-frame baroque'), but when you can penetrate the translated text, he often offers remarkable montages of the social and cultural life of the 20th century city.

Of present-day travel writers, Jan Morris has engaged most fully with the world's cities. Over a period of fifty years she has published books on Oxford, Venice, Hong Kong, Sydney and Trieste as well as essays on other cities as diverse as Cairo and Chicago, Leningrad and La Paz. She has often returned to the same city at different times. Her approach is impressionistic, drawing on history, politics and culture as well as personal observations and encounters. She is as interested in people as much as buildings, the feel as much as the look of the city. Her style is visual and rich, often over-rich with simile, alliteration and complicated syntax. But she always gets places right.

Old and new cities

Urban history also provides insights. In the Middle Ages there were three regions in the world – in Asia, the Middle East, and Europe – which each had

Jan Morris on:[7]

Hong Kong in the 1950s

'More people live in Hong Kong than in all the rest of the world put together, and they make more noise than a million electric drills, and they work like automation, and their babies are beyond computation, and their machinery chitter-chatters away for twenty-five hours every day, and in their markets they sell every fish that was ever caught, and every shrimp that ever wriggles, and every crab that ever pinched, and their excellent shirts cost fourpence-ha'penny apiece, and there are five million Chinese for every European in the city, each one of them more energetic than a power station: and all these unbelievable paradoxes of prolixity and profusion are a lesson in the impermanence of power and the mutability of history.'(Morris admits that these are wildly imaginative statistics.)

Soweto in the 1970s

'There is nowhere else in the world like Soweto. It is something like a disused exhibition, something like an open prison, something like a gypsy encampment, something like a construction camp, and something like a slum. With a population of more than a million – twice the size of Johannesburg itself – Soweto is one of the great cities of Africa, but it does not feel like a city at all, for it has no centre. Mile after mile, in interminable geometrical lines, curves and circles, the shabby little brick houses of the blacks extend across the treeless veld, linked by rutted mud roads, unkempt, unpainted, each section indistinguishable from the next, the whole seeming to possess no recognisable shape or limit.'

Sydney in the 1990s

'The cosmopolitanism of Sydney is of a decidedly European kind. A century ago James Bryce called Manhattan "a Euro city, but of no particular country", and the description now fits Sydney just as well. Of course, its substratum is aboriginal, its structure is still British, and like all English-speaking cities it has American overtones. More and more of its citizens are Asians. However, for the moment its superficial flavour. seems to me vaguely Mediterranean, Italianate, Greekish, Portuguesy, Lebanese-like – cappuccino after its oysters, street cafes, the lights of fishing boats passing beneath the Harbour Bridge in the dark – tinged, though, with the Irishness that has been so potent a part of it since the beginning.'

148

'an archipelago of cities.'[8] In contrast there was little in the way of cities in the Americas and in Africa. It was trade that bound these medieval cities together. Trade by land and sea also connected these groups of cities across the then known world, carrying precious commodities like silk and spices, pilgrims, slaves, even the Black Death of the mid 14th century. Cities like Hangchow and Canton in China, Calicut and Benares in India, Samarkand and Bukhara in central Asia, Basra, Damascus and Cairo in the Middle East, and Venice, Bruges and Krakow in Europe were already important by this time. They were 'merchant cities' and any of today's world cities have grown from these ancient trading origins.

A later kind of new city were capitals of emerging states, the homes of royal courts and their governments. In Europe, London, Paris, Antwerp, Madrid and others rose to pre-eminence in this way. Elsewhere in the world newly dominant dynasties, like the conquering Mughals in India and Manchu in China, also created new urban seats of power. Likewise, the colonisations of the Western powers in Latin America and Asia. These were cities dominated socially by governing elites, usually in the service of absolutist rulers. They can be called 'prince's cities'. Their growth was often planned, either by royal fiat or through capitalist property development, to create new residential quarters for the well-to-do, impressive palaces for the rulers, offices for government, sometimes all contained within grandiose layouts of streets, parks and monuments. The poorer residents, providing goods and services for the rich, were left to squeeze themselves into the gaps.

Starting in Western Europe in the 19th century, another kind of new city emerged: 'the industrial city'. It spread across the globe, into Eastern Europe, Russia and into North America in the later 19th century and into much of the rest of the world thereafter. It was principally the site of industrial manufacturing, all undertaken on a hitherto unknown scale in factories producing goods at high speed and low cost through new mechanical technologies. These cities rose quickly above a population of one million in size. Economically and socially they were characterised by a decline of artisanship, self-employment and homeworking, the loss of many old skills and customs and the learning of new ones, the development of a waged working class, and the growing importance of investors and managers. Class divisions became sharper, and these divisions were reflected in the changing structure of the city: massive extensions to accommodate its new businesses and their workers, a greater separation between homes and workplaces, new modes of public transport to connect them and more socially homogeneous city districts.

The 20th century saw the creation of yet other kinds of new city. These can be called 'migrants' cities'. Of course, immigration had historically always been a factor in the dynamism and growth of cities. But in the last century there was an explosion of such population movements right across the globe, different in their scale, in their geographical range, and in the diverse motivation of the migrants. This arose from the growing ease and cheapness of travel, growing knowledge of urban worlds beyond migrants' home patches, not least through the media, and growing aspirations for the better life that others are seemingly enjoying elsewhere. Such migration has a cumulative effect as word gets back from the cities to the sources of migration.

The 20th century cities most obviously built on migration are the resorts. The growth of resorts has been largely a phenomenon of the global North – though it has European precursors in the spa towns at home and the 'hill stations' of the colonies. Warm climate, the attractive scenery of coasts, mountains, or deserts, cheap property and easy access from wealthy countries have kickstarted the growth of many of these places, but they quickly acquire all sorts of other attractions like clubs, casinos, golf courses, health farms – and like-minded residents. Their growth frequently damages the natural landscape that was their original rationale, a process evident all along the Mediterranean and Florida coastlines.

Occasionally people of shared faith or ethnicity have migrated in such numbers to a specific place that they have effectively created a new émigré city in their own image. Salt Lake City in Utah, founded as their spiritual home by Mormons in the mid 19th century, was an early example – reportedly Brigham Young, Mormon's founder, declared 'This is the place' when he arrived there. In the last century Tel Aviv has been since 1909 a focus for Jewish immigration to Israel (and acquired a fine collection of Art Deco buildings in the process). These are successful, prosperous emigré cities. There are other, far more numerous cities in Latin America, Africa and Asia to which poor people, driven by war, natural disaster, or poverty or drawn by hope of a better life, have migrated and built themselves homes. These are the shanty towns which, while often built on the edge of existing cities, are often so enormous that they are cities in themselves. These are the biggest and most numerous modern cities in today's world. Thus, as the geographer Mike Davis observes:

'the cities of the future, rather than being made out of glass and steel as envisioned by earlier generations of urbanists, are instead largely constructed out of crude brick, straw, recycled plastic, cement blocks and scrap woods. Instead of cities of light soaring towards heaven, much of the twenty-first century urban world squats in squalor, surrounded by pollution, excrement and decay'.[9]

Resorts, émigré cities and shanty towns are mostly spontaneous creations. There are also new kinds of 20th century city which have been planned to attract migrants. Some are satellite cities built to accommodate urban growth not by the continued peripheral expansion of existing cities but by new free-standing settlements. Governments have also created new cities to accommodate the enterprises and workers needed to exploit new resources. Cities were built for heavy industry in the socialist states of the 20th century: the growth of Novosibirsk, now Russia's third largest city after Moscow and St Petersburg, was boosted by Stalin's industrialisation policies despite its remote location – some called it the 'Chicago of Siberia'. Company towns have also been built by businesses, though rarely on a large scale. The motor industry in the 1930s provides two examples with contrasting fortunes: Fordlandia, which was built by the Ford Company in the Amazon jungle, very much in small town American style, both in its architecture and its mores (ID badges to be worn! Alcohol prohibited! Regular hygiene checks compulsory!), to support an ultimately failed attempt to create major rubber plantations; and Wolfsburg in Germany, built to house workers at the new Volkswagen car factory and still the company HQ. Otherwise governments have stimulated city development by offering tax breaks to developers and businesses: like Dubai in the Gulf or the Shenzen 'special economic zone' in China. Shenzen, on the mainland north of Hong Kong, has grown from a small fishing village in the late 1970s to a city of ten million today, to become one of China's main manufacturing centres and one of its most prosperous cities, with 5 star hotels, a Gucci store, flashy restaurants and hectares of factories and blocks of flats.

Globalisation and cities

Contemporary analysts have become very preoccupied with the place of the city in an increasingly global economy. London, New York and Tokyo are today

151

clearly global cities, connected not just with their local hinterland but, probably more importantly, with other cities around the world. Their global pre-eminence is based largely on their role in financial services, especially from the way in which their stock markets operate successively through the twenty-four hour day. But other cities have claims to a global role in other terms – as locations for the headquarters of multinational corporations, as important centres of political power or even as international tourist destinations. The globalisation of cities is thus part commercial, part political and part cultural.

Some analysts argue that globalisation is not entirely new. Long distance trade has connected cities together for centuries: along the Silk Road in central Asia from before Christ, through coastal shipping from the Baltic to the Mediterranean in medieval Europe, across the Atlantic and Indian oceans with the Spanish, Portuguese, Dutch, French and British Empires from 1600 onwards, and through railway networks across most continents in the last two centuries. In Fernand Braudel's world history, *Civilisation and Capitalism, 15th to 18th Century,* he explores the role of successive 'world economies' each with a city as its 'logistic heart'. Over these centuries world dominance passed from Venice to Antwerp, Genoa, then Amsterdam and finally to London.[10]

What's different about global connections today is that they function at greater speed, on a much larger scale and with broader scope. New technologies have speeded up communication. Transport of goods and people around the world has been eased by motorways, railways and air travel – the day trip for business, the overnight delivery, the distant weekend break are now routine. Information can be transmitted instantaneously by phone, fax, email, text, Facebook or Twitter. In terms of scale, these connections are now far more pervasive: most places in the world are networked to most others and these connections transcend not just national boundaries but other historic divisions between East and West, North and South, First and Third Worlds. And the scope of global connections is now vast. Historically it was the trades in raw materials and manufactured goods that were dominant: the spice trade, the textile trade, the trade in precious metals were emblematic of earlier globalisation. Now it is many kinds of goods, services, people, capital, information, ideas and culture that flow around the world, often at the behest of international organisations such as Sony, McDonalds, GlaxoSmithKline, PriceWaterhouseCoopers, the World Bank, UNESCO, even the Mafia. Other such enterprises – like airlines, Microsoft, Vodafone, Google, Western Union, DHL – provide the universal means of communication.

One consequence of these shifts in the speed, scale and scope of global connections has been the emergence of new kinds of place across the world. One example is the so-called regional command centres of the global economy, cities like Singapore, Sydney or Brussels, where multinational organisations have their regional HQs. Another is those cities acting as gateways to major economies: Hong Kong as gateway to China is the supreme example, but others are Mumbai to India, Miami to the Caribbean and Latin America. But there are other less obvious examples of globally connected places, such as export processing zones using cheap labour to produce trainers, assemble computers or staff call centres; high-tech districts, like the original Silicon Valley in California and its many imitators in other countries; banking locations, as traditionally in Zurich but now also in the Cayman Islands, Guernsey or wherever tax and regulatory costs are low; and mass tourist or retirement destinations such as the resorts of the Mediterranean, the Caribbean, Thailand and Florida.

These dispersals of activity were thought by some analysts to signify the decline of big cities and the accumulation of people and activity within them. Some spoke of the 'death of distance', of the emergence of the 'non-place urban realm', of a new form of virtual 'cybercity'. In reality, the global city has emerged as another kind of new place, one that services international trade and investment through its financial markets and banks and the professional services provided by lawyers, accountants, media professions, marketing and management consultants.

Analysts note two outcomes. First, the emergence of a competition between cities for globally footloose resources, most evidently investment capital but also corporate HQs, highly skilled people, and even events like international conferences or the Olympic Games. This produces winners and losers, not just between countries but within countries. In many countries historically dominant cities have done well, as have London, Paris, Buenos Aires, Sydney and Bangkok. But some have been displaced by upstarts: thus in Brazil Sao Paulo is now the global city rather than Rio de Janeiro or Brasilia, in China Shanghai rather than Beijing, in India Mumbai rather than Delhi.

Secondly, within cities, the dominance of global over local connections has produced a greater polarisation between haves and have-nots. Among the affluent minority are the entrepreneurs, professionals and managers in global business, politics and culture, many from other countries, often on short sojourns sponsored by their multi-national employers. Among the poorer

153

majority are those in support work, working for low wages as cooks and waiters, maids, security guards, prostitutes, construction workers and chauffeurs, many of them immigrants to the city drawn to better paid work than at home. This polarisation has commonly been played out in the restructuring of cities. The contrasts are often very evident and extreme on the ground. In Shanghai the shining new skyscrapers of Pudong, financed, built by and housing international corporations, contrast with the small houses of the poor that they are progressively replacing. In London the financial district 'The City' merges to its west with the 'West End' of government, business, retailing and high-class residential areas but to its east it abruptly adjoins the city's 'East End' of poor, in some parts immigrant, communities.

Close-up and distant views

At a city anywhere in the world, compare the experience of coming in to land by plane in daylight or at nighttime. In daylight what you see below is like a map on which large and small buildings, roads and railways, parks and other open land, rivers, ports and airports are on show. The view is rich in detail and variety; colour helps to enliven the scene. You get a sense of the city as a place, its composition, its look, its density, even its character. If a visitor you may be eagerly looking for that first impression which precedes your ground level encounter with the place. By contrast, landing at nighttime what you see is more abstract, poor in detail and variety, mostly monochrome, but strongly delineated. Much depends on the illumination. Roads show up from their street lights and the vehicles on them, whereas railways may appear as dark strips with, maybe, trains snaking along them. Parks, their openness and greenery so evident in daylight, are now voids, closed for the night; docks and goodsyards may also be blanks. But floodlit sportsgrounds are often bright beacons. Overall, among the city's predominantly dark industrial and residential areas, there are crescendos of light in the centres where window displays, lights on for office cleaning, floodlighting, neon adverts and streetlights blaze together. The sense you get is of the city's spatial pattern, a diagram more than a map.

Both are valid, only different, perspectives. So it is with analysts' takes on time and space in the city. Sometimes what is offered is a close-up: lively, detailed, full of vitality, warts and all, maybe quite bewildering and needing interpretation. We may respond empathetically as much as intellectually to this kind of analysis. Then again, sometimes what analysts offer is a more distanced view: strongly patterned, conceptualised, maybe quite abstract, possibly harder to relate to and intellectually challenging, but, once understood, providing fresh insights of an underlying order in the complexity of the city.

10.

Metamorphosis: Tokyo's renewals and reinventions

Venus Fort 2011. *We are having lunch in the Piazza del Duomo: Parma ham, followed by Pizza Capricciosa, a glass of red wine, an excellent Panna Cotta and an espresso. All around us are Japanese couples and families. But they are not tourists, they are locals. For our Italian lunch is in Tokyo's Venus Fort shopping mall, designed as an Italian town of streets, alleys and piazzas, facades with colonnades and balconies, all in warm-coloured stone, with the cathedral next to our restaurant as its highpoint, its clock striking the hour. Above us a blue sky changes – on an hourly cycle – from sunrise to daylight, then dusk and nighttime. The mood is all very Mediterranean, not Japanese. But the outlets in this replica Italian town in Tokyo are mostly familiar global brands – Tommy Hilfiger, Starbucks, Burberry, Zara, McDonalds, Diesel. Tokyoites clearly love this stuff.*

Looking west

In 1853 Commodore Matthew Perry sailed his ships into Tokyo (then called Edo) Bay to deliver a letter from US President Millard Fillmore, demanding trading rights. After a brief stand-off the shogun rulers of Japan finally agreed. The ban on outside contact that had prevailed since the early 17th century ended and Japan entered the modern world. In the subsequent century and a half, Tokyo has had a love affair with the Western world that today – as Venus Fort shows – still persists. It is evident in the look and habits of the city.

In architecture, locals first imitated Western styles while using traditional building techniques. Later English and German architects came to Tokyo to practice. The most eminent was Josiah Conder, who arrived in 1877 and was employed by the government to teach a new generation of architects at the university. He was a highly eclectic designer, he and his pupils employing many different styles in their banks, hotels, mansions, palaces (including the imperial Akasaka Palace – like Buckingham Palace outside, Versailles inside, according to one guide book[1]), museums, railway stations (the main Tokyo station resembles that in Amsterdam) and offices. Few of these buildings survived subsequent fires or earthquakes. The exception was the Imperial Hotel, opened in 1923 and designed by American Frank Lloyd Wright in 'Mayan Revival' style. Architectural eclecticism still prevails. In 1958 the Tokyo Tower – an imitation of the Eiffel Tower in Paris – was built. Among recent eye-popping buildings, are the Tokyo International Forum (meeting and concert halls accessed through a 60 metre high inverted boat-shaped foyer), the glass bubble of the new Prada store which has become a tourist attraction in its own right, the Lego-like Fuji TV HQ (with a gold spherical observatory on top) and the soaring towers of the new Tokyo Metropolitan Government Centre in Shinjuku, these last two by Tange Kenzo, Japan's pre-eminent modern architect. More than any of my other iconic cities, Tokyo has become a playground for the fantasies of international architects. Donald Richie, a lifelong Tokyo resident and observer, comments damningly that 'Tokyo in its entirety resembles Disneyland on a mammoth scale...'[2]

Western styles crept into other aspects of the city's life. For men, Western dress was initially expensive, but the Western haircut was not and by the end of the 19th century only the rare eccentric man still sported a topknot; for women, it was not until the flapper styles of the 1920s that they cut their hair shorter and let it down. Today you will see most Tokyoites in Western dress, though traditional dress for both men and women will have an outing for relaxation at home or on special occasions. Rich Tokyoites are still ardent fans of Western brands: many such firms have Tokyo alongside New York, Los Angeles, Milan, London and Paris as the locations for flagship stores advertised on their bags and storefronts. But Tokyo's teenagers are something else when it comes to dressing up. Visit Harajuku district on a Sunday for the strangest fashion parade of all. This is when the *kosupurai* (costume play) kids gather on the bridge over the railway tracks dressed up in outrageous outfits – referenced to favourite rock bands, cartoon characters, porn videos or militaria – which are certainly creative, if weird. Other Western customs were adopted gradually: reading print from left to right, time measured in minutes and hours, beer replacing *sake* as the national drink, school uniforms, baseball as the national sporting obsession, eating beef, coffee shops replacing tea houses.

All this went beyond imported customs and styles. Tokyo also led Japan's embrace of Western technology in the early 20th century. 'Japanese spirit, Western technology' was a government slogan of the day. Large corporations, commonly family-owned, grew in new manufacturing industries like vehicles, electrical and electronic goods and chemicals, often with integrated finance and trading businesses. They followed a common path, starting with imported technologies, often on licence from firms like Siemens and General Electric, but soon investing heavily in their own research and development and diversifying into new product lines. Strong government support was in place from the start. From these beginnings sprang Japan's later export successes.

For Tokyo's relationship with the West has not been all one-way. In the decades that followed the opening of Japan to trade with the West there was a craze in Europe and North America for Japanese arts, crafts and culture. Artists like Monet, Van Gogh and Degas became influenced by Japanese art. In Paris, Berlin, London and New York new galleries imported ceramics, prints and lacquerware for collectors to buy – the early reputation of the Liberty store in London, founded in 1875, rested on these imports, displayed in its basement Eastern Bazaar. Also in London, in 1885-7 a Japanese Village was built as an exhibition in Knightsbridge and attracted over a million visitors. Advertisements for it in the *Illustrated London News* declared that 'Skilled Japanese artisans and workers (male and female) will illustrate the manners, customs and art-industries of their country, attired in their national and picturesque costumes. Magnificently decorated and illuminated Buddhist temple. Five o'clock tea in the Japanese tea-house. Japanese Musical and other Entertainments. Every-day Life as in Japan.' In 1885 too Gilbert and Sullivan's comic operetta *The Mikado*, its libretto based in Japan, had its premiere. Later, in 1904, Puccini's opera *Madame Butterfly*, with its tale of the American naval officer Pinkerton's duplicity in abandoning his Japanese mistress Butterfly and his child by her, provided a more tragic take on Japan's relations with the West.

Tokyo's economic success, giving it now the largest Gross Domestic Product among world cities[3], has largely been a consequence of its export trade. Vehicles and electronics are the products and corporate finance the service that come most to mind: Honda, Sony, Toshiba, Nomura are global brands. But there are others, such as the fashion houses of *Comme des Garçons* and Issy Miyake, Shiseido cosmetics, and more generally the popularity overseas of karaoke, manga comics, karate and judo, sudoku puzzles and sushi cuisine. In recent years a curious example of a global export was the tamagotchi, a portable computer game created in 1996 that became a must-have craze for children. It was a virtual pet, shaped like an egg (*tamago* in Japanese) that you watch (*gotchi* being a homonym for this English word).

Tokyo's exports

Capital – Tokyo ranks with New York and London as a leading financial centre. Its stock exchange opens and closes daily in synch with theirs.

Designer clothes – in the 1980s Japanese fashion designers from Tokyo made a splash internationally with their unconventional treatments of fabric: Rei Kawakuo's label *Comme des Garçons* pioneered distressed fabric, Issy Miyake worked with pleating, Yohji Yamamoto with draping. These and other Japanese labels have diversified and flourished since to become part of the international fashion scene. At the lower end of the market Uniqlo casual clothes have expanded from their Japanese base into Singapore, Seoul, New York, London, Paris, even Moscow.

Honda vehicles – until the 1970s Europe or the USA dominated world markets for cars, trucks and motorcycles. Then, Japanese manufacturers – including Honda with its HQ in Tokyo – broke into these markets with models that were affordable and reliable. They are still world leaders.

Karaoke – the singalong machine, invented in the 1970s: literally the word means 'empty orchestra.'

Manga – this cartoon style of comics and movies has greatly influenced graphic design outside Japan in the last two decades. Its roots are in traditional art, but with US cultural influence from the occupation of Japan after World War Two.

Muji – the producer and retailer of minimalist household and consumer goods has stores, and loyal followers, across southeast Asia and Europe.

Seiko and Casio watches – Hattori Kintajo, following apprenticeship to a watch dealer, set up a street stall and in 1885, as his Seiko brand prospered, he bought the premises in Ginza where the firm's flagship store has been ever since. Casio produce cheaper watches and calculators.

Sony Walkmans – Sony produce a range of consumer electronic products, introducing in 1979 the first portable cassette and later CD player which dominated the world market until the Apple iPod came along.

Toshiba laptops – famed for introducing laptops in the 1980s, the company was formed in 1939 from the merger of the Shibaura Engineering Works Corporation (founded in 1869) and the Tokyo Electrical Corporation (founded 1890).

Sushi – cooked and vinegared rice (the word means 'it's sour'), topped with or put into rolls with other ingredients, commonly seafood; its popularity round the world has created endless non-Japanese variants.

Tamagotchis – this electronic virtual pet became a worldwide craze for a few years in the late 1990s and early 2000s.

Once activated to give birth and named, it required constant attention: pressing buttons to feed it, to medicate it, to dispose of its excrement, to play with and discipline it, to put it to bed. If not fed enough, it died on you; if ignored, it became delinquent; if looked after, it reached adulthood and could mate. Seventy million were sold worldwide. Video, film and music spin-offs followed. By 2009, the craze had largely passed.

Tokyo was the first Asian city to become westernised in these ways. Where it has lead, others – notably Hong Kong, Singapore, Shanghai, Seoul – have followed in the last half century. But among the world's big cities it remains comparatively un-cosmopolitan. There are some foreigners working for local branches of multi-nationals, fewer for Japanese corporations. There a number of Koreans, Chinese and Philippinos in low paid work. But Tokyo is not the magnet for migrants that other cities have become. Despite the determined modernisation of the last century and a half, Tokyoites remain ambivalent about the wider world. They talk of 'the double life', meaning being both foreign and domestic, bound to both tradition and change, conversing in Japanese and English or even a hybrid 'Japlish'. For them 'The double life is at best an expense and an inconvenience… at worst a torment, leading to crises of identity…'[4] As a Western visitor, you frequently experience a sense of dislocation that leaves you uncertain how to interpret – as familiar or strange? – the evidence of your eyes, ears or taste buds. This was captured well in – and nicely expressed in the title of – Sofia Coppola's film *Lost in Translation* (2003), where in a luxury Tokyo hotel Bob, an aging American movie star here to film a Suntory whisky commercial for $2million, encounters and exchanges experiences of the city with Charlotte, a young Yale graduate accompanying her celebrity photographer husband on assignment.

Four traumas

That today Tokyo strikes you as so modern – certainly more so than Venice or even Paris and New York, among my iconic cities – is not just because of this century and a half of Westernisation. It is also because in that short history it has suffered a succession of traumas, necessitating new starts in the life of the city. The Great Wave, a woodblock print made around 1830 by the artist Hokusai (which has become one of the most reproduced artworks in the world), vividly captures the sense of trauma as its three fishing boats, returning to Tokyo with Mount Fuji shown in the distance, are about to be overwhelmed by the sea. This now seems like a foresight of the real life traumas that Tokyo would suffer in the next 200 years. The 1923 Tokyo earthquake is well-known. There was, too, its destruction by aerial bombing at the end of World War Two, almost as complete as the destruction of the cities of Hiroshima and Nagasaki by atomic bombs. But human events have also had their impact on the city as political regimes have come and gone, as business has boomed and bust, often bringing calamity in their wake. These traumas have successively reshaped Tokyo.

The first trauma was political: the Meiji Restoration of 1868 when the Tokugawa shoguns, the feudal strongmen who had ruled Japan since 1603, were defeated by the forces of the seventeen-year-old Emperor Meiji. The fifteenth and last shogun, his aristocratic supporters, bureaucrats, servants, concubines and hangers-on fled the city. Their mansions were burned, dismantled or left to decay, the population of the city halved in size, its economic life came to a standstill. The Emperor moved his permanent residence from Kyoto to Edo, which was renamed Tokyo, meaning 'Eastern Capital'. Slowly the city revived

Hokusai's *The Great Wave* – a foresight of Tokyo's traumas

161

as the royal, political and, in due course, commercial capital of Japan. It is in these years that the origins of many of the city's major businesses can be found. Construction of the new Imperial Palace was completed by 1889 and wider rebuilding got underway. 'Civilisation and Enlightenment' became the watchword of the new regime in the following decades. Universities, department stores, horse-drawn carriages and trolleys, and industrial factories arrived in the city.

This progress came to a sudden halt with the second trauma of the Great Earthquake of 1923. The epicenter was in the bay southeast of the city. It hit 8.3 on the Richter scale. Over three days from 1st-3rd September there were 1,700 quakes. More than 100,000 people died, most from fires, some from drowning, few crushed by collapsing buildings. When it was all over more than half the buildings in the city, many still of timber construction, had been destroyed or seriously damaged and millions were homeless. After the earthquake, the damaged city districts were rebuilt piecemeal on the old street pattern. But for some businesses the trauma created an opportunity to relocate and rebuild, and the city accelerated its expansion westward across the plain and away from the bay. In this period Tokyo aspired to be not just a national but also an imperial city. Japan's rulers had come to believe that Imperialism was an essential aspect of Westernisation. They annexed Manchuria in 1931, invaded China in 1937 and conquered much of southeast Asia after entering the World War Two, on the side of the Axis Powers, with the surprise attack on Pearl Harbour in 1941.

This imperial adventure ended badly and brought upon the city its third trauma. In 1944-45 the US air force made over 4,000 bombing raids on Tokyo before Japan surrendered. The city was largely reduced to rubble. Its government collapsed (excepting the Emperor who, for reasons of *realpolitik*, the victorious Americans left on his throne) as did its economy and society. Of the city's seven million residents, four million left and whole districts were depopulated. David Peace's detective novels *Tokyo Year Zero* (2007) and *Occupied City* (2009) capture the chaos of this time. This is a city in which ruined buildings and makeshift shacks must make do as premises for home and work; its famous department stores are only trading from their ground floors; the Imperial Palace is destroyed. Repatriated Japanese from newly liberated parts of Asia swell the population. Road vehicles are scarce (Peace's Inspector Minami and his colleagues have to walk as they go about their business), the occasional trains and trams are packed to capacity, with broken windows, running to and from derelict stations. People are starving. There are 60,000 black market stalls, where much of the emergency food aid is ending up, controlled by rival gangs. Typhoid, cholera, smallpox, alcohol and drug abuse are widespread. Prostitution is rife, not least to serve the Victors.

The Americans' occupation of 1945-51 brought to Tokyo a mix of democracy, capitalism and New Deal welfare. Slowly the city got back on its feet. Hosting the 1964 Olympics was a symbolic celebration of its resurgence: 'No longer a defeated nation in disgrace, Japan was respectable now. After years of feverish construction, of highways and stadiums, hotels, sewers, overhead railways, and subway lines, Tokyo was ready to receive the world with a grand display of love, peace, and sports.'[5] The new bullet trains from Tokyo to Osaka, running at speeds of 300 kilometres per hour were the envy of the world. Boomtime continued in Tokyo through the next three decades. Credit was easy, property prices reached dizzying heights, construction was relentless, consumption was unbounded, lifetime jobs were secure, Japanese management styles were widely praised and copied abroad. But in the 1990s, the city suffered its fourth trauma: the financial bubble burst, shares and property lost value, corruptions scandals unseated politicians, in 1995 a terrorist group released deadly sarin gas on commuter trains, bankruptcies grew in number and suicides climbed to over 30,000 people a year. Some of the city's manufacturing shifted overseas and some of its financial businesses relocated to Hong Kong or Singapore. What followed became known as Japan's 'lost decades'. Since then Tokyo has only slowly reclaimed its role as a world city.

In 2011 an earthquake and tsunami struck 150 kilometres north of Tokyo. This time the city remained intact, despite the tremors, but concern spread about radiation leaks from a damaged nuclear plant and there was panic buying of food and drugs. Some people, especially foreigners, left the city for other parts of Japan or overseas. A fifth trauma was averted, but Tokyoites were reminded yet again of the fragility of their city.

Low City, High City

Greater Tokyo is enormous; the world's biggest city. Thirty-five million people live here – about a quarter of Japan's population. The city spreads over an area about 90 kilometres from east to west, from Tokyo Bay towards Mount Fuji visible on the western horizon, and 25 kilometres from north to south. Its major airport at Narita is 66 kilometres out from the city centre. (In comparison JFK in New York is 19 kilometres out, Charles de Gaulle in Paris 25 kilometres out.) Administratively Tokyo contains the twenty-three special wards of the former Tokyo city, twenty-six other cities in the suburbs, five towns and eight villages, each of which is to some degree self-governing, all overseen by the Tokyo Metropolitan Government. The fragmentation of the city has long been noted by Western visitors: the Victorian traveller Isabella Bird remarked in 1889 that the city was a mere 'aggregation of villages' and 'lacked concentration'; in 1930 the author Peter Quennel saw it as 'a huge extension of a single neighbourhood' and the sociologist David Riesman in 1976 declared Tokyo to be 'a metropolis superimposed on a series of villages.'

Visiting Tokyo today – with its skyscrapers, metro trains, freeways, neon signs and noise – 'village' hardly seems the right descriptor for its districts, but the impression of a city of many parts remains. Tokyo has a cellular structure, its inner and outer parts equal in importance, not the former dominant over the other, its transport routes not radial but loosely rectangular, its districts modular repeats of each other with commonly a railway station and a department store at their core. In these respects it is, among my iconic cities, most like Los Angeles, having expanded organically with relatively little overall planning. It is, of course, of a comparable youth, both being largely the creation of the late 19th and 20th centuries.

The leading historian of Tokyo, Edward Seidensticker, gave his 1983 book the title *Low City, High City*.[6] This distinction is partly topographical, partly historical. The Low City districts were originally built in the late 19th century on the flatlands of the Sumida River delta alongside Tokyo Bay and contain most of the few old buildings that have survived the city's traumas. The High City districts occupy hillier ground to the west, largely developed in the 20th century. But this simple duality only tells part of the story. To the south are industrial and port zones and after them Tokyo merges into the neighbouring city of Yokohama. Away to the west on the Musashino plain are most of the city's modern suburbs. Offshore in Tokyo Bay are new districts on reclaimed land.

Symbolically, the Imperial Palace is the centre of the city. It is set in 115 wooded hectares and open to the public only twice a year, for them to give greetings to His Imperial Highness at New Year and on his birthday. It's decidedly not a public green space, like Central Park in New York or Hyde Park in London. The cultural commentator Roland Barthes noted the paradox that Tokyo 'does possess a center, but this center is empty. The entire city turns around a site both forbidden and indifferent, a residence concealed beneath foliage, protected by moats, inhabited by an emperor who is never seen, which is to say, literally, by no one knows who.'[7]

Asakusa to the north is the nearest Tokyo comes to an old town district. At its heart is Senso-ji, the city's most venerable Buddhist temple, and around it developed the city's principal popular entertainment district of theatres, cabarets, cinemas, bars and restaurants. In its heyday it was like Montmartre in the 1890s or Times Square in the 1940s. The 1945 bombing wiped it out and since then such trades have largely moved elsewhere. Some gentrification is now underway.

South of Asakusa and east of the Palace lie the districts that, in the early stages of modernisation, became the new commercial centre of the city. Ginza was a busy and prosperous district of artisans and small shops that went up in flames in 1872. The city rulers decided that the city must be fireproof and the new Ginza was the place to start. An English architect, Thomas Waters, was hired to oversee the rebuilding. A grid street pattern, provided with streetlights and planted with trees and lined by brick buildings with shops and the new department stores with residences above, was decreed – it became known as Bricktown. Locals were initially uncertain about its North American appearance but Ginza became, and indeed has remained through subsequent rebuilding, a fashionable place to see and be seen – such that 'Ginza' is the name in many other Japanese cities for their fashionable shopping district.

Between Ginza and the Imperial Palace is Marunouchi. Here the shogunate courtiers had had their mansions, but after the Meiji restoration many were abandoned and the area became mostly wasteland. In 1890 it was sold as a whole to the Mitsubishi enterprise, which made its early fortune providing transport and supplies to the Meiji army. Over the next three decades Mitsubishi built it up with brick buildings on a street grid in an architectural style reminiscent of Marylebone or Kensington – so it was known as Londontown. The building of Tokyo's main railway station on its eastern edge in 1914, with the main entrance facing west into Marunouchi (towards the palace out of respect for the Emperor, it was said) assured its status as a business district. It was in Marunouchi that, after 1945, the American victors set up their HQ, symbolically alongside the Emperor's palace. Today it has high-rise office blocks with shopping arcades in their basements and restaurants at the top. Those dining expensively there can, for the first time, see more of the Imperial Palace and its grounds than had ever before been visible to Tokyo's residents. In Marunouchi, bank and insurance company executives are the modern heirs of the shogunate.

But while Ginza and Marunouchi and nearby districts next to the palace have been built and rebuilt over a century or so, other districts in the city well away from there have become vibrant new centres for Tokyo life. Some of these originated as post stations on the four great highways connecting the city with the rest of Japan: they were at Shinagawa, Shinjuku, Itabashi and Senju. Here travellers rested before entering or leaving the city and to serve them inns, hostelries, tea houses and brothels thrived – creating what locals called *ukiyo*, 'the floating world' of transient pleasures. Not all of these traditional locales have been transformed into modern centres. What made the difference was the coming of the railways and later the freeways as new entry routes to the city. Itabashi and Senju were bypassed and lost out; Shinagawa and Shinjuku benefited.

Shinagawa, 8 kilometres south of the palace, now has most embassies in the city, a big group of luxury hotels, upmarket residences and is also a fast-growing business centre. Its skyscrapers cluster around the railway station, which is a stop on the bullet train line to Osaka. Shinjuku, 5 kilometres west of the palace, is likewise built around a railway station, one that is claimed to be the busiest in the world with nearly four million passengers every day, either terminating or transferring here. Shinjuku has developed in a few decades as a very typical Tokyo mix of glitz and grot: to the west of the station is the glossy Shinjuku of fashion stores, high-rise apartments, restaurants, cinemas and theatres and concert halls, offices and hotels; to the east is a grotty Shinjuku of hostess bars, love hotels, strip shows and street food. It was to east Shinjuku that, it is claimed, film director Ridley Scott came, looked around, then went home and designed the street scenes for his movie *Blade Runner*.

Other districts are centres for particular trades: Shibuya for youth fashion, Omotesando for more upmarket fashion (its main avenue known as 'the Champs Elysées of Tokyo'), Akihabara for electronic goods with over 600 shops shifting 10% of national sales; Ueno for museums and the city's most spectacular cherry blossom display in April. In recent decades property developers have been busy creating further new centres, known as 'cities within the city', extensive in scale, with mixed residential, commercial and cultural uses, accommodated in spectacular architecture. Yebisu Garden Place fills the former site of the Sapporo brewery with a thirty-nine storey tower, a glossy hotel, shops and bars and restaurants galore (with a top-notch French restaurant in a *faux* chateau), and the city's photography and beer museums, all connected to the nearest railway station by a covered moving walkway. Odaiba in Tokyo Bay, an island reclaimed with landfill, has grown as a shopping and entertainment destination with a strange array of attractions: Tokyo Big Sight (a conference and exhibition centre), Toyota City Showcase (with all the car maker's current models), the Wonder Wheel (a ferris wheel), an artificial beach, and the Venus Fort shopping mall (named after the fortress in the bay that failed to deter Commander Perry in 1853). A monorail and the spectacular Rainbow Bridge (colourfully lit at night) connect Odaiba to the city. Roppongi Hills is the latest new centre, developing former military lands into a mixture of commerce and culture with plentiful greenery – what its developer fancifully called an 'artintelligent city.'

All these Tokyo districts, old and new, are well connected by the city's transport system. There are freeways, frequently congested, often squeezed tightly between buildings. But it is the dense subway and surface rail networks that keep the city on the move. One guide book describes the subway route map as 'like a messy plate of noodles'.[8] You quickly find the system easy to navigate and impressively efficient: fourteen colour-coded lines, stations numbered, many interchanges and, above all, frequent and reliable trains – though the numerous exits can confuse you. Surface railways move massive commuter flows between the suburbs and the major city termini. These, and the subway lines, are connected to the 34 kilometres long Yamanote line that loops around inner Tokyo, with trains every few minutes, running both clockwise and anti-clockwise, stopping at twenty-nine stations and taking an hour for a circuit. The loop connects the older eastern Low City and newer western High City centres of Tokyo as well as the termini for the lines bringing commuters in from the city's far-flung suburbs.

It is these western districts that are now dominant in Tokyo. Modern Tokyoites regard Shinjuku as the city's real centre. The opening here in 1990 of the new forty-five storey HQ of Tokyo's metropolitan government seemed to symbolise its new status. Donald Richie observes that Shinjuku 'is, in its way, a microcosm of Tokyo itself. Big, sprawling, forever metamorphosing, packaging all the advantages of over-crowding with all the charms of free enterprise. Noisy, forever under construction, Shinjuku is not (despite its share of rip-off joints)

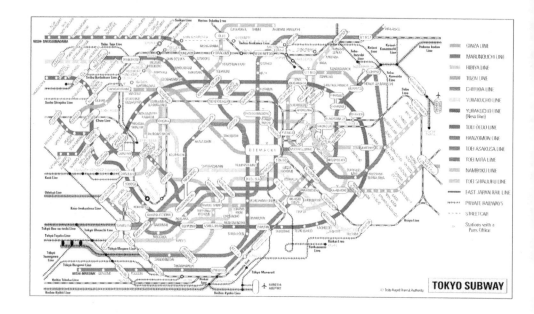

Tokyo's metro system – like a messy plate of noodles.

hostile or (money-grubbing though it is) cynical. It is massive, crammed, bewildering, but it is also warm and filled with the wonderful innocence of just being alive.'[9]

Technology and touch

In these many centres the nighttime cityscape is ablaze with light from street advertising. Whereas other cities have one such neon-soaked district – Times Square in New York, Piccadilly Circus in London, for example – Tokyo has many. Akihabara, Ginza, Shibuya and Shinjuku are the most spectacular, but there are others across the city. When night falls, Tokyo seems to be built of light rather than steel, glass or concrete. Buildings are lined vertically with strips of neon, often flashing on and off or changing colour; across some run electronic ticker messages or they carry vast screens showing adverts with soundtracks, or maybe they have images projected onto their facades; atop them are enormous neon hoardings, some revolving. Even some streetlamps have illuminated columns. Clubs and bars export their music through outside loudspeakers. This sound and light show goes on for street after street in districts that attract nighttime crowds bar-hopping, film-going, eating out, shopping or just strolling with friends.

But neon is only one of Tokyo's technological wonders. Vendomats are found on almost every street corner. They sell an amazing range of products: not just drinks, snacks and cigarettes (the latter requiring age verification with an identity card), but also hot coffee, pot noodles, underwear, DVDs and magazines (including porn), films, toiletries, underwear, condoms and sex aids, flowers, fresh meat and eggs. Some vendomats will speak to you ('Thank you for your custom' or 'Please come again'), some serving cold drinks can

Nighttime Tokyo – ablaze with light

adjust their price according to the outside temperature. Then there are pachinko parlours where up to one hundred people – all sorts: men and women, young and old, smart and shabby – sit in rows facing slot machines, testing their skill and maybe winning modest prizes of chocolate, fruit or tobacco; the noise of the steel balls whizzing round is deafening. Equally loud is karaoke which, though now a worldwide phenomenon, has its home in Tokyo.

Kapital of kitsch

The concept of 'kitsch' originated in Germany, but today the Japanese have made it their own. With kitsch something pretends to be something else. Tokyo is full of it: plastic versions in a window of the dishes on offer in restaurants, Mount Fuji as a tissue box with the paper as the volcano smoke, temples built in steel and concrete but pretending to be timber, new buildings in classic Italian, French or American style. And it's not just kitsch objects, it's customs too: like every station on the Yamamote line having its own musical theme to accompany announcements; like the 'maid cafes' where the waitresses are dressed in themed costumes as schoolgirls or nuns or nurses (and the 'butler cafes' that dress waiters for a female clientele). 'In Tokyo the ostensible is the real' – Donald Richie again[10].

Even weirder are the sushi bars where the food passes your table on conveyor belts with colour-coded dish prices (now copied elsewhere in the world); the capsule hotels where the rented 'room' may be no more than 2 metres long by 1metre wide and high with just a bed, TV and internet connection while luggage is stored in a locker, washrooms are communal and check in and check out are totally automated; or – in more upmarket hotels – toilets with heated seats, built-in bidet, automatic flush and hot air bum drier, all controlled from a panel beside you. All these technological wonders lead William Gibson, the sci-fi author, to describe Tokyo as 'the global imagination's default setting for the future.'[11]

But Tokyo also offers you more personal service than you might expect in a large city – high touch as well as high technology. Enter a restaurant, or even just a cafe, and you will be loudly greeted by the servers; and thanked when you depart. On metro station platforms are staff, dressed in fancy uniforms with caps and braid, to assist the loading and unloading of passengers, including some shoving in the rush hour. In the classier department stores there are staff accompanying the lifts, not just inside announcing the floors but outside directing you to the next available lift – and bowing deeply as the doors close. You quickly learn that hands together and a slight incline of the head is an essential day by day civility in personal contacts. For the business traveller the ritual of the business card must be learned: giving and receiving it with both hands, name side up, with script facing the recipient. The paradox of personal service and advanced technology side by side in Tokyo is captured by the routine of the city centre parking garage. From the street you will be guided by polite, uniformed staff who will wave you in when space is free, tell you where to stop and then open your door for you and help you and your bags out; then your car will be whisked away mechanically by ramps and lifts to its storage space. All this mutual politeness and respect also plays out in the low rates of street crime, vandalism or litter in the city.

But sometimes this reliance on the personal touch strikes you as perverse – as with the Tokyo system of property addresses. You will mostly look for a street name and number in vain; instead you must identify the district (by name), the streetblock (by number), the lot (by number) and the property (by number), but the sequence of lot numbering within the block is geographically quite random, possibly related to when the buildings went up. Thus the address of the Tenmaru restaurant in Ginza is Chuo-ku 6-9-2. That's no problem for the postal service, but strangers seeking it require advice from a local, maybe from one of the police boxes that in busy areas can be found at most major street junctions.

Transience

All cities mutate in response to the shifting pressures placed upon them. Their economies and communities as well as their buildings and infrastructure change all the time, replacing old with new. Tokyo expresses this propensity to change more than many other cities. The city is transient.

The paucity of old buildings strikes any visitor; the city is even short of monuments and other such landmarks. The massive destructions of the 1923 earthquake and the 1945 bombing largely explain this obliteration of the past.

171

But traditional timber construction was never designed for durability – a forty year life span for a house was the norm – so an expectation exists that the city's buildings will be frequently renewed. Even in a district like Marunouchi, which has been a commercial district for over a century, most plots have been rebuilt several times, including twice or more since 1945. In other districts, where functions have been more volatile, new buildings replace old ones at speeds that can leave the returning visitor quite disoriented. This frequent renewal has rarely been the occasion for grand city planning – fragmented land ownerships, weak planning laws, even a lack of political vision has conspired against such ambitions.

Tokyo has also been constantly reinventing itself. In its brief history as a major city – as short as that of Los Angeles and Mumbai – Tokyo has seen itself in three roles: as a national capital of an emergent country in the late 19th and early 20th century, then as an imperial capital in the period of national aggrandisement and war in the 1930s and 1940s, and finally as a world city (and the world's largest city) in the late 20th and early 21st century. These role shifts were spurred by the natural and man-made traumas that the city has suffered.

Much of city life here seems ephemeral. The nighttime sound and light shows in the central districts are turned on and off every day and its commercial content is regularly updated. Fashion – in clothing, in restaurants (the city has more Michelin-starred restaurants than Paris or New York), in youth culture, in districts – is a potent influence on the lives of well-to-do Tokyoites. Amusements that pass time like pachinko and karaoke have many devotees. And then there is sex, for which the city provides its famous love hotels with rooms rentable by the hour. All this can be seen as a modern variation on that traditional 'floating world' of transient pleasures.

11.

Efficiency and order: cities as machines

London 1970s. These days London is an occasional target of terrorist bombs from the Irish Republican Army. Living there we become used to taking precautions – looking under the car before you get in and drive off, asking out loud whose is the suitcase seemingly unattended on the train or bus, even avoiding crowded pubs or shops. The circumstances also, unsurprisingly, raise awareness of anyone speaking with an Irish accent, for they are the outsiders who threaten daily life. On a radio programme an Irish woman, a lifelong London resident, is asked whether this hostility makes life difficult for her. "Not really" is her reply, because most of her daily transactions outside her immediate neighbourhood are now mechanised. She can pass through the city – getting cash from an ATM, accessing transport through an automated ticket machine and barrier, buying goods in self service shops with checkouts – without breaching her anonymity. Nobody needs to hear her voice and know that she is Irish.

London 2000s. Fast forward three decades and her movements could be observed by CCTV, recorded through her use of a debit card or tracked by the GPS on her mobile. All minute by minute, in what we now call 'real time'.

Increasing tempo

This mechanisation of city life is historically a product of industrialisation. In his 1829 essay *Signs of the Times,* Thomas Carlyle declared: 'It is the Age of Machinery, in every outward and inward sense of that word; the age which, with its whole undivided might, forwards, teaches and practises the great art of adapting means to ends. Nothing is now done directly, or by hand; all is by rule and calculated contrivance.'[1] He had a point: power machines were replacing handwork in farming, manufacture and transport and new ways of providing urban life's necessities – water, food, energy, transport, information – were being invented. Carlyle also argued that 'Not the external and physical alone is now managed by machinery, but the internal and spiritual also.' Thoughts and feelings, as well as behaviours, were being reshaped by these new mechanical technologies. Economic, social and domestic life was getting more organised and thus more reliable, more predictable, more efficient and more standardised. These changes affected, very directly, life in Britain's Victorian cities and later in other cities.

The most radical impact came from altering people's experience and perception of time. Traditionally, the passage of time was observed daily through the rising and setting of the sun and annually through the seasons and the movements of the stars. Sundials, candles and hourglasses served as timepieces. Then from the 13th century onwards rich people started to have mechanical clocks in their houses. Public clocks appeared on church towers, guildhalls and city gates. Many of these survive; some as big tourist attractions, like the 15th century clock on the town hall in Prague with its hourly dumbshow in which the Apostles shuffle past, bowing to the audience, and a cockerel pops out flapping its wings just before the clock chimes.

The need for ordinary citizens to always know the time really arose with industrialisation and the consequent regular working and trading hours. Getting to work on time, knowing whether the shops are still open, catching a train became daily concerns. City life had become timetabled: this new discipline is one still forcefully felt by rural immigrants to cities today. Punctuality became important, not just to the hour but to the minute – the familiar remonstrance 'You're late' entered the language. Reliance on public clocks no longer sufficed, domestic and portable timekeeping was needed. The alarm clock, the pocket watch, then the wristwatch became essential urban accessories, along with the pocket diary. Today, for some of us the smartphone has replaced the watch and the diary for organising our time.

This increase in the tempo of city life was much deplored at the end of the 19th century. Conservative social critics were full of regretful jeremiads and dark prognoses, seeing rises in crime, madness and suicide as a direct consequence of the pressures of urban life. Some argued that the tensions of modern city living produced chronic exhaustion – neurasthenia was then the common description. This 'degeneratist' school of psychiatry has long been discredited professionally, but its theories persist as a popular belief. In contrast, others found the fast life all very exciting. The characters in Proust's *A la Recherche du Temps Perdu* (published 1913-27) congratulated themselves on living in an 'age of speed' and observed the necessity of rapid change in all aspects of life. Gertrude Stein, also writing in Paris in the 1920s, claimed that her prose imitated the sound of the streets and the movement of the automobiles.[2] (It was pretty monotonous.)

Among painters and illustrators, the French Cubists, Russian Constructivists and British Vorticists all found inspiration in the modern city. But it was the Italian Futurists – a loose association of painters, poets, illustrators, musicians and architects – who were the greatest enthusiasts. They declared a love of speed, technology and violence, and saw the plane, the car, electricity, the telephone, photography and the industrial town as the welcome triumph of people over nature. In 1909 one of its leaders, Filippo Tommaso Marinetti, published his *Manifesto of Futurism*, a barely articulate rant rejecting Italy's inherited culture: 'We today are founding Futurism, because we want to deliver Italy from its gangrene of professors, archaeologists, tourist guides and antiquaries.' In its place, it declaimed: 'We want to sing the love of danger, the habit of energy and rashness…We declare that the splendour of the world has been enriched by a new beauty; the beauty of speed'[3]. Futurist painters commonly captured the energy of the modern street scene. Umberto Boccioni was the greatest of them and his painting *The City Rises* conveys the bustle and the struggle of city life – the crowds, buildings, steam engine, and enormous red horse galloping into the construction site in the foreground, all expressed in energetic, swirling forms. Art critics regard it as one of the essential paintings of the modern world.

The tempo of city life has increased further over the last century. Much of our concern nowadays is to get ourselves somewhere on time – to school, to work, to the sports match – by one means of transport or another. Time has shortened and space has shrunk, so that we expect, and are expected by others, to travel vast distances across the city in relatively short spans of time. This is most evident in daily commuting: in cities around the world people often transport themselves distances of up to 50 kilometres, taking up to two hours to do so, getting themselves from home to workplace and then back again five or six days a week. Also, most cities are now busy – shops and bars and cafes open, public transport running, traffic congested, ATMs operative, streets lively – both day and night, weekday and weekend: the so-called 24/7 society. Communication has become potentially instantaneous: through radio and TV, the email or text message, the website, the mobile phone, the blog or tweet, we can receive words, data, sounds and images of 'breaking news' in any part of the world within seconds.

175

Umberto Boccioni's *The City Rises* 1910

But ambivalence about the tempo of city life persists to this day. For some city people the fast pace is immensely exciting, offering richer information, more consumer choices, larger social networks, new work and leisure patterns. They just pack more and more into each twenty-four hours. For others all this just adds new kinds of pressure to city life, such that the malady of 'stress' has become the contemporary equivalent of the 'neurasthenia' of the late 19th century.

On the move

Over time ways of moving people, goods and information around cities have multiplied. Until the last two centuries, only human and animal power was available. Most people just walked around their city. The richer few might ride horses or donkeys. Animal-drawn carts, cabs and carriages could carry more people, and goods as well, but in small numbers and only at slightly faster speeds than pedestrians. Horse-drawn trams on rails were more efficient, needing fewer horses to pull more passengers; they appeared in New York in 1832, Paris in 1855 and London in 1870. But it was the invention of the bicycle that brought machines to city streets for the first time. Bicycles became popular in the 1880s, with the adoption of wheels of equal size, efficient braking and pneumatic tyres. They caused a furore. Some thought them unhealthy, their riders prone to bicycle 'stoop' (from the riding position) and bicycle 'face' (from moving against the wind at high speeds). They were too fast; they spooked horses and caused accidents. Should they be on the carriageway or the pavement? In time, of course, they became accepted. (Today rollerblading incurs similar criticisms.)

Power – using steam, electricity or petroleum – brought a whole range of new mechanical transport into cities. From the 1830s onwards in Europe and North America, the steam railways pushed their lines into the big cities, building major termini and connecting the centre to new suburbs and places beyond. The concept of commuting was born and cities spread rapidly outwards. In cities with rivers or canals steamboat ferries were introduced. The first electric tram in Europe operated in Berlin from 1879, Sarajevo followed in 1885, the same year as in the USA in Baltimore. The first underground railway line was earlier in London in 1863 running on steam; electrification followed in 1890. Other big cities in Europe and North America quickly followed suit in building underground or overground urban railways. In recent decades, cities in Asia and South America have also built metros. Today there are nearly 200 such systems around the world moving, day in, day out, millions of people going about their business across their cities.

Internal combustion petrol engines made individual mechanical transport – a car, van, lorry or motorbike – possible. Now the word 'driving' (as in 'Did you drive here?') usually means driving your own vehicle. Car ownership and use only really took off in the 1920s with mass production by Ford in the USA, Morris in Britain, Citroën, Renault and Peugeot in France, and Opel in Germany. As with bicycles there was an initial panic reaction and low speed limits were imposed. Petrol engines also made motorised cycling possible and motorbikes appeared. Petrol or diesel-driven buses and taxis were added to urban traffic. In the cities of the North, buses and taxis are now two clearly different modes of travel: shared versus exclusive occupancy, large versus small capacity, with fixed routes and stops or taking the passenger to any chosen destination. In the cities of the South there is a less clear distinction and far more variety, including rickshaws (a punishing form of human carriage still found in some Asian cities), cyclos or pedicabs (the cycle version), autorickshaws (the motorbike version), motorbike taxis (you ride pillion), taxicabs (but the driver may feel free to pick up other fares on the way), minibuses that stop anywhere along a given route (called colectivos in Latin America, poda podas in Sierra Leone, jeepneys in Manila, based on ex US Army jeeps, or songthaews in Thailand, where they are adaptations of pickup trucks) as well as regular buses and trams with fixed routes and stops.

Mechanisation also speeded up vertical movement. Stairs and ramps were traditionally how you went up and down, so few buildings in frequent use exceeded five storeys. The Otis Company, founded in 1853 in New York, changed all that with the invention of the safety elevator (safe because it locked the car in place should the cables fail) that made taller buildings possible. Escalators came later – they made their debut, and were a sensation, at the 1900 Paris Exposition – bringing a capacity to move more people over shorter vertical distances. With elevators and escalators cities could now spread underground, with deep basements, subways and tunnels, and upwards, with high-rise buildings, as well as outwards. The modern cityscape – of which Manhattan is still the iconic exemplar – was created.

Urban transport remains an attractive challenge for futurologists. Among their dream machines are jetpacks (personal rockets strapped to your back to carry you over the crowds), hoverboards (skateboards using hovercraft technology to speed you along just above the ground), flying cars (that simply take off when congestion looms ahead), smart roads (for guiding vehicles independently of the driver, increasing capacity by bunching them in convoys) and intelligent speed control (automatically stopping you exceeding the speed limit). There are also less fanciful, proven transport technologies that some once thought would find wide application in cities. The moving pavement is one, but it is still only found in transport terminals. Monorails have only been used for fast communication to airports or expositions. Pedestrian decks, providing circulation routes above the traffic, have been features of urban renewal schemes, but earlier ambitions to make over whole city centres in this way failed. The helicopter is another technology that has not become much used for travel within cities, though Sao Paulo in Brazil is an exception. Here nearly 500 helicopters fly around the city, many of them taxis for hire, commonly used by the rich business class for daily or weekly commuting from their distant homes, thereby escaping the traffic congestion on the roads and – probably just as important – avoiding the dangers of passing near the poor shanty towns below.

Novel urban transport

In various cities around the world are innovative, even weird and wacky, transport systems, many since copied elsewhere.

In *Bangkok,* an overhead railway called Skytrain rides on heavy concrete columns above the main streets, in places double or triple-decked, casting the street beneath into sunless gloom.

Havana has Camello (camel buses), attached to an articulated truck front and so called because the passenger space, for as many as 300 people, has two humps and a dip in the middle – another of Havana's improvised responses, like its famous preserved Cadillacs, to the longstanding US trade blockade.

In *Lisbon* a public lift, the *Elevador de Santa Justa,* whisks you up 32 metres from the central Baixa district to the older Barro Ailto district on the western hillside. The lift rides inside a latticework metal tower, created in 1902 by a disciple of Gustav Eiffel.

At *London's Heathrow* airport, guided pods on tracks carry business passengers from the carpark to the terminal.

In *Medellin*, Colombia, new aerial cable cars connect residents in the remote hillside *barrios* to the city centre.

Montreal has the world's largest underground network for pedestrians known as the *RESO* (from the French *reseau*, 'network'): 30 kilometres long, it links the centre's public buildings, shops, offices, train and metro stations, the bus terminal and car parks. It helps the locals escape the harsh winters and hot summers.

The Mayor of *Paris* has supplied the city with thousands of rental bicycles, called *Vélibs*, free for the first half hour, charged thereafter, to be picked up and dropped off at racks throughout the city. Other European cities have followed suit.

In *Perugia*, Italy, with its hilltop city centre, escalators weave through ancient subterranean passages and cellars to transport visitors from the car parks on the lower slopes to the central Piazza Italia.

Tokyo originated the traffic lights at crossroad junctions that hold all vehicles on Stop to allow diagonal pedestrian flows.

Valparaiso in Chile has many funicular railways, climbing and descending inclined tracks, that form the backbone of the hilly city's transport system. The oldest dates from 1883. Other cities with funiculars include Budapest, Hong Kong and Naples, this last underground.

Some cities have found novel solutions to their local transport problems – among them funiculars, cable cars, shared bicycles. There have also been inventive adaptations of transport technologies to better fit urban conditions. Visiting Italian cities you see lots of their small cars and vans and their motor scooters, seemingly sized for the narrow streets of their historic centres. Fiat originated the 'city car', with small dimensions for manoeuvring and parking in tight spaces, a low purchase price and low running costs, and a top speed sufficient for urban driving. The Fiat 600 was first produced in 1955 and successor models have been in production ever since. The motor scooter had its debut with the first Vespa model at the 1946 Milan Fair. Its features – the small wheels (for easy turning), front shield (to protect everyday clothing), the platform area for feet (no need to sit astride and OK in a skirt), and low running costs – make it attractive for getting around cities. Both city cars and scooters are now by no means just found in Italy. They have been sold around the world and and indeed are made around the world, either the Italian originals manufactured under licence or local variants. Non-polluting, electric city cars are the latest invention.

But, whatever the technology, traffic congestion has characterised cities throughout history. In Caesar's Rome the traffic became so intense that he declared a daytime ban on chariots, except those supplying temples and other public buildings. In medieval cities, laws or tolls were often introduced to limit the entry of travelling merchants. Speed restrictions for carts were common. As horse-drawn carriages became more numerous, the main routes sometimes got blocked with traffic, pedestrian deaths increased and the streets became filthy with horse shit. Today there is no city in the world in which traffic always moves freely. The terms 'traffic jam' and 'gridlock' have entered our vocabulary.

While traffic congestion is a universal phenomenon, what varies is the particular mix of people and vehicles[4]. The description of Delhi traffic could apply equally in Cairo, Saigon or Mexico City and dozens of other cities of the South. In US cities less than 10% of journeys are made by foot or bike; in Europe, Asian, Middle Eastern and Latin American cities the proportion is around 30%, in African and Chinese cities it rises to 50% and above, with people walking to work, often over large distances, unable to afford fares even where public transport is available. Everywhere in the world vehicles have taken over the streets. In Asian cities motorcycles outnumber cars – their affordability, manouevrability and capacity (sometimes cramming whole families onto them) have made them the ideal vehicle for middle income people. In cities elsewhere cars, vans and increasingly SUVs are the preferred mode of private transport

Traffic in Delhi

'By day, the mayhem is revealed as true chaos. Delhi's streets play host to a bewildering stream of zigzagging green-and-yellow auto-rickshaws, speeding cabs, weaving bicyclists, slow-moving oxen carts, multi-passengered motorcycles conveying helmetless children and sari-clad women who struggle to keep their clothing from getting tangled in the chain, and heaving buses, which are often forced out of the bus-only lane because it is filled with cyclists and pedestrians, who are themselves in the lane because there tends to be no sidewalk, or "footpath" as they say in Delhi. If there is a footpath, it is often occupied by people sleeping, eating, selling, buying or simply sitting watching the traffic go by. Limbless and young hawkers converge at each intersection, scratching at the windows as drivers study the countdown signals that tell them when the traffic lights will change. Endearingly, if hopelessly, the signals have been embellished with a single word: RELAX.'[5]

and they are on the increase too in the cities of the South. Good public transport – buses, trams and trains – ameliorates this trend in some cities. Even then, there is often a duality with two transport systems existing side by side, most evident in South Africa's cities: cars and taxis for richer (in South Africa predominantly white) people and buses and walking for the majority of poor (black and mixed race) people.

Over the last century and a half many ways of managing the press of urban traffic have been devised. London was often in the vanguard. A 10 miles per hour (16 kilometres per hour) speed limit was introduced there in 1861, later reduced to 2 miles per hour with a man and a red flag walking in advance of the motor vehicle to give warning to horse riders. The first traffic light was installed in London in December 1868, with red and green gas lights that were turned manually to face the traffic; unfortunately it exploded on 2nd January 1869 injuring the policeman who was operating it. More reliable, electric, automated versions arrived in the 1920s and are today totally computerised, their phasing connected together over whole swathes of the road network. Pedestrian crossings arrived in the 1920s. In British cities different kinds of pedestrian crossing have been given animal names: Zebra crossings (so called because of the wide black and white stripes on the road) came first, supplemented by Pelican crossings (with lights for both pedestrians and vehicles), Puffin crossings (mnemonically Pedestrian User-Friendly Intelligent crossing, button-operated and with kerbside detectors), Toucan crossings (for bicycles as well as pedestrians) and even Pegasus crossings (for horses). Bus-only lanes came relatively late to London in 1968 – Hamburg had one in 1962 and other German cities had quickly followed. Cycle lanes have been introduced since. And in 2003 London introduced the 'congestion charge', a £5 per day fee (since increased to £10) for vehicles entering its central area. Singapore had got there first in 1998.

Restrictions on traffic are contentious political issues in many cities. In post-reunification Berlin, even proposals to phase out the little man with a hat on the pedestrian crossing lights in erstwhile East Berlin caused an uproar. More generally, every one of the traffic management measures – from the earliest speed limits to the latest road charging – has been opposed by vehicle drivers. The voices of the majority pedestrians and public transport users in cities always seem weak in comparison. But most cities now realise that they cannot be totally motorised, that transport policies of 'predict and provide' can never give lasting relief from traffic congestion. The more new road space that is provided, the more vehicles will be attracted onto it, through extra trips, rerouted trips, retimed trips or diversion of travel from other modes. Quickly the degree of congestion is back where it started. Conversely, when road space is reduced – to create bus lanes or pedestrian zones or by removing parking spaces, for example – the result is not the often predicted 'traffic chaos' because the same kinds of adjustments of travel behaviour occur in reverse. Where urban transport is concerned demand follows supply.

Support systems

The population of Imperial Rome reached over a million people in the 1st century AD. The city covered 30 square kilometres. It was the biggest metropolis the world had seen. Feeding and watering the city was a triumph of technology and logistics.

Rome subsequently declined and shrank in size. Not until the 19th century in Europe and North America did the challenge of supporting million plus cities arise again; then new technologies came into play. Advances in food preservation (with canning and freezing) and transport (by trains and planes as well as by sea and road) extended the sources for a city's food across the globe. Food processing and retailing became major economic enterprises: every large city

Feeding and watering Imperial Rome[6]

In its early days most Romans had been farmers tending their land and livestock in the surrounding countryside. But as the city grew, and became richer and politically ambitious, it needed soldiers, administrators, merchants and engineers to secure its food supply. The engineers built the infrastructure that brought food and water to Rome; the soldiers conquered and defended the territories from which they were drawn; the merchants and administrators managed their distribution to the population. Food was imported from around the Mediterranean – grain from Egypt, North Africa, and Sicily, pork from Spain, fish from all the coasts, honey from the Balkans, olive oil from Greece and Spain, wine from France, salt, pepper and spices from Asia Minor and the Levant. All were shipped to the port of Ostia, then transferred to barges which were towed 35 kilometres upstream along the Tiber to the city's food markets. Grain imports alone required about ninety bargeloads per week. The first aqueduct to bring water into the city, the *Acqua Appia,* was built in the 4th century BC. In time, Rome had eleven aqueducts, totalling 400 kilometres in length, providing the city with over a million cubic feet of water daily, supplying 700 basins, 500 fountains, 130 reservoirs, and 170 public baths. The writer and statesman Pliny boasted that 'there has never been anything more remarkable in the whole world.'

now has its wholesale and retail markets, its distribution centres, fleets of vehicles, supermarkets and corner shops to put daily food on city tables. For richer city people food supplies – in great variety, at all seasons – are assured. For poorer city people much of this may not be available at prices they can afford, with the consequences of poor diets and hunger.

Water – clean and abundant for drinking, cooking, washing and waste removal – is the other essential urban life support. Water from rivers and wells and rainwater can supply small amounts; water sellers can provide drinking water, but at high cost. What the large numbers of people gathered in cities need is piped water, pumped into the city from distant reservoirs and distributed to private or public taps, and waterborne underground sewerage; in short, a mechanised water system. In the modern cities of the North we take the existence of such infrastructure for granted. In the cities of Latin America, Africa and South Asia, this may be true of the districts where richer people live, but there are large areas of cities where water may be supplied only to public taps, bodies and clothes must be washed in streams, pissing and shitting done in public or in rare, shared latrines, while the contaminated water flows in open ditches. Consequently, digestive tract diseases arising from unclean water and poor sanitation – diarrhoea, enteritis, colitis, typhoid – are a leading cause of death in these cities, especially among small children.

People in cities need more than food and water. Energy is also basic to city life and livelihoods. Traditionally, wood and coal were burned on open fires but their supply and delivery was small scale and their use in dense urban areas potentially hazardous. With the invention of manufactured gas in the early 19th century, energy became available for the first time at the turn of a tap – it became known as 'town gas'. London had it from 1807, Dublin from 1818, Paris from 1819. By the mid-century every town and city in Europe, North America and Australia had a gas plant and a gas supply network providing metered energy to homes and businesses. This made radical changes to daily life: well-lit streets, night shift working, more time for reading and writing, warmer homes and a whole range of domestic gas appliances. At the mid 20th century natural gas, piped from offshore or overland, mostly replaced town gas. But by then electricity had come along and had become the standard energy source for lighting, heating and motive power in cities around the world. Initially both gas and electricity supply were provided by local utilities, often bearing the name of their city, sometimes owned by the municipal authority. In time, these local urban suppliers became integrated into regional and national networks, either in public or private ownership.

Information has become another essential urban life support. Before the 19th century, up-to-date news passed essentially by word of mouth. Then, over that century, most large cities acquired daily or weekly newspapers, getting cheaper with advances in printing technology and finding new demand from increasingly literate populations. In London *The Times* was founded in 1785, the *Daily Telegraph* in 1855, the mid-market *Daily Mail* in 1896, and the downmarket *Daily Mirror* in 1903. Also in the 19th century postal services started to speed up personal written communication. Standard rates, postboxes for collecting mail and daily deliveries to homes and workplaces – in some cities several times daily – put people in touch with each other at a new frequency. In London, telegraph services (transmitting messages along wires by Morse code to be delivered by telegram) started in 1870, telephone services (introducing person-to-person voice communication) in 1912. Today every city in the world has its newspapers, postal service and telephone system; also its TV and radio stations. And now the majority of city people in both North and South carry a mobile phone giving them access to contacts and to vast new sources of information to help them with their daily lives: aside from phone calls and text messages they can get addresses, street maps, music, traffic alerts, photos, entertainment listings, transport timetables, health advice, personal banking, news updates, weather forecasts, pollution alerts and every year more and more such applications.

The Roman satirist Juvenal said its citizens only wanted two things: bread and circuses. Entertainments like circuses can be readily contrived; maintaining supplies of bread and other necessities is more problematic. Rulers know how supply failures can turn popular sentiment against them, even drive them from office. 'Food riots' have recurred throughout history when shortages or price hikes have created hunger among market-dependent city populations. In modern times failures in both water and energy supply have also been the cause of public unrest. Deregulation, privatisation and mergers of producers have been common in the water, energy and telecommunication sectors. In the cities of the South these policies have been urged by the World Bank as part of the 'structural adjustment' of struggling national economies. Often the result has been a mix of 'cherry picking' – high quality services for the rich few – and 'social dumping' – a declining, residual service for the poor; in cases even rationing for everyone. But the richer cities of the North are not immune from the occasional collapse of their supply systems. In particular, power blackouts, usually short, are common every year in a city somewhere. There were major cases in New York in 1977 (lasting two days with much looting), in Auckland, New Zealand in 1998 (lasting several weeks in the city centre) and also that year in San Francisco; in London in 2003; Chenzhou, China in 2008 and in Rio and Sao Paulo at the same time in 2009. Phone and internet connections also crash from time to time, often from the pressure of overloading. The sophistication and complexity of city supply systems – for energy, information, food and water – make them vulnerable, like all machines, to occasional inefficiencies and breakdowns.

Engineering cities

The designers of cities – architects, engineers, planners – seek to create order. So they prescribe street patterns, water supply systems, energy networks, transport regulations, land use zones, building height restrictions, high or low

185

densities, even aesthetic rulebooks and trade licensing. These kinds of measures have been imposed on cities throughout history and across the world: for example, in the city building of the Roman Empire, in the Baroque cities of 17th century Europe, in the cities created by European colonists in Asia, Africa and the Americas, in the urban improvements of the 19th century industrial city, in the garden cities and new towns of the 20th century. The rationalisation offered is usually functional: the orderly city will be more efficient, healthier, better looking, or even more equitable for its citizens.

The machine concept provides an attractive template for this work. A machine has interlinked parts that work as a whole, operating in simple cause and effect ways, always reliably subject to the same laws, driven by some motive power, seemingly neutral and value-free. Machines can be engineered, designed purposefully to achieve a given purpose; and they can be controlled. It was the physicist Isaac Newton who first articulated a model of mechanical order in the late 17th and early 18th centuries. The writer Bryan Appleyard rightly declares that the model's importance 'lies not in its exact laws and calculations, but rather in its general nature and imaginative power.'[7] But the language of machinery only really entered the urban designer's vocabulary in the early 20th century. In the 1910s the Italian Futurist architect Antonio Sant'Elia offered a vision of a highly industrialised and mechanised *Citta Nuova*, comprising a vast megastructure of tower blocks, elevators, triple-tiered traffic routes and an airport on top of the railway station. He did not get to build it, but a fictional version can be seen in Fritz Lang's 1927 film fable *Metropolis*.

It was the Swiss architect Le Corbusier who later expanded this view. He famously declared that 'a house is a machine to live in.' His approach to the design of cities also reflected this mechanistic viewpoint. (He was the son of a watchmaker, which may explain his obsession with clockwork order.) His 1925 plan for the total rebuilding of Paris north of the Seine would have substituted eighteen uniform, 200 metre high towers for what stood there before, with the exception of a few monuments including, revealingly, Place Vendôme which he liked as a symbol of order.

The city council did not buy this proposal. Nor did Algiers, Rio de Janeiro, Moscow or Buenos Aires, where he proposed similar high-rise structures. In his writing Le Corbusier claimed practical reasons for his prescription to decongest cities by building at higher densities: thereby traffic circulation would be improved, open space increased, work and residential areas would be separated and so healthier. But to make all this work there should also be social

Le Corbusier's *Plan Voisin* for Paris

segregation and collective services for cooking, learning and childcare. Many of these precepts were enshrined in the Athens Charter, adopted by the 1933 *Congrès Internationale d'Architecture Moderne (CIAM)*, which promoted functional urban design and became a manifesto for many mid 20th century architects.

This approach was influential in the rebuilding of many European cities after World War Two: cities in Britain, Sweden, Italy and France all acquired high-rise towers of flats as new social housing. As did those US cities committed to public housing projects. The design for Brazil's new capital of Brasilia in the 1950s followed the fashion virtually to the letter. As in the same decade did that for Chandighar, a new capital for the Punjab, largely designed by Le Corbusier himself. But despite this commitment to function determining form, there was never much empirical basis for how these designers proposed to reshape cities. Le Corbusier himself said: 'The harmonious city must first be planned by experts who understand the science of urbanism. They work out their plans in total freedom from partisan pressures and special interests; once their plans are formulated, they must be implemented without opposition.'[8] These self-styled experts were not really interested in how people in their cities wanted to live their lives. In time, the residents had their revenge. In both Brasilia and Chandighar, unplanned settlements grew alongside and finally outgrew the planned, functional city. In Britain and the USA, the tower blocks proved so unpopular and became so poorly maintained that many were demolished within a few decades of construction.

But the lure of engineering cities persists. Architects and planners, commissioned to create new neighbourhoods, big urban renewal schemes or new cities, invariably come up with 'grand designs', usually claiming some functional – rather than purely aesthetic –rationale. Three or four decades ago efficient circulation was the design priority, leading to ingeniously geometrical road networks, often separating buses, cars, cyclists and pedestrians. Then planning pursued social engineering, seeking to create communities that provided economic opportunities for all and harmonious social relations. These days the design is almost certain to have an ecological flavour through, for example, attractive public transport, energy conservation, minimal resource consumption, open space and greenery for the water cycle, minimal journeys to shops and schools. There may be some evidence and analysis to underpin these prescriptions. But one is still left with the feeling that the motivation for thus mechanising the city is less to do with functionalism than with power – the godlike urge of professionals and politicians to decree how we should live our city lives.

Hardware and software

All these supply systems require networks connecting people, connecting activities, connecting supply and demand for food, energy and information, connecting parts of the city and connecting the city to the world beyond. The most visible networks in the city are the surface streets, the freeways, the vehicles that travel on them, their parking spaces, the trams and trains and their tracks, stations and depots, streetlights and signs, and the pylons, poles and overhead lines for power and phone. Invisible, below ground, are tunnels, ducts, pipes and cables through which traffic, water and sewerage, gas, electricity and digital information move. And also invisible, because intangible, are the radio waves of telecommunications systems coursing through the air.

This is the hardware of the modern mechanised city. But all this technology is brought into practical use by organisational arrangements, financing regimes, social customs, behavioural norms, personal skills and states of mind – metaphorically the city's software. It is the interaction between hardware and software that matters. For new urban technologies succeed not just as a response to established social and economic practices but rather by helping to shape them. That reshaping – of both city forms and processes – is not technologically determined in some simple cause and effect way. Rather the reshaping proceeds over time in a recursive manner. Cities adapt to motor vehicles through traffic engineering in the street, designing buildings to accommodate them and by relocating activities to make them more accessible. But the motor vehicle also adapts to its use in cities through cleaner fuels, smaller vehicles, taxi services and traffic regulation. Remote services from banks and retailers are possible not just because of the technology of phones, computers, ATMs and delivery services, but also through familiarity of usage, the ownership of cash and credit cards for payment and – not least important – a sense of public trust in the probity of such remote transactions. In all such cases there is, in cities, an interdependence between the technology and social behaviour that validates – and humanises – the machine.

12.

Variety: the contradictions of Paris

Montparnasse 1997. A Parisian friend tells us that she is moving with her partner to a new apartment. They will be setting up a small advertising business there. She had been born and bred and lived most of her adult life in the 6th arondissement, Montparnasse, a very respectable district near the Luxembourg Gardens. We are surprised when she says they have found a new place in the 10th Arondissement, in the clothing district near the Gare de l'Est. She says it is very 'populaire.' My interpretation of this is in terms of London estate agent's use of the term 'popular' to indicate districts that are getting gentrified by the young middle class. But it turns out that our friend is not happy in her new district, irritated by dirty streets, workshops spilling onto the pavement, noisy neighbours, spicy smells from the Arab restaurants, episodes of minor street violence. I realise then that by 'populaire' she had meant proletarian. After a while she rejected the raffishness of the 10th and moved back to the bourgeois comforts of the 6th.

1789 and all that

In 2005 and 2007 there were major riots in Paris when the young, unemployed, immigrant inhabitants of the vast public housing schemes in the suburbs trashed buildings and vehicles. After a week or so the disturbances were contained and no political upheaval followed. Across the world, watching these events on your TV screen, you might well – if you are over sixty – have had a sense of *déjà vu*. For, forty years before, in May 1968 students had similarly rioted in central Paris. The immediate cause was their dissatisfaction with how their universities were run, but their protests, soon joined by workers, were expressive of a deep-seated antagonism to the hierarchy, rigidity and conservatism of the French economy, society and polity. Parisians had taken to the streets many times before: in 1870, in 1848, in 1830 and in 1789. French politics has been remarkably volatile over the last two centuries or so – a 'see-

190

saw history of alternating conservative and liberal regimes, interspersed with a series of violent revolutionary outbreaks.'[1] Paris, the capital city, was always in the forefront of these revolutions that replaced one regime by another.

There was the original French Revolution of 1789 and the years that followed. The capture of the Bastille Prison by Parisians on 14th July 1789 was highly symbolic. Told of this, King Louis XVI asked one of his advisers 'Is it a revolt?', to be told 'No, Sire, it is a revolution.' Three days later, the king travelled from his palace at Versailles outside the city, modestly dressed and accompanied, to a ceremony at the Hotel de Ville, where he pinned the revolutionary tricolour cockade to his hat in recognition of his new status as a constitutional monarch. But it was not to last, and within three years a republic was declared and the king and queen lost their heads on the guillotine. The French Revolution sent shock waves across Europe, its promotion of *Liberté, Egalité, Fraternité* plunging the continent into a more profound and protracted crisis than it had ever known. It was like an earthquake and Paris was its epicentre. The Parisians of 1789 can claim to have originated the modern concept of revolution, that is, not a mere *coup d'état* but popular action to overthrow a whole system of government together with the destruction of its social, economic and cultural foundations. Its influence was universal and persistent. Zhou Enlai, the Chinese Communist leader, when asked in the 1970s about the significance of the French Revolution, reportedly said that it was too soon to say.

The avant-garde

It is not just in politics that Parisians have led and others have followed. Its culture – painting, writing, film, architecture, clothing – has been frequently and contentiously avant-garde. In modern times art led the way. In 1876 a critic observed that 'an exhibition has opened at the Durand-Ruel's gallery that purports to be of paintings… five or six loonies, among them a woman, have been given appointments to display their work… A dreadful spectacle of human vanity lost in folly.'[2] On show were the first Impressionists. Their preoccupation was with light, attempting to capture its fluidity in time and space and, in doing so, playing fast and loose with conventional notions of representation. Their work was genuinely disturbing. Thereafter from the artists came one wave of innovation after another: after Impressionism came Post-Impressionism,

Pointillism, Symbolism, Fauvism, Cubism, Surrealism. All were condemned initially. But today these artists – Manet, Degas, Cézanne, Monet, Renoir, Gauguin, Van Gogh, Matisse, Picasso – are more widely recognised, highly prized and highly priced than almost any others in history.

For these painters, Paris was important. It was where most of them lived, some born there, others drawn to it from the provinces, even – as with Van Gogh and Picasso – from abroad. In their *quartiers* the artists were close, sharing rooms and studios, drinking and dining together, doing drugs (opium for preference), having affairs, exchanging opinions and ideas, viewing each other's work in progress, in touch with galleries and dealers, sometimes off on joint expeditions to the coast or countryside, and thereby reinforcing their view of themselves as outsiders. They lived and worked in each other's pockets. The city and its life were often their inspiration. They were attracted to portraying everyday life in the city, subject matters that had seemed too banal before. They painted city life in the raw, the product of 19th century industrialisation and urbanisation, scenes like railway stations, cafes, cabarets and theatres, workers' suburbs, horse-races, picnics, brothels, and the people who populated those places, not excluding addicts, artistes, prostitutes and punters.

The inventiveness and iconoclasm shown by the Parisian artists of the late 19th and early 20th century have appeared time and again in other cultural forms. In the late 1940s, existentialism became the defining mood of a generation of young people. Philosophically, as given expression by Jean-Paul Sartre, Simone de Beauvoir and Albert Camus, it was a development of German nihilism, emphasising the freedom and responsibility of the individual to act outside any pre-determined system of belief. Its focus of activity was Saint Germain des Près on the Left Bank. There it had as much to do with style as with philosophy. *De rigeur* clothes were black, casual, and unisex, with the polo neck sweater and the duffel coat as key fashions; jazz was the favoured soundtrack; drinking, dancing and sex were central to its image. It became one of the first manifestations of universal pop culture. When Sartre died in 1980, 50,000 people thronged the streets for his funeral procession to the Montparnasse cemetery. The Café des Deux Magots and Café de Flore have now become tourist haunts from their past association with the Existentialists.

At the end of the 1950s a group of Parisian filmmakers burst onto the scene quite as alarmingly as the painters and writers had done in earlier decades. They were labelled the *Nouvelle Vague* (New Wave). In embracing new ways of film making and new subjects for film they were rejecting much of what had gone before, cutting loose from fifty years of accumulated style and methods, presenting themselves as *auteurs* working in very personal manners. Francois Truffaut's *The 400 Blows* of 1959 and Jean Luc Godard's *Breathless* of 1960 were the first of their films to gain international recognition. They quickly inspired filmmakers in other countries. In terms of technique they used long tracking shots, jump cutting, natural light, dislocations of space and time – all known before but never used to such effect. These technical choices were underpinned by a radical view of the potential of film. For them, movies were not just vehicles to carry stories; they were also a sensory experience like, say, sitting in a cafe watching the world go by. This philosophy, with the help of superfast film, handheld cameras and lightweight sound equipment, led them to shoot in the streets and interiors of the city, rather than in the studio. Paris became a live character in their films.

The Eiffel Tower

Gustav Eiffel was an engineer from Alsace. His experience designing metal bridges and viaducts led him to propose a tower as the centerpiece of the 1889 Paris Exposition, itself planned to mark the centenary of the French Revolution. It was to be a '300 metre flagpole' and the tallest building in the world. The city bought the proposal. 300 steeplejacks worked for two years running it up. Unsurprisingly, it had its critics. A group of artists, calling themselves the Committee of Three Hundred (one for each metre of the tower), wrote to the press:

> '[We] protest with all our force, with all our indignation, in the name of unappreciated French taste, in the name of menaced French art and history, against the erection, in the very heart of our capital, of the useless and monstrous Eiffel Tower… Is Paris going to be associated with the grotesque, mercantile imaginings of a constructor of machines, to be irreparably defaced and dishonoured?'[3]

To which question the answer of history has been 'Yes.' The tower has become a symbol for the city, its image reproduced endlessly. In 1986 the floodlighting was replaced by internal illumination, so that at night it now has a filigree quality.

In Paris, architectural novelty has expressed itself less in 'new waves' than in 'grand projects'. At first glance, the city, in its central districts, gives an

impression of conservative uniformity. Certainly, compared with other iconoc
cities – New York, Tokyo, Los Angeles – the fabric of Paris remains remarkably
little touched by 20th century development or warfare. But there are
exceptions that illustrate a Parisian taste for novel, even weird and wacky,
buildings. The most recent are the so-called *grands projets* of President
Mitterand from the 1980s – the *Louvre* pyramid, the *Grande Arche* office
building at *La Défense*, the Opera house at *Place de la Bastille* and the new
National Library – all undertaken in determinedly modern style. His
predecessor Pompidou promoted the building that carries his name, the *Centre
Pompidou* in the Marais that opened in 1977 and became that rarity, a modern
building that is an instant visitor attraction. It has a predecessor, of course, in
the Eiffel Tower, erected for the 1889 International Exposition, which – while
condemned at the time by the cultural elite – was an immediate hit with the
public and has remained so.

The 1889 Exposition was one of a series held in Paris – in 1855, 1867, 1878,
1889, 1900, 1925, 1931, 1937 – celebrating new commodities and experiences
and thereby showcasing the city as the acme of modernity. It was from the 1925
Exposition Internationale des Arts Decoratifs et Industriels Modernes that the style called
Art Deco took its name. It characterised china, furniture, and jewellery and also
influenced architecture, fashion and the visual arts. It was an opulent style,
possibly expressing a reaction to the forced austerity of the years around the
World War of 1914-18. It spread rapidly to become an international style of the
1930s but Paris remained the centre for its more upmarket products.

As with *Art Deco*, so with *Haute Couture*, the French have the word for it. It
translates literally as 'high dressmaking.' Its wider meaning is of fashionable,
bespoke clothing, expensive too because of the quality of materials used and
the hand sewing. By extension the term applies not just to the clothes
themselves but also to the designers and makers of such clothes and the
businesses that employ them. Paris's pre-eminence in European fashion dates
from the 18th century when the Versailles court was a trend-setter for the
European aristocracy. Visitors would buy in Paris and have copies made back
home. As travel became easier the fashion-conscious rich would do serious
shopping in Paris. The first couturier to establish an international reputation
was Charles Frederick Worth in the mid 19th century. Following in his footsteps
in the early-mid 20th century were the houses of Patou, Lanvin, Chanel,
Balenciaga and Dior; the 1960s saw the rise of Yves Saint Laurent, Pierre
Cardin, Andre Courreges, and Christian Lacroix; and more recently non-

French designers established themselves there. Today's couture houses are mostly owned by business conglomerates and make their money from ready to wear clothing, perfumes and accessories. But their bi-annual catwalk shows still attract enormous, worldwide publicity for the businesses, their products and the concept of 'Paris fashion'. Though Paris must now share its pre-eminence in fashion with other cities, it retains its distinctive style: a common view in the trade is that while Milan does sexy fashion, New York commercial, London creative, Paris still does pretty.

Quartiers

Distinguishing the Left Bank and the Right Bank is the most well-known way of describing the geography of Paris. Largely because of the cultural history of the last century and more, the Left Bank – that is, south of the Seine – has come to symbolise the bohemian side of the city's personality. Here are the Sorbonne university, the Eiffel Tower, the garret in which the heroine of *La Bohème* starved. The Right Bank – north of the river – symbolises the bourgeois side. Here are the Presidential Palace, the Stock Exchange, the Louvre Museum and most of the department stores.

The arondissements

In most cities, ask residents where they live and they will tell you the name of a district. Ask a Parisian and they will reply with a number: 'the 5th' or 'the 16th.' The twenty numbered *arondissements* into which the city of Paris is divided carry far more meaning than the postcodes in other cities. They serve that modern purpose but are in fact far more ancient. They were first created in 1795, perhaps as a political step by the National Convention to weaken the revolutionary power of the city, for the central municipality was abolished at the same time. Initially there were twelve *arondissements,* later increased, with the 1859 extension of the city boundary, to the present twenty. They have retained that pattern to the present day. The numbers spiral out anticlockwise, starting with the 1st Arondissement around the Louvre and then making three circuits of the city and finishing with the 20th Arondissement in the east where the *Père-Lachaise* cemetery stands. Each *arondissement* has a mayor, a council and an administration – it is the citizen's first port of call for official business.

The *arondissements* provide a social and cultural map of Paris. The Marais, comprising most of the 3rd and 4th, is now firmly part of visitors' Paris. But until its rediscovery and renovation from the 1960s onwards it had been a rundown area, where ancient buildings, dating back to its heyday as an aristocratic quarter in the 17th and 18th century, were in multiple occupation. Now it is the residential area of choice for media, arty and gay Parisians, its character spilling over eastwards around *Place de la Bastille*. In the northeast the 11th is Belleville, a traditional working class quarter of mixed housing and trade, that is now also home to a rich melange of immigrant communities. Montmartre in the 18th, around the hill from which the church of *Sacre Coeur* dominates the northern Paris skyline, and Montparnasse in the 14th, where the modern *Tour Montparnasse* is equally dominant in the south, are both associated with the artistic revolutionaries of the late 19th and early 20th century. Today, their social characters are very different: Montmartre remains very mixed socially whereas Montparnasse is more exclusively bourgeois. The Latin Quarter, in the 5th and 6th with Boulevard St Germain as its spine, has traditionally been seen as home to bohemians and dissidents but, as so often happens, tourism has followed in their wake. Away to the west of the city, in the 7th, 8th, 16th and 17th Arondissements are the posh residential areas like Invalides, Etoile and Passy.

Aside from this local detail, there is in Paris – as in many cities – a distinction between a poorer east and a richer west. Historically, rich people and poor people in Paris lived closely together in a way that surprised visitors. The private houses of the nobility, before the 1789 revolution, were often H-shaped with a courtyard at the front concealed behind a high wall and gate with a garden behind, with the owners and their servants living in the middle wing but letting off the side wings to less than noble tenants. Examples of these *hôtels particuliers* remain in the Marais. Blocks of flats, designed from the outset for multiple occupation, first appeared in the late 17th century and became the dominant dwelling type after the Revolution. Even then, there was often a social mix – shopkeepers and craftsmen on the ground floor and maybe stables in the courtyard, grand apartments on the first floor and tenants of diminishing means on the upper floors, with the rooms in the roof reserved for servants. In the 19th century, as the city expanded, Paris acquired a geography of class. Increasingly the bourgeoisie moved to live in the new quarters in the west, the workers in the east.

Then, as the city spread outwards new suburbs of varying quality were created – some with classic, leafy villas, the majority with poor class housing mixed up with industry, often no more than shanty towns. By the 1930s the suburbs were as populous as the city. Later, from the 1950s onwards, a public commitment to better housing was realised through redevelopment schemes within the city and further suburban expansion. The latter comprised the so-called *grands ensembles* that now ring Paris, projects containing 30-40,000 residents, built with high-rise towers and slabs, together with parks, schools and shopping, occupied for the most part by lower income families and now very much the home for many immigrants from North and West Africa. So rapid was their growth that by 1970 a sixth of the population of the Paris region lived in the *grands ensembles*.

In its social geography Paris is now different from most other large cities. More significant than differences between Left and Right Bank, east and west, is that between city and suburbs. The central City of Paris remains predominantly middle class, surrounded by a ring of industrial and working class suburbs, surrounded in turn by clusters of equally working class, strongly immigrant, *grands ensembles*. It is the central core that is the iconic Paris.

The boulevards

In this core the boulevards, the bus routes on them and the Metro underneath them hold the city together. These boulevards are commonly thought to be the creation of Napoleon III and his Prefect Haussmann in the mid 19th century. Many were, but the first boulevards were built in the 17th century when old, redundant fortifications were removed. Here were created the inner ring of boulevards, running eastwards from the Madeleine Church to the *Place de la Republique* and on to the *Place de la Bastille*. A century or so later, another wall was built further out, not for defensive purposes but to channel traffic through customs posts. Sixty grand gates were planned, though only forty were built. Roads flanked the inner and outer side of the wall, so that when it in turn was pulled down, the broad double carriageways of the outer boulevards were formed, running eastwards from the Etoile at the foot of Montmartre to the present day Place Stalingrad, across the river to Place d'Italie and on to Montparnasse, crossing the river again west of where the Eiffel Tower would later stand and back to Etoile. These two rings of boulevards were largely built through open land, though flanking development followed. Later there was a third set of fortifications built yet further out in the 1840s; in time these too were razed and today's six lane freeway, the *Boulevard Périphérique*, replaced them.

Haussmann's mid 19th century boulevards were different from their predecessors in both their geography and purpose. They pierced through the city rather then bounded it. One project was the creation of a *grand croisée* with major north-south and east-west routes intersecting at the *place du Châtelet*: the east-west axis involved the eastward extension of Napoleon Ist's *Rue de Rivoli*, the north-south axis the creation of the *Boulevards Strasbourg* and *Sebastopol* on the Right Bank, the *Boulevard du Palais* across the *Ile de la Cité* and the *Boulevard St Michel* on the Left Bank. Another Haussmann project was a makeover for the *Avenue des Champs Elysées,* bringing it to its present appearance with lawns, trees, walks and benches flanking the city's grand processional way known as *La Voie Triomphale*. Other boulevards created new connections from the centre of the city to its newly developing quarters further out.

Haussman boulevard

The boulevards of Paris give the city a strong mental map. They are still the main traffic arteries for – with a few exceptions like the road tunnels inserted with the redevelopment of the *Les Halles* market area — there has been no later major road building inside the city boundary. So the bus network mostly runs on the boulevards and the underground Metro was mostly built, by cut and cover method, to follow them – accounting for the sharp, shuddering turns that you experience travelling on it. It is the boulevards that also provide the characteristic image of Paris. Before the Haussmann boulevards there had been a boom in building arcades, inserted as pedestrian connections between streets, using iron and glass roofs and later gas lighting to create airy, but intimate spaces. They were lined with upmarket cafes, restaurants, shops – bookstores, milliners, *patisseries*, tobacconists, toy makers and the occasional novelty entertainments like panoramas and dioramas. Once there were 150 such arcades and many survive, albeit often rather run-down; for fashionable street life had passed to the new boulevards.

Haussmann's boulevards created a wholly new urban form by adding together dense building, commerce, greenery and spaciousness. It has been copied – a Paris fashion – in cities on all continents – you will find them in Moscow, Teheran, Saigon or Manila. Characteristically, the Parisian boulevard is straight and wide, sometimes with an important building as a distant focal point: the *Opéra*, the *Gare de l'Est*, the church of the *Madeleine*, the *Arc de Triomphe*. It is flanked by buildings of a consistent six or seven storey height, with facades incorporating characteristic deep windows, balconies and mansard roofs. At street level there are shopfronts, sometimes with goods on display outside as well as through the window, punctuated by large, handsome doors opening on to the rear courtyards. In front of them are wide pavements, furnished with streetlamps, trees, benches, advertising pillars and kiosks – selling newspapers and magazines, tobacco, confectionery, lottery tickets, travelcards, postage stamps. (The once familiar *pissotières* have been removed.) At the main junctions are the outdoor tables of cafes and *brasseries* and the entrances to the Metro, many still in the original *Art Nouveau* style.

Above all, the boulevards are lively with people. Look at photos of the same boulevard taken one hundred years apart and they look remarkably similar – the townscape and the street life seem common, only the road vehicles and the clothing seem to have changed. The growth of wheeled traffic, and particularly its petrol fumes, has somewhat diminished the attraction of the boulevards as a setting for street life. As in other cities, the more pedestrian-friendly back streets have been rediscovered. But whether in its passages, its boulevards, its places or its gardens and parks, Paris and Parisians retain a capacity for public

199

display. It is indeed curious how many of the necessities and pleasures of city life across the world have French words for them and French, often Parisian, origins: bistro, boulevard, cafe, disco, metro among them.

Paris pleasures[4]

Arcade – a covered passage with arches along one or both sides. Origin late 17th century French, from Provencal *arcada* or Italian *arcata* based on Latin *arcus,* 'bow'.

Artiste – a professional entertainer, especially a singer or dancer. Origin early 19th century French.

Bistro – a small, inexpensive restaurant. Origin 1920s French, perhaps related to *bistouille*, a northern colloquial term meaning 'bad alcohol', or perhaps from Russian *bystro* meaning 'rapidly.' The latter derivation relates to a story that Russian soldiers occupying Paris after the defeat of Napoleon would shout '*bystro*' when ordering their food.

Boulevard – a wide street in a town or city, typically one lined with trees. Origin mid 18th century French, a 'rampart', later a 'promenade' on the site of one, from German *Bollwerk.*

Brasserie – a restaurant in France or one in a French style. Origin mid 19th century French, originally 'brewery' from *brasser*, 'to brew.'

Cabaret – entertainment held in a nightclub or restaurant while the audience drink at tables. Origin mid 17th century denoting a French inn. In 1881 two entrepreneurs Emile Goudeau and Rodolphe Salins started the Chat Noir, the world's first modern cabaret, in the Boulevard Rochecouart.

Cafe – a small restaurant selling light meals and drinks. Origin early 19th century French from *café*, coffee house. The Café Procope on the *Rue de l'Ancienne Comedie,* founded by a Sicilian in 1670, is still there.

Disco – a club at which people dance to recorded pop music. Origin 1950s from French *discothèque*, 'record library.'

Hotel – an establishment providing accommodation, meals and other services for travellers. Origin mid 18th century from French *hostel.*

Latin Quarter – a neighbourhood associated with artists and intellectuals. Origin in the Left Bank area of Paris where the Church and Schools, which spoke Latin, were dominant.

Metro – an underground railway system in a city. Origin early 20th century French from *métro*, an abbreviation of *Chemin de Fer Métropolitain,* 'metropolitan railway.'

The character of the *flaneur* is prototypically Parisian. It emerged in the early 19th century. The *flaneur* walked the city streets, occupied its cafes and restaurants, enjoying the anonymity of the crowd, drinking in appearances and experiences, but ready for exchanges of glance or comment when acquaintances were encountered. The character appears in much writing about Paris of that time. But the *flaneur* was not just a hedonist, he sought also to understand the city that he observed. Balzac mused: 'Ah! To wander in Paris! Adorable and delectable existence. To be a *flaneur* is a form of science. It is gastronomy for the eye.'[5] The density and compactness of Paris means that it remains a very walkable city in which the *flaneur* experience persists.

Americans in Paris

North Americans have long had a love affair with Paris. They arrived in large numbers in the latter half of the 19th century, especially artists like John Singer Sargent and James Whistler, drawn to what they saw as the world centre of the new art. Writers came in later years, notably Henry James, Edith Wharton, Gertude Stein, Ernest Hemingway and James Baldwin. Musicians too, especially from the French embrace of jazz. Writers, artists and musicians found inspiration in Paris as a place and as a society. Others have shared this fascination with and love of Paris. It has always been a place to which émigrés gravitated – 'the natural European home of the disinherited intellectual'[6]. Karl Marx, Heinrich Heine, Guiseppe Mazzini and Alexander Herzen all lived here at some point in the 19th century; it was one of the destinations for Russian émigrés after the 1917 Revolution, followed by opponents of the post 1945 Communist regimes in Central and Eastern Europe; Francophone intellectuals from North and West Africa have also found their home here. In consequence the *Père Lachaise* cemetery has become one of the city's tourist destinations – for here are the graves and monuments for Oscar Wilde, Gertrude Stein, Isadora Duncan, Modigliani and Jim Morrison, all foreigners who had settled in Paris.

Where the cultural elite led, mass tourism has followed. Today, Paris is the world's premier tourist city. Its great sights – the *Sacre Coeur* church in Montmartre, the *Centre Pompidou*, the Eiffel Tower, the *Arc de Triomphe* – are familiar the world over. Part of its appeal is an association with romance – as the Cole Porter song *I Love Paris* says. Photography has played a strong part in this, particularly the images created by Robert Doisneau, Henri Cartier Bresson and Brassaï, who all achieved a poetic realism in their portraits of the city and its people. Above all, Paris is so Parisian. Jan Morris remarked that 'in Paris I sometimes feel that every street, every event, every gesture is dedicated to some aspects of Parisness. Elsewhere civic generalisations are generally out of date, overtaken by shifting styles and standards. Here they remain almost disconcertingly valid.'[7]

I love Paris by Cole Porter[8]

Everytime I look down
On this timeless town
Whether blue or grey be her skies
Whether loud be her cheers
Or whether soft be her tears
More and more do I realise that...
I love Paris in the springtime
I love Paris in the fall
I love Paris in the winter when it drizzles
I love Paris in the summer when it sizzles
I love Paris every moment
Every moment of the year
I love Paris, why oh why do I love Paris?
Because my love is near.

The persistent appeal of Paris is that it manages to be both bourgeois and bohemian, orderly and revolutionary, conservative and radical, cerebral and sensual, comforting and challenging. This ambivalence is nicely expressed in the proposition by the writer Adam Gopnik, himself an American in Paris, that some come to Paris for the food, some for the drink. Those who come, so to speak, for the food are drawn to the comfort and pleasure and learning and beauty – walking in the Luxembourg Gardens, visiting the Louvre, buying fashionable clothes, studying and, of course, eating in the restaurants. Those who come for the drink are there to be dazzled by new art, nightlife and new experiences and maybe in search of romance. But, 'the two kinds of visitor often end up swapping roles and tastes...The people who come for the drinks stay for the dinner, and the people who come for the dinner are often the ones who go home drunk...The Parisian achievement was to have made, in the nineteenth century, two ideas of society: the Haussmannian idea of bourgeois order and comfort, and the avant-garde of *la vie bohème*.'[9]

13.

Power: rulers' cities

Berlin 1990. *A few months after the demolition of the Wall that had divided the city for thirty years, strange evidence of the former regime can be seen throughout the eastern part of the city, previously the capital of the communist German Democratic Republic. Smashed filing cabinets still litter the courtyards of some government buildings. The former Parliament building carries the ironic graffiti 'Autonomes Zentrum'. Everywhere there are new copyshops (they had been restricted by the old regime and people need documentation under the new regime) and car sellers offering Western models for the first time. At the Brandenburg Gate there are stalls selling fragments of the Wall and various items – badges, caps, watches – from the Stasi, the former secret police. It seems weird that objects used so recently to oppress the people of East Berlin have now become tourist trinkets. Also on sale are a version of the classic Russian wooden doll in which the outer doll is Gorbachev and the inner dolls successively Brezhnev, Khrushchev, Stalin and Lenin. Some American visitors are haggling over the price with the articulate young Berliner running the stall. Finally, in exasperation, he says 'C'mon guys, just pay up, we're not dealing with fucking Russians now.'*

City fathers

In cities someone is always in charge. Such rulers are sometimes known as 'city fathers'. The term gives an impression of benign care for the city and its citizens, but also a sense of authority that may – as with fathers in families – be exercised in ways that are either liberal or dictatorial. The plural 'city fathers' clearly implies oligarchy and this is indeed one way in which some cities have been ruled: witness the Doges of Venice, the Shoguns of Tokyo, Tammany Hall in New York. Other cities were and are ruled by autocrats, their power conferred by *coup d'état*, dynastic inheritance, conquest or appointment by state government. But increasingly in today's world, most cities – like most states –

are ruled more or less democratically, their leaders chosen through elections. Many now have directly elected Mayors.

However rulers gain power, that power is ephemeral; clearly so where constitutions limit tenure, likely too where autocrats are at risk of overthrow – even hereditary monarchs and self-proclaimed 'Lifetime Presidents' die sooner or later. So, rulers are often vainly concerned about their legacy, and a construction – a monument, a palace, an entire new city – is the most visible and permanent kind of legacy. Some wit called it the 'edifice complex.'[1] On his deathbed, Roman emperor Augustus boasted 'I found Rome a city of clay; I leave it to you a city of marble.' But it is not just about legacies. While alive and in power rulers can believe that new buildings symbolise their values: their authority, their modernity, their superior aesthetic taste. Such public buildings become part of the iconography of a dominant regime and its epoch.

These buildings are predominantly in cities. They are designed as showcases for old or new institutions: government itself, the state religion, universities, museums, opera houses and theatres, sports arenas. They may also be the places where the rituals of power – military parades, state visits, anniversary celebrations – are acted out. These buildings get a lot of attention as you pass them, going about your daily life. They are also what city tourists go to see. And the global media regularly display them. Note how such buildings serve as visual backdrops to daily TV coverage of world news, as with the use of Big Ben in London for news from the UK, or the dome of the Capitol building in Washington or the Kremlin Palace in Moscow.

Rulers always need professional help in this city building. Traditionally they employed architects and engineers to design the buildings, financiers to raise the money and administrators to create and manage the institutions. Today they also worry about PR, so additional skills are needed, like publicists, web designers, events organisers and educationists. These acolytes have sometimes become more strongly associated with the cities they helped to build and run than the rulers they served. The imperial architect Sinan, born soon after the Ottomans' conquest of Constantinople in the 15th century, designed over 300 buildings for them, of which eighty-five still stand including the Mosque of Sultan Suleiman the Magnificent that from its hilltop site still provides a landmark for the city. Christopher Wren masterminded the reconstruction of London after the Great Fire of 1666 and gave the city St Paul's Cathedral and another fifty new churches, most of which are still there, now squeezed between the office buildings of the financial district. The transformation of Berlin into a capital city in the early 19th century is known as the work of Schinkel, its Director of Public Works, more than of the Kaiser who appointed him. Similar fame followed Haussman's later restructuring of Paris, Edwin Lutyen's creation of New Delhi and Robert Moses' road-building in New York. Sinan, Wren, Schinkel and Lutyens were architects, Moses and Haussmann were administrators. In each case their role was not just that of professional adviser, more that of commissar personally chosen by the ruler and given the power and money for ambitious city building. Today, such city professionals often pursue international careers: leading architects, theatre and museum directors, transport managers move from city to city, in the service of various regimes.

New capitals

Monarchs or presidents often built grand palaces for themselves in the country, as with Louis XIV's Versailles outside Paris, Hitler's Berghof in the Bavarian Alps (complete with bomb shelters) or Mobutu's Gbadolite in the Congo jungle (abandoned by his successors and now overrun by vegetation). There is also a long tradition of rulers building new capital cities. In the 18th century there was Peter the Great's founding of St Petersburg at the head of the Baltic Sea as Russia's 'window on the west' in 1703, and the building of Washington as the capital of the new United States of America in the 1790s. The 20th century saw the creation of Canberra as the capital of post-1901 independent Australia, New Delhi as the capital of British India after 1911, then in post-imperial India Chandighar as capital of Indian Punjab and Islamabad as a new capital of Pakistan; and, perhaps the most ambitious of all, the building of Brasilia in the Amazon jungle from the 1950s onwards. Today rulers are still building new capitals, especially in newly-independent states. In Africa Dodoma became the capital of Tanzania in 1973 and Abuja, in the centre of Nigeria, became the federal capital in 1991. Astana, since 1998 the capital of post-Soviet Russian Kazakhstan, is one of the world's greatest building sites, with new ministerial buildings, a massive Presidential Palace and numerous parks and monuments, all funded by state oil revenues. Naypyidaw, deep in the Burmese jungle, is the latest example, nominated in 2005 by the nation's long-ruling military junta as the new capital of Myanmar.

Rulers usually justify building their new capitals on entirely practical grounds – such as reducing congestion in older cities, moving politicians and officials to healthier climates, making government more efficient, or choosing a more central location. But there is always a deeper, unspoken rationale. A new capital city, with its unique and singular purpose, symbolises the ruler's power – hence the particular attraction of new capitals for autocrats. It may also express the regime's dominance of rival political interests, some with attachments to older, existing cities. So in 1561 Philip II chose the small garrison town of Madrid, smack in the middle of his newly unified Spain, as its capital. The creation of St Petersburg implied a rejection of the ancient capitals of Russia – Novgorod, Kiev and Moscow. Washington's location was part of a deal struck between the northern and southern states of the Union after the War of Independence. It, like Canberra and Brasilia and Abuja subsequently, was built on territory administratively separate from the nation's federal states.

All this leads inevitably to the choice of grand designs for new capital cities. Budgets and timetables are usually exceeded. Leading architects are employed and given a free rein. In the design competition for Brasilia the winner Lucio Costa just submitted 'freehand drawings on five medium-sized cards: not a single population projection, economic analysis, land use schedule, model or mechanical drawing. The jury liked its grandeur'[2]. Characteristic of these new capital cities is a prominent disposition of key buildings – palace, parliament, ministries, supreme court, theatres, temples and churches. Then there are wide axial highways, often with monuments as their end points and intersecting to create places or squares or circuses, creating a network designed more for ceremony than for circulation, and certainly not for pedestrians. All of this is laced with generous greenery, including wide strips flanking the highways, landscape settings for buildings, and many parks, gardens and lakes, often needing extravagant irrigation to keep them going. Overall it is more spacious and less dense than a traditional city. Everything is often designed in monumental style with massive buildings, symmetric layouts, using expensive materials – a style aped by (or derived from?) sets designed for Hollywood costume movies about ancient Babylon or Rome. In the case of Brasilia 'its plan was variously described as an airplane, a bird or dragonfly: the body, or fuselage, was a monumental axis for the principal public buildings and offices, the wings were the residential and other areas. In the first, uniform office blocks were to line a wide central mall leading to the complex of governmental buildings. In the second, uniform apartments were to be built in Corbusian superblocks … everyone, from Permanent Secretary to janitor, was to live in the same blocks in the same kind of apartment.'[3] Brasilia is now a UNESCO World Heritage site – the only modern city to have this status.

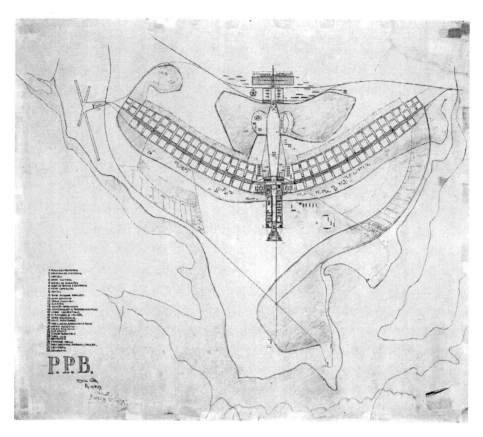

The master plan of Brasilia

These new capitals were designed to house politicians, bureaucrats and their personal staff. Ordinary city life was rarely allowed for. In every case, unsurprisingly, it forced itself in and the city's pristine plan gets subverted one way or another, the grand design becoming frayed at the edges. In Washington, The Mall, designed as a great park running for more than a mile from the Capitol to the Potomac River, became common pasture, was occupied in part by commercial uses and in 1870 a railway was built across it. It only took its present form in the 1920s. Meanwhile, Washington had become what it remains today, predominantly a city of poor, black families whose forbears had migrated from the South, its government functions and grandeur largely confined to the city centre and its rich northwest districts. In New Delhi shanty towns now fill out the city, some packed into the open spaces designed to flank the ceremonial routes. In Brasilia the original plan declared that there would be no such *favelas* anywhere in the Federal District; but equally there was no provision in the plan for cheap housing. The city population was planned as 500,000. But migrants turned up, squatted land, found work and created satellite cities. Now these house the majority of Brasilia's population of over two million people.

Occasionally capital cities are abandoned by rulers. St Petersburg, for two centuries the capital city of the Tsars of Russia, was where the Bolshevik Revolution of October 1917 started. It was to the Finland Station there that Lenin returned and the city was later renamed Leningrad after him. But a rivalry with Moscow persisted: Leningrad tended to think of Moscow as unsophisticated and primitive, while Moscow despised Leningrad as corrupt, effete, even unreliable in its support for the Revolution. The Bolsheviks moved their capital to Moscow. In a similar break with the past, in 1924 the Turkish republic that succeeded the Ottomans moved its capital from Constantinople to Ankara. There is symbolism in the demotion as in the creation of capital cities.

Monuments and makeovers

All the world's cities are chock-full of monuments to past rulers. Most are barely noticed, just part of the street scene, but they can occasionally stir strong emotions. Some are unloved, as is the enormous *Vittoriano* in Rome that honours the first king of united Italy, Vittorio Emanuele of Savoy: 'a piece of nationalistic kitsch that outdoes anything dreamed up by the ancients' is the view of one current guide book[4]. Ruler's statues are occasionally pulled down – the fate of Stalin, Saddam Hussein and Muammar Gaddafi in recent time. But other monuments are loved, even revered as shrines: in St Petersburg young couples still leave flowers, after a wedding, at the Bronze Horseman memorial to Peter the Great; a statue of Tamerlaine is similarly honoured in Samarkand. Loved or hated, monuments serve rulers' purposes in many ways.

Monuments are not the only kind of memorial to history. Cities, their streets and places may be named in commemoration of people or events. These names may become embarrassing when the tide of history turns. India has seen a wave of post-imperial substitutions, including Mumbai for Bombay and Kolkata for Calcutta. In Russia Stalingrad became Volgograd when Stalin was denounced and Leningrad has reverted in post-Communist times to its earlier name of St Petersburg. In 2011 the name of fallen dictator Mubarak disappeared

The purpose of monuments

'A monument is intended to call forth fear or wonder in the observer: to remind him of the antiquity of the dynasty, the power of the regime, the wealth of the community, the truth of its ideology, or of some event – a military victory or successful revolution – that demonstrated such wealth, power, or truth. To succeed in its aims, a monument needs to jolt the individual out of his mundane concerns – catching the 5:37, remembering to renew a driver's licence, buying postage stamps – to remind him that life involves more than such concerns, and that he is fortunate to be the citizen of such a splendid metropolis, a subject of such a benevolent ruler, an adherent of the one true faith.' [5]

quickly from streets, hospitals and metro stations in Cairo (though those of his predecessor autocrats Sadat and Nasser remained). Even in London the naming of Trafalgar Square and Waterloo Station in celebration of British victories over Napoleonic France has been challenged as chauvinistic; though Paris in turn has the *Gare d'Austerlitz* in celebration of a French victory of that time.

Regimes often carve out for themselves a private enclave in the city. Here their leaders live in style, their court functions, supporters and servants are housed, the innermost business of government is conducted, and the elite's spiritual and bodily needs are satisfied; all this behind high walls and guarded gates, their shenanigans concealed from their subjects. Such were the Alhambra in Granada, the Forbidden City in Beijing, the Kremlin in Moscow, the Imperial Palace in Tokyo. Similar enclaves accommodated colonial rulers and merchants in conquered territories. In the ten Chinese 'treaty ports' established after the Opium Wars of the 1840s, the victorious Western powers made their foothold concrete in such ways. In Shanghai there was an International Settlement from which Chinese law, business or people (except as servants) were excluded. In present-day Baghdad the so-called Green Zone fulfils this purpose. Originally its 10 square kilometres were home to the villas of government officials, some ministries and a number of palaces for Saddam Hussein's clique. Since his defeat it has been occupied by the new Iraqi government, its supporters and advisers, including the HQ of the US-led coalition forces, all heavily protected by 3 metre high, 50 centimetre thick blast walls topped with barbed wire and with restricted access in and out. Critics of the 2003 invasion of Iraq described it ironically as a 'crusader castle'.

In the last century some rulers have had great ambitions to remould their capital cities in their own image. Moscow under Stalin, Teheran under the Shahs of Iran, Pyongyang in North Korea under Kim Il Sung, Manila under the Marcos regime all had big makeovers. In Mao's Beijing, Tiananmen Square was extended to an enormous 40 hectares (the size of thirty-five football pitches) flanked by the Museum of the Chinese Revolution, the Great Hall of the People and, in its centre, the Monument to the People's Heroes. But the 20th century's other major tyrant, Hitler, achieved little of his grandiose ambitions for Berlin, or his more modest plans for Munich, his home town, or Linz, his birthplace.

Some cities are built and rebuilt over long periods of time by dynasties, shaping them as decisively as climate or geography or economics. The Ottoman dynasty ruled over Constantinople as the capital of its vast empire from 1453 to 1924, producing a city that functioned 'on every level: political, military, naval, religious (both Muslim and Christian), economic, cultural and gastronomic.'[7]

Germania[6]

After seizing power in 1933, Hitler came to believe that Berlin was not sufficiently impressive as the capital of his Third Reich. 'Berlin is a big city, but not a real metropolis' he complained. It compared unfavourably with Paris and Vienna. Albert Speer was appointed Inspector General of Buildings for the Renovation of the Federal Capital. His brief from Hitler: 'My simple ambition is to present the new German Reich with buildings it need not be ashamed of... but, above all, this new German republic is neither a boarder nor a lodger in the royal chambers of bygone days.' The project for the reconstruction of Berlin into a new capital to be called Germania was born. Speer's designs for grand avenues, squares, buildings and monuments were in neo-classical style but longer, bigger, taller, wider than in other capitals. So the new railway station would be bigger than Grand Central in New York, the great domed *Volkshalle* could accommodate St Peter's in Rome several times over. The centrepiece was to be a crossing of north-south and east-west thoroughfares, both wider and greener than the *Champs Elysées* in Paris. Of this only the east-west route, extending from the Brandenburg Gate through the *Tiergarten*, was built; it was unveiled on Hitler's fiftieth birthday in 1938 with a four hour long parade. As for the rest of the plan, war intervened. But Hitler and Speer reportedly whiled away many an hour in the Bunker rearranging the model of the rebuilt Berlin that was not to be.

Other dynastic rule of cities in Europe was only slightly less long-lived: Vienna under the Hapsburgs from 1556 to 1918, Paris under the Bourbons from 1589 to 1792, Berlin under the Hohenzollerns (as Kings of Prussia and later Emperors of Germany) from 1701 to 1918, St Petersburg under the Romanovs from 1703 to 1918. Outside Europe, the Mughal emperors ruled in Delhi from 1526 to 1857, when they were deposed by the British, and the Chakri royal dynasty has ruled over Bangkok in Thailand (the only Southeast Asian nation never to have been colonised) from 1782 to the present day.

The dynasties built up these cities as capitals of their empires. They could achieve this largely because they were autocratic, for these were cities where power was held and wielded by only a few hands. That power became very evident in the fabric of the city and remains so today. Here we find not just royal palaces – usually in the plural as successive dynast's tastes and preferences changed – but also the numerous smaller palaces of the nobility. As well, the grand churches, temples or mosques of the state religion which conferred legitimacy on the ruler and the fortresses, parade grounds and prisons of the army and police essential to their control of the citizenry. It should not be forgotten that the architectural splendours of St Petersburg, Vienna or Constantinople were achieved in part through the exploitation of subject peoples.

Dynastic cities were also created in the 19th-20th centuries in the Asian, African and Latin American colonies of Western powers. In the earlier stages of imperialism, from the 16th century onwards, trade in high value commodities like gold, tea, spices, silk and sugar was the focus; only barracks, warehouses and small new European quarters were built, commonly in appropriate Dutch, Spanish, French or British architectural style. It was from the mid 19th century, as the colonial powers tightened their grip (excepting Latin America, where independent states had already succeeded the Spanish and Portuguese empires), that each imperial dynasty sought to shape its colonial cities as their economic, political and military HQs. In part this produced similar modernisations to those in the home country: railway stations, docks, government buildings, universities, churches, parks and villas. Also some specific colonial requirements, notably clubhouses and hotels – many of the latter acquiring glamorous reputations like Shepherd's in Cairo, Raffles in Singapore, and the Metropole in Hanoi.

These colonial cities were diverse both socially and ethnically. The European population had expanded to include lower class employees as clerks in trade and government; expatriate non-Europeans – Indians, Chinese or Arabs

– had arrived as craftsmen and traders; and the indigenous population did the manual work. For example, in Rangoon at the start of the 20th century, only a third of the population was the local Burmese, whilst two thirds were immigrants. Ethnic separation became a feature of these colonial cities and was planned into the creation of new districts, which then varied greatly in the quality of buildings, infrastructure and amenities. The imperial masters lived in style in the European Districts, in India called the Civil Lines, while the locals lived in more primitive Native Quarters. In some places this separation transmuted into formal segregation policies backed by the force of law. Since colonial rule has been thrown off in the last half century, the new political elites – the liberators and their successors, their expatriate associates and advisers – have commonly occupied the better, formerly European districts of these cities, grabbing private and public money to maintain their higher standards. The rest of the city has become occupied and extended with shanty towns by massive numbers of rural immigrants.

Dynasties are still shaping cities today. Shanghai and Dubai are two of the most rapidly growing cities in the world: the product of two quite distinct dynasties. Shanghai, under Communist rule since 1949, has been actively promoted since 1991 as China's leading port and business centre. Dubai has been ruled by Sheiks from the al-Maktoum family since the mid 19th century, and they have latterly conceived an ambition to make Dubai the trade hub and financial centre of the Middle East – in their words, with a nod to history, 'an Arab city of global significance, rivalling Cordoba and Baghdad.' In these modern versions of dynastic cities you will not see just the palaces, parade grounds, mosques or cathedrals of the older dynastic cities. As well you will see skyscraper flats, offices and hotels, shopping malls, and the airports, freeways and metro systems that serve them. All this is funded by state corporations in partnership with international capital offered generous tax breaks. And it is achieved on the backs of vast armies of immigrant labour: in Shanghai about a third of the population are migrant workers drawn from the countryside; in Dubai the migrant workers, mostly from India, Bangladesh and Pakistan, are more than half the population.

Public works

Rulers' city building may start as self-indulgence but in time the places they create for their private pleasure often pass into public ownership: hunting grounds, forests and parks are opened to the masses, theatres become commercial enterprises, private art collections are gifted to or confiscated by popular governments, palaces are turned over to administrative or cultural uses. This is common after revolutions, though also a product of more gradual democratisation. But rulers – both autocratic and constitutional – are also given to philanthropy. In London, for example, Hyde Park was originally purchased by Henry VIII from the church in the 16th century and opened to the public in the 17th century; the Banqueting House in Whitehall was constructed as part of a never-completed new palace for Charles I at about the same time; the National Gallery was created in 1824 by parliament.

But the massive growth of cities in the 19th century in Europe and North America impelled their rulers to embark on more ambitious and extensive public works. Migrants from the countryside poured into European cities, emigrants from Europe poured into the new cities of North America. They were poor, frequently unemployed, living in overcrowded housing with little sanitation, bad diet and too much alcohol, prone to epidemics and often the victims of crime. In London one family to a room was common and that room might also have to accommodate homeworking. Paris and Berlin were smaller but denser and more congested; in the latter tightly packed five storey tenements called *Mietkaserne* (rent barracks) were the norm. New York and Chicago were so crowded that a single street block could house 4,000 people. Most 19th century Old and New World cities shared these conditions. Journalists and campaigners raised awareness among the better off. In response, rulers promoted improvements, not just from a sense of philanthropy but also undoubtedly from fear of insurrection.

The public works of Haussman, Napoleon III's Prefect in Paris in the 1850s and 1860s, were one kind of action. His creation of new boulevards through the old, dense street pattern of the city was its hallmark, but better water supply, drainage and the creation of parks were also part of his programme. The logistics of property purchase, demolition, construction of roads, drainage and parks, and then leasing the new frontages to builders was achieved by the exercise of draconian state powers. Hausmann's and Napoleon's motives have long been debated. At the time the official justifications were the clearing away of poor quality property, ventilation of unhealthy neighbourhoods, providing sewerage and drainage, increasing the city's open space, easing the flow of traffic and creating grander settings and vistas for the city's prominent buildings.

Undoubtedly, as critics then and now noted, the result was also a city layout with wide, straight and long streets suited to the rapid deployment of military force and the use of cannon fire to deal with the Parisians' persistent inclination to riot.

Many cities in other countries were restructured similarly at the time. Cities in which French influence or power was strong – like Bucharest, Casablanca, Saigon – were obvious candidates for new boulevards. Vienna also acquired its *Ringstrasse*, lined by public buildings, parks and new apartments, on the line of the old city fortifications. London engaged in a pragmatic mix of slum clearance, new street building and drainage improvements. Some North American cities took inspiration from Europe – successfully in Chicago, where a reclaimed lake front with a new City Hall, museums and galleries, and boulevards radiating out from the centre all sought to create order and beauty from chaos; unsuccessfully in San Francisco, where, despite the opportunity for rebuilding after the earthquake and fire of 1906, only a new Civic Centre in *Beaux Arts* style was realised.

Improvement of urban housing was another commitment. In Britain the 1885 Royal Commission on the Housing of the Working Classes – including among its members the heir to the throne, a cardinal, sundry peers and a few philanthropists – argued the case. It was not pure coincidence that at about that time the 1884 Reform Act extended voting rights to a large part of the male working class; Charles Booth reported in 1887 the first results of his mammoth survey of the lives of the poor of East London; and in 1888 the London County Council, the city's first democratically elected government, took office. A new tradition of the provision of social housing became established and continues across the world to this day. In different cities and at different times it has taken different forms. One has been slum clearance, the demolition and replacement of older dwellings by new in order to improve public health. Building anew has been another form, sometimes as suburban extensions to cities on their edge, sometimes in new towns away from the overcrowded cities. And there are many variants on the upgrading of existing housing by repair work, installation of new services, sometimes thinning out property to improve road layouts or provide parks, schools, shops or workplaces.

In North American cities in the late 19th century, new public transport systems started to reshape cities. Initially there were buses and street trams, later railways on separate surface routes and then underground or overground lines in the city centres. Chicago showed the way with radial street trams connecting into the downtown elevated railway, known locally as the 'El', that still winds between the skyscrapers – as fans of the TV series *ER* will know. These new transport systems operated with franchises from the city authorities, but were privately funded and run for profit, the income often coming not just from fares but also from related property development. In time, public transport corporations took over the early private operators, either to save them from going bust or to achieve more integrated networks. Many other cities acquired new public transport systems: London's first underground railway line opened in 1863, the Paris Metro opened in 1900, around that time Los Angeles created a system of electric streetcars, and Moscow's underground system – noted for the glamour of its marble halls and chandeliers – came later in 1934. Today, you can travel by bus or taxi in every major city in the world, by tram or streetcar as well in many and by overground or underground metros in some.

Chicago's elevated railroad

The later development of urban motorways – restricted access roads with multi-level junctions – was dependent on public money from the start. Again US cities led the way. In New York, Robert Moses built freeways (the US term for the roads) on Long Island in the 1920s to connect the city to the suburbs and beaches, later extending them into Manhattan with the Henry Hudson Parkway on the west side that can claim to be the first true urban motorway. The first Los Angeles freeways were built in the late 1930s. Only in the 1950s did freeway building in other North American cities get underway. Then a conscious decision was taken that the Federal Government's new interstate highways system should not just connect the cities but also penetrate, rather than skirt, them, thereby improving accessibility to downtown and removing blighted areas – a repeat of the arguments used by Haussmann and his boulevard building imitators elsewhere a century earlier. Many European cities prepared plans for new urban motorways and some were built in the 1970s and 1980s, but popular opposition defeated many others and rulers' enthusiasm for them has waned. Even in North America, city freeway building has largely ceased, and some existing freeways in New York and San Francisco have been closed and dismantled. Urban motorways are, though, still getting built, in response to rising private transport, in the cities of the Gulf, Asia and Latin America.

In recent decades urban renewal has become a new focus for public works in many cities. Changing functions have made some existing parts of cities redundant: warehouse districts, railway goods yards and docklands have offered opportunities for large scale development, sometimes with waterfront locations or historic buildings as added attractions. Partnerships between city governments, state agencies and property developers are the common organisation for renewal. Early examples were the old wholesale market of Les Halles in Paris, Baltimore Harbour, London Docklands, and the Cape Town Waterfront. Now such projects are commonplace all round the world – and all rather alike, with multiplex cinemas, cafes and restaurants, offices, conference halls, upmarket flats, shops and yet more shops as the familiar ingredients.

Sometimes these grand urban renewal projects are keyed into celebrations or events. For the last twenty years the European Capital of Culture award has provided a stimulus to renewal in some of the recipient cities, most recently Maribor in Slovenia and Guimaräes in Portugal (2012), Turku in Finland and Tallinn in Estonia (in 2011) and Essen and Istanbul (2010). Similar schemes operate among cities in the USA and the Arab world. On a world scale it is the Olympics Games that have come to be the great prize. Ever since the Barcelona

Olympics in 1992 the potential stimulus to urban renewal has become an important part of their rationale. Before then the Games more often left the host city near bankrupt and with unwanted sports facilities. Since then the effect of the Games in raising a city's profile, attracting visitors, providing an excuse to spruce up the place, and justifying investment in transport systems, parkland, housing as well as the sports venues, has attracted city fathers to compete for hosting the Games. However, there are always downsides: the diversion of resources from other public investments, large displacements of residents to make way for building works, and frequently a smaller longterm boost to the city economy than promised. For Beijing, in hosting the 2008 Games, both these upsides and downsides were apparent, but there was also a political payoff in the acknowledgement of China's new role on the world stage.

Beijing's Olympics

The city got a lavish makeover in preparation for the 2008 Games – a 80,000 seat stadium, new media centre, hotels galore, the world's biggest airport, 300 kilometres of new roads and doubling the extent of the metro system. Much of it was on land cleared of traditional low-rise hutong housing with over 300,000 dwellings demolished and over a million people relocated. Before and during the Games, car travel in the city was severely restricted, power plants and factories closed, construction work ceased, all to improve the city's air quality. Beijing residents were also groomed, with language classes for the police and taxi drivers, etiquette training for hotel staff, a campaign to improve public manners with a crackdown on spitting – and the threat of restrictions on internet access, political protest, vagrancy and begging. 100,000 extra police were recruited and 300,000 surveillance cameras installed; anti-aircraft missiles were even in place next to the main stadium.

This tradition of public works by city rulers is not always benign in its effects. Frequently the benefits from investment in housing, transport or urban renewal have been skewed towards the well-off. Public money for housing ends in the pockets of landowners or landlords. Transport investment favours road building for cars and lorries, neglecting or even worsening conditions for walking, cycling or bus travel that most city people rely on. Urban renewal creates upmarket flats, glossy retailing and high-tech jobs way beyond the means of existing residents,

218

while destroying existing homes and work without providing adequate substitutes or even, in cases, fair compensation. All too often the poor of the city are the losers.

Worse still, rulers' public works may be undertaken in pursuit of partisan agendas: restriction of political opposition, confiscation of land and property, pocketing foreign investment or development aid, even just impressing foreign visitors. When Imelda Marcos was the self-appointed Governor of Manila, a tarted up parade route was provided for the 1974 Miss Universe pageant, the 1975 visit of US President Gerald Ford, and the 1976 World Bank meeting; to achieve that 160,000 people were dispossessed and dumped on the city outskirts.[8] For Pope John Paul's visit in 1981 she commissioned the Coconut Palace – so-called because the tree and its products featured strongly in its design and construction – but the Pope declined to grace such ostentation. Later in the 1980s Juan Balanguer, the Dominican Republic's elderly autocrat, set about rebuilding swathes of the capital Santo Domingo in preparation for the quincentenary of Columbus's discovery of the New World and another visit from the Pope. The tradition continues: in 2003 St Petersburg was expensively spruced up by local-boy-made-good President Putin for the G8 summit.

Public works also too easily provide scope for corruption among the city's ruling elites. Design and construction contracts, appointments to public bodies, salaries and expenses for real or imaginary employment, inflated prices for property, bribes and backhanders can all be in the gift of rulers for themselves, their relations and friends, advisers and political supporters. More than that, these benefits to corrupt rulers may not just be incidental: creating such pay-offs may be the prime purpose of some projects. The world's most notorious kleptocracies of recent time – the regimes of Suharto in Indonesia, Marcos in the Philippines, the Duvaliers in Haiti, Mobutu in Zaire, Sani Abacha in Nigeria, Milosevic in Yugoslavia, to name some of the biggest crooks – have done this big style for their own enrichment. Most cities in the world, and mostly more than once in their history, have seen public works – and the public money that supports them – perverted in these ways.

Command and control

From time to time rulers seek to restrict the growth of cities. In 1580, Elizabeth I proclaimed a prohibition on 'any new buildings of any house or tenement within three miles from any of the gates of the said city of London.'[9] Communist China sought to control immigration to the cities between 1949 and 1978 through registering households as either 'city dwellers' or 'peasants.' Such restrictions may be driven by a belief in the virtues of rural life, by concern at the social and economic costs of city growth or – just as likely – by political fear of the urban masses. They may be pursued through schemes to retain people in rural areas or to divert them into colonising new agricultural land, at home or overseas. More often they are sought through penal action against city immigrants: requiring permits to move to the city, restricting immigrants' rights to work or education or healthcare, even by harassment, evictions and property demolition where newcomers have settled.

Beyond that, regimes commonly seek to impose rules of conduct in cities. Mostly these regulate how you behave in public, sometimes they extend to behaviour in private. There are many kinds of public misdemeanour that are often prohibited or restricted in cities. As well there are generic offences like 'anti-social behaviour' or 'public indecency' or 'disrespect.' How tightly your behaviour is restricted varies from place to place: sometimes it may just be subject to social disapproval, other times it may be illegal, even then the vigour of enforcement may vary. You can jaywalk with impunity in most European cities, but not so in North America. Bans on spitting or littering are fiercely enforced in Singapore. Dress codes for women in public – requiring them to cover the body, the hair, even the face – are increasingly common in Islamic cities.

Public misdemeanours

abandoning vehicles	gambling	shitting
advertising	graffiti	shouting abuse
assembling in groups	grazing animals	skateboarding
begging	improper clothing	sleeping
busking	jaywalking	soliciting for sex
cooking	kissing	spitting
drinking alcohol	littering	squatting
drug taking	making music	stalking
drunkenness	nudity	swearing
eating	photography	trading
uncovering arms or legs	pissing	vandalism
flyposting	political speeches	walking pets

Democratic as well as autocratic city rulers are often tempted to adopt such measures. Some may be justified as safeguarding public health, others in terms of maintaining widely accepted social norms, but some are clearly intended to curb freedom of expression in words or behaviour. The theory of 'zero tolerance' – that punishing minor misdemeanours discourages more serious crime – is also used as justification. Surveillance has long accompanied such restrictions. Public spirited citizens – as parents or neighbours or teachers – are enjoined to take on the task of reporting transgressions to the authorities. Now CCTV provides a new technology of surveillance. In shopping centres, car parks, schools and colleges, building forecourts and foyers, at road crossings, on public transport, in sports grounds, and sometimes right across the city, cameras scan the scene and capture footage in which daily lives are recorded and monitored by unseen officials for evidence of crimes and misdemeanours. In some cities the number of cameras now runs to many thousands. For the most part city dwellers seem to take comfort rather than fright from this.

The coercive power of rulers operates in cities in many other ways. In most cities at certain times rulers impose restrictions on free movement: curfews keep people off the streets, usually in the hours of darkness, bans restrict access to certain localities, there may be checkpoints. More insidiously, police powers may exist for arbitrary stopping, searching and even detention of people suspected of misdemeanours or just failing to have the required ID. This reached an extreme in the cities of apartheid South Africa, where black South Africans over the age of 16 had to carry a 'passbook' containing their name and address, a and evidence of employment. Some rulers adopt more aspirational approaches to improved behaviour. In 2006 the Governor of St Petersburg issued a list of 793 desired standards for her city, to be achieved by 2008: among them, each citizen should produce no more than 340 kilograms of refuse each year, should aim to live eleven months longer than the current life expectancy of 67.4 years, should need to walk no further than ten minutes to reach a bus stop, wait no longer than seven days for a plumber; there should also be only one alcoholic out of every 2,000 residents and an upper limit of 1,420 tramps in the whole city. We do not know how many of these standards were met.

Then there is the more formal regulation of city life: rules on shop opening times, permits for street selling or busking, censorship of what may be published or performed or taught, permissions for public meetings or marches, licensing of taxis and buses, their fares and routes, regulation of water and energy supplies, building and land use controls for new construction. The practice of zoning, whereby public authorities determine the acceptable scale and use of buildings in city districts, originated in its modern form in late 19th century Germany. It was enthusiastically espoused by US cities in the early 20th century and later by cities elsewhere in the world. Its combination of restrictions on land use, building height and density effectively determines the kind of activities – and so the kind of people engaged in them – in a district. It thus became a powerful tool of social segregation. A US commentator declared: 'The basic purpose of zoning was to keep Them where They belonged – Out. If They had already gotten in, then its purpose was to confine Them to limited areas. The exact identity of Them varied a lot around the country. Blacks, Latinos and poor people qualified. Catholics, Jews and Orientals were targets in many places. The elderly also qualified, if they were candidates for public housing.'[10]

These forms of command and control have been a fruitful theme of fictional urban dystopias. In Fritz Lang's 1927 film *Metropolis,* the population of the city has been divided into the Planners or Thinkers, who live above the earth in luxury, and the Workers, who toil underground to sustain these privileged lives – as one character in the film remarks: 'the dreams of a few had turned to the curses of many.' In George Orwell's 1949 novel *Nineteen Eighty-Four* the hero, Winston Smith, lives in Airstrip One, a frontline province of the totalitarian superstate Oceania, itself locked in permanent war with the other world superstates of Eurasia and Eastasia. The cities are all in ruins, apart from the four bomb-proof Ministries of Peace, of Plenty, of Truth and of Love which control, under the leadership of Big Brother, every aspect of the citizens' daily thought and action. In Ridley Scott's 1982 film *Blade Runner,* the hero's task of hunting down the escaped bio-engineered replicants is in the service of the mysterious Tyrell Corporation that controls the city from its skyscraper HQ.

Cities where their rulers systematically oppress their populations in these ways are, sadly, not unknown in reality. By definition, slaves have always been subject to tyranny, and even today there are people in cities who work and live in conditions of near slavery, powerless before employers or bureaucrats: domestic service, construction work and manufacturing sweatshops are where they are often to be found. That apart, people in cities are rarely treated with total equality. Citizens differing from the majority in their nationality, ethnicity or faith are more likely to be abused for suspected disloyalty. Gypsies, Jews and immigrants generally have a long history as victims of such discrimination. Some rulers extend their viciousness more indiscriminately. Military regimes have a particular habit of 'disappearing' people, as happened notoriously in Buenos Aires and Santiago in the 1970s and 1980s. In Cambodia under the Khmer Rouge, oppression reached an extreme. On taking power in 1975 the regime immediately evacuated the entire two million plus population of the capital Phnom Pehn and other cities by force, sending people to work in the country for their 're-education'. 1.5 million people, about a fifth of the national population, died of starvation, illness, torture or execution. The Khmer Rouge regime fell after four years and survivors slowly returned to the cities.

Love and fear

In his 1532 book *The Prince,* Niccolo Machiavelli offered advice to the rulers of the city states of Renaissance Italy. He identified two ways in which rulers can secure the support of their citizens – love and fear – and expressed his preference: 'it is far better to be feared than loved, if you cannot be both.'[11] Although 'love' and 'fear' may seem rather extreme expressions, they do represent two kinds of relationship between rulers and those they rule over. Historically, rulers have been wise to be wary of the cities. Their populations were large, often well informed and with high aspirations, and could be rapidly mobilised in opposition. Maintaining a climate of fear – through close surveillance, restrictions of dissent, shows of force, exemplary punishments – seems the obvious means of control. But history also shows that such measures, when excessive, can act to provoke rather than prevent revolt. So love is also sought by rulers – by attending to minor grievances, improving living conditions through public works, providing entertainments, building uplifting monuments.

Such rulers' tactics of inculcating both love and fear is only part of the story of the relationship between rulers and citizens. Alexandra Richie's history of Berlin is called *Faust's Metropolis*[12] because she sees, in the city's troubled history, traces of a Faustian bargain between Berliners and their successive rulers, a willingness to sell their souls for the fame and fortune, security and success that the rulers promised, if not always provided. There is a general truth to this proposition about cities dominated by their rulers, particularly autocratic rulers. There comes to be complicity between the ruling elite and the citizenry that inhibits civic development. For the mass of the population, deference and dependence seem easier options than autonomy and enterprise. Taking Berlin again as the exemplary case, it was Lenin who said that it was impossible to stage a revolution in such a city where the mob refuses to disobey the 'Keep Off the Grass' signs.

14.

Modernity: Los Angeles' rise and fall

Beverly Hills 2000. At a drinks party, to which we are invited as friends of friends, it is difficult to contribute to LA small talk. On the problems with maids and gardeners, the risk of further fires or earthquakes, the latest fashionable restaurant, we are ill-equipped as visitors to join in. When conversation turns to foreign travel there seems more possibility. Where had we been? Could we recommend a hotel in Prague? Were the locals friendly in Morocco? Did they speak (really meaning understand) English in Turkey? These are questions we can handle. One lady is wondering about vacationing with her husband in Italy. But she has one question we find unanswerable: 'Do you have to walk a lot in Italy?'

Mobility

Ask an Angeleno how far it is to a destination in the city and their answer will be expressed in time, not distance. 'From San Bernardino to the International Airport will take about an hour outside rush hour.' 'From Long Beach to Hollywood it's half an hour at best, but over two hours at worst.' 'From Santa Monica to Disneyland allow forty minutes.' And so on. The means of travel implicit in these measures remains unspoken. It's the freeway, the 400 kilometre-long network of roads that laces the city together, with four, six or even eight lanes each way, spanned by enormous direction signs, connecting to tributary streets through entry and exit ramps, busy with traffic day and night. The freeways are one of the characteristic sights of Los Angeles – like the canals of Venice or the boulevards of Paris. They make sense in getting around because the city is so vast, extending over 100 kilometres from north to south and from east to west. Its travel pattern involves multiple origins and destinations, criss-crossing the place, not strongly focused – as is common in other cities – on radial movement to and from a city centre. But it wasn't the freeways that made it this way. They came relatively late in the city's development and are more a

225

consequence than the cause of its quintessential dispersed character. Rather it was earlier forms of transport that shaped LA; the freeways are the fourth transport system superimposed on the city[1].

By world standards Los Angeles is – like Tokyo – a new city; by North American standards it is quite old. It started with the village of *Pueblo de Nuestra Senora la Reina de Los Angeles de Porciuncula,* founded in 1783 by Spaniards and Mexicans coming up from the south to establish missions and ranches. Over the 19th century settlers colonised other places in the surrounding area, between the enclosing mountains and the Pacific Ocean to the west. By 1900 there was a number of small towns, separated by fields and orchards, some of them farm communities, some resorts, some railroad centres, some just speculative property developments. Ventura, Riverside, Pomona, Pasadena, Anaheim, Santa Monica, Long Beach, all now familiar parts of Greater Los Angeles, date from this time.

For transport, steam railways and horse-drawn streetcars came first. In the 1870s the Southern Pacific Railroad Company created a network joining the towns together and connecting them to its new intercontinental railway. Within the towns there were horse-drawn cars running on tracks in the streets. Then these two were combined, with electric streetcars running in the streets within built-up areas and on their own tracks between. They were known as the 'interurbans.' To succeed they required long term, monopolistic franchises from the municipalities and financially they relied as much, if not more, on the profits from associated land development as on fare revenues. So they were commonly built in anticipation of demand. This was a risky speculation and many of the early ventures failed. One man, Henry E Huntington, succeeded – and made the fortune that endowed the art gallery, library and botanical garden in San Marino that still bears his name. In 1901 he merged seventy streetcar systems into one and, through a string of companies, combined extending the interurbans with water supply, utility provision and land development. By the 1920s the 'Big Red Cars' of his Pacific Electric Railway Corporation reached all fifty odd communities in Greater Los Angeles, with nearly 2,000 kilometres of track, running 600 scheduled trips daily. It took forty-five minutes from downtown LA to Pasadena, fifty minutes to Long Beach, about an hour to Santa Monica. It was one of the finest public transport systems in the USA.

But already in the 1920s car ownership in Los Angeles was reaching levels that would not come to other North American cities until the 1940s and to Western Europe until the 1980s. In 1915 there was one car for each eight residents, by 1920 one per 3.6, by 1930 one per 1.5, meaning that virtually every adult, able-bodied Angeleno had a car. In 1921 a car dealer declared: 'The automobile is 10 per cent pleasure, 90 per cent utility and 100 per cent necessity.'[2] The interurbans slowly lost custom, the network shrunk, services deteriorated, annual deficits became routine and ruinous, though it wasn't until 1961 that the last streetcar ran. Since then there have been attempts to resurrect public transport in the city: many reports and plans but little action, just the skeletal subway and light rail system and more comprehensive bus services now run by the Metropolitan Transit Authority. Today, public transport in LA is mostly just for poor people.

Travel by car took over. At first widening streets, synchronising traffic lights, banning left turns, restricting on-street parking and increasing off-street parking sought to keep congestion at bay. By the 1930s the idea of an additional network of super roads was being floated: they would be exclusively for motor vehicles, separated from existing streets, with limited access points and called freeways or occasionally parkways. In 1938, the first short stretches were built. In the 1940s successive plans sketched what was to become, over the following decades, the city's present-day freeway system. Building them destroyed the homes of a quarter of a million people.

Thus Los Angeles changed from a city of interurban streetcars to a city of automobile boulevards and then to a city of freeways. All this was closely bound up with property development. It provided both motive and reward. The open land – whether desert, farmland, orchards or hillsides – could be transformed by improved transport access into valuable commercial and industrial real estate; public relations and marketing would then attract the customers to occupy it. The geographer Peter Hall observes that this was the reversal of all previous experience in cities where new urban transport was built to meet existing demand. In the growth of Los Angeles, the basic industry was not steel or ships or textiles, but property development.[3]

Five and a half ecologies

In 1971 Reyner Banham, then Professor of the History of Architecture at University College London, wrote a book called *Los Angeles: The Architecture of Four Ecologies* that celebrated the city's form, its townscape and its buildings. LA had had its previous fans. The dustjacket of Banham's book reproduced the artist David Hockney's *A Bigger Splash* painting of 1966, showing a glass-fronted, single storey house, two palm trees and a swimming pool with diving board, revealing the artist's fascination with the place. Hockney, newly settled in the city, declared that 'In Los Angeles I actually began to paint the city round me, as I'd never – still haven't – done in London.'[4] Earlier still, in 1964 a Berkeley academic Melvin Webber had argued that town planners should abandon their bias against the non-traditional urban form that Los Angeles represented and which he called a 'non-place urban realm', functionally coherent while physically fragmented.[5]

Banham had a different take on the city. He argued that the topography and history of Los Angeles bound its diverse architectures into a comprehensible unity. Understand that context and you will see unity, not monotony, and variety, not confusion. This had escaped other critics because the city is unique and so without any handy terms of comparison. How, then, to bridge this incomparability? Banham's answer was that 'One can most properly begin by learning the local language; and the language of design, architecture and urbanism in Los Angeles is the language of movement. Mobility outweighs monumentality there to a unique degree. So, like earlier generations of English intellectuals who taught themselves Italian in order to read Dante in the original, I learned to drive in order to read Los Angeles in the original.'[6]

Banham defined what he called four ecologies of the city in which the context has shaped a defined character. He called them Surfurbia (the Pacific Coast and beach towns), the Plains, the Foothills, and Autopia (the freeways). All four can still be recognised in today's Los Angeles. But forty years have passed since Banham wrote and the city has developed apace, extending eastward into the Low Desert (to create a new fifth ecology) and partially renewing (as a half ecology) its Downtown. Within this pattern of city ecologies, you can also find a wild variety of buildings and spaces – a hetero-architecture.

From Malibu in the north to Laguna Beach in the south are 100 kilometres of coast, mostly white sandy beaches with occasional ports, energy and industrial sites, all backed by the Pacific Coast Highway. Only Rio de Janeiro and Perth have comparable city shorelines. Unlike them, Los Angeles did not originate as a coastal city, rather ports like Wilmington and resorts like Newport Beach and Santa Monica developed independently before being connected by rail and road to other parts of the city. But like Rio and Perth, in LA the beach is part and parcel of city life. Along this coastline are some of the city's most famous locales: Malibu Colony, a gated community with the beach homes of movie stars and

LA's freeways

other glitterati; the fabulously well-endowed Getty Museum; then Santa Monica, reputedly laid-back and liberal; south of that is Venice, laid out in marshland in 1905 as a fantasy replica of the real Italian thing, plus a beach and boardwalk that's now LA's premier public place for bodily display; then some less exotic beach towns and Long Beach, with the old *Queen Mary* ocean liner berthed as a tourist attraction; and finally upmarket Huntington Beach, Newport Beach and Laguna Beach.

Inland from the Pacific Ocean stretch the vast plains that lie at the heart of the city. They provide the classic view of LA looking south from Griffith Park Observatory, with Vermont and Western Avenue stretching dead straight some 30 kilometres to the south, and crossed by the 25 kilometre long east-west Wilshire Boulevard. The plains also extend away to the east in the San Gabriel Valley, to the southeast in Orange County and to the northwest in the San Fernando Valley. On the plain is a repetitive pattern of streets,overlain with the supergrid of the freeways. Filling it in are mostly detached, single family, single storey houses, with some multi-unit residences nearer the freeways and trailer parks on scruffier sites. This cityscape is laced with commercial strips of shops,

LA's hetero-architecture

The architectural critic Charles Jencks coined this term to express the variety of building types and architectural styles that are characteristic of Los Angeles. Not all originated here, nor are all now unique to the city or indeed just to North American cities. But they are part of the city's iconography in fact, fiction and film.

Drive-ins – the idea that one could do business without parking or leaving the car had obvious appeal to Angelenos: drive-in gas stations came first, the first drive-in bank in 1937, drive-in fast food followed. Drive-in cinemas appeared later in the 1950s and 1960s but demanded too much space to survive economically.

Food courts – an eating place with multiple retailers and shared tables, it had its origin in the Farmer's Market on Fairfax Avenue, created in the 1930s as an outlet for local producers who started serving prepared food as well as selling produce: it still sees 40,000 visitors daily.

Modernist houses – wherever there is a good view, on the coast or in the hills or the desert, and money to buy it, Angelenos and their architects have created some stunning modernist houses, open-plan glass and steel structures with surrounding terraces and pools, inside which their owners lounge drinking cocktails.

Motels – the first motor hotel opened in Los Angeles in 1921; they then spread rapidly along the main highways, offering cheap, anonymous accommodation, the location for discreet trysts or bloody murders in many Hollywood movies.

Shopping plazas, supermarkets and malls – the first small shopping plazas appeared in the 1920s as a row of single storey shops, set back from the road, often in a U-shape with its own parking lot in front. Supermarkets, with all business under one owner and one roof and with the parking behind or at the side, appeared in the 1930s. The larger shopping malls, with multiple shops in enclosed pedestrian areas and surrounded by the parking lots, were built from the 1950s onwards.

Theme parks – Walt Disney is credited with the invention of the modern theme park, opening Disneyland at Anaheim in 1955, though borrowing ideas from earlier amusement parks like the Tivoli Gardens, Copenhagen and Coney Island, Brooklyn as well as previous World Fairs. Disneyland has attracted over 500 million visitors since then. LA now has many other theme parks.

Trailer parks – trailers or mobile homes are the cheapest kind of single household accommodation, commonly squeezed into unattractive sites; their low status is epitomised by the expression 'trailer trash' for their residents.

restaurants and fast food outlets, with small industrial and commercial zones, and is occasionally punctuated by a shopping mall, a multiplex cinema, some offices, a cluster of public buildings, an airfield, a university campus or maybe a theme park. This is where Los Angeles is most like other North American cities. In contrast, the foothills – Banham's third ecology – are unique to Los Angeles. Some of the streetcar lines ran along the edge of the plain where the foothills of the Santa Monica, San Gabriel, Santa Ana and Verdugo mountains rise. These slopes became attractive locations for the better off – the higher up, the richer the residents. Large houses, lush vegetation, the swishing of sprinklers, curving roads, security guards and dogs, immigrant maids and gardeners and expensive cars are what you see in these foothill places, some of whose names – Pasadena, Hollywood, Bel Air, Beverley Hills, Pacific Palisades, Palos Verdes – are known around the world, not least because this is where most LA celebrities live.

The Low Desert in the east of Los Angeles has been one of the fastest growing parts of the USA in recent decades. Palm Springs is its original and main community, but other places have developed through the length of the Coachella valley: Cathedral City, Indio, La Quinta, Rancho Mirago among them. Palm Springs was known from the 1930s to 1950s as 'the playground of

Nighttime view of LA from Griffith Park

the stars' when Hollywood actors, directors and producers had houses there. Since then the Low Desert has attracted large numbers of retirees and visitors, drawn particularly by its climate of over 350 days of sunshine and less than 6 inches of rain annually. It also has a large gay and lesbian community. Leisure is a dominant pre-occupation and industry: the area has numerous resort hotels, natural spas, medical centres, more than 200 golf courses and many classy casinos, some run by local Native Americans on their tribal lands.

In LA the freeway is where you spend a large part of your daily life, hence its identity as a separate ecology. LA people know the freeway pattern as readily as people in other cities know their metro map. For visitors, the experience of freeway driving can be confusing and scary: the routes have names as well as numbers, but both can change along their length; they intersect in two or three level interchanges, even an eye-popping four levels in 'The Stack' in Downtown, where several freeways meet; exits and entrances follow each other in quick succession; freeway merges need courage and acceleration and some exits demand quick responses to tight curves; everywhere traffic weaves constantly between lanes; and there is always the risk of getting trapped in gridlock, so you must keep tuned to the radio for traffic updates. But, once mastered, freeway driving can become addictive. The travel writer Jan Morris observed: 'To most strangers they suggest chaos, or at least purgatory. There comes a moment, though, when something clicks in one's own mechanism, and suddenly one grasps the rhythm of the freeway system, masters its tribal or ritual forms, and discovers it not to be a disruptive element at all, but a kind of computer key to the use of Los Angeles. One is processed by the freeways.'[7]

Finally, there is the half ecology of downtown Los Angeles. It was here that the city originated in the Spanish-Mexican pueblo. Major institutions, like City Hall, Union Station and the law courts were built and remain there but, with the rise of car travel, other metropolitan functions abandoned it for less congested locations. The completion of the freeway system boosted its accessibility and this, together with the removal of building height restrictions and the boom in business services, have stimulated successive renewal schemes in the last few decades. The new Downtown has grown upwards with new high-rise developments and shifted several blocks westwards, alongside the Harbor Freeway, leaving the old Downtown to transmute into the Latino centre of the city.

Angelenos

Today Los Angeles has a very diverse population. It is home to people from over 100 countries, speaking more than 200 different languages. The Hispanics – from Mexico and other Central and South American countries – are the most numerous, making up over 40% of the population. Another 40% of the population are so-called Anglo-Americans, that is, non-hispanic Whites. The other population is 10% African-American and 10% Asian, the latter with substantial Korean, Chinese, Japanese, Vietnamese, Thai, Cambodian and Filipino communities.

The earliest immigrants in the 1870s and 1880s were from elsewhere in the USA, predominantly white Anglo-Americans from the Northeast which they judged to have been spoiled through overcrowding by immigrant newcomers. The transcontinental railways, opened in the 1880s, offered them cheap transport. For them, southern California was a promised land, a New Eden, and for most the promise was of farming rich agricultural land. The original Spanish-Mexican ranches were divided into smaller farmholdings for growing citrus fruits, vines, wheat and corn. 'No happier paradise for the farmer can be found than Los Angeles County' declared the Southern California Immigration Association, the first of many boosters in the city's growth. In this period twenty new municipalities were established.

From 1890 onwards, industrial work became an additional attraction to immigrants. The film industry established its foothold; oil was discovered and exploited; aircraft design and production were established by local entrepreneurs Douglas, Lockheed and Northrup; and the ports of San Pedro and Long Beach came to dominate the Pacific Coast trade. It was also a period in which more and more young Americans were rejecting their rural upbringing and moving to the cities to seek better lives. Many came from the Midwest, both well-off families, profitably selling off their farms and businesses, and impoverished families leaving all behind them, like those whose bitter experiences John Steinbeck's 1939 novel *The Grapes of Wrath* recounted.

Other kinds of immigrant also arrived. The film industry pioneers were predominantly Jews from the East Coast. African-Americans were leaving the rural South in large numbers, and many of them found their way to Los Angeles. Even larger numbers crossed the border from Mexico, many planning to stay a short while but frequently settling permanently – in 1930 the Bureau of the Census reclassified them as non-white. From beyond the continent, the city drew immigrants from Asia, especially from Japan after its government lifted restrictions on emigration. And from Europe, but, as elsewhere in the USA, the main source shifted from north and west Europe to south and east Europe, and Los Angeles acquired Italian, Polish and Russian communities. Forty new municipalities were created in the first two decades of the century. By the 1930s Greater Los Angeles had grown to be a city of 2.5 million people, the fourth largest in the USA.

The long economic boom in the second half of the 20th century was intense here. High-tech aerospace, electronics and weaponry – much stimulated by defence expenditure – and low-tech clothing, furniture and jewellery were added to the local economy; professional, public and personal services expanded; and tourism grew. In broad terms an ethnic division of labour emerged: Anglo-Americans in business and entertainment, Asians in professions and high-tech industry, African-Americans in public services, Latinos in low skill service and assembly work. The population continued to grow from new immigration and from the natural growth of its youthful population. The city extended ever outwards – northwest into the San Fernando Valley, south into Orange County and east into the Low Desert around Palm Springs. Between 1940 and 1970 another sixty municipalities were created.

Today, like most US cities, Los Angeles remains strongly segregated. Many parts of the city are predominantly White or Hispanic or Black or Asian. The hills, beachside and desert neighbourhoods are predominantly White; those around Downtown are Hispanic; those in South Central and Watts are Black; Asians are found in smaller enclaves such as Old Chinatown, New Chinatown, Koreatown, ThaiTown, Little Tokyo and Little Saigon. But members of all these groups are also found spread across the city, as their more well-off families have moved outwards, like the Whites before them. Thus, in the last few decades, Hispanics have largely replaced blue collar Whites in the northeast San Fernando Valley, the western San Gabriel Valley and northern Orange County. They have also superceded African-Americans on the east side of South Central, so that Central Avenue, formerly the main street of Black Los Angeles, is now predominantly occupied by Hispanic businesses. The city's ethnic geography is kaleidoscopic and ever-changing.

Hooray for Hollywood[8]

For most of the world's population, Los Angeles is less well-known than one locale within it: Hollywood. Its iconic status is confirmed by the use of derivatives – Bollywood in India, Nollywood in Nigeria – to identify other countries' filmmaking. Like them, Hollywood is both a place and an industry. As such it is also something of a myth, because only a fraction of the film business in Los Angeles has ever been concentrated there. Even so, Hollywood is seen as the entertainment capital of the world. The 20 metre high HOLLYWOOD sign, standing since the 1920s in the hills above the place, is – on the evidence of postcards you can buy – one of LA's most symbolic sights.

Before 1910 freelance film producers were converging here and by 1920 most of the major film studios had become established. They constituted a new kind of industry, mass producing films for a mass audience. That audience had already been created by the nickelodeons in US cities, offering films – then silent, so suited to polyglot immigrants – as cheap entertainment. It was largely men in this distribution business who turned themselves into producers and who moved to Los Angeles. Many reasons are offered for why they came here: year round sunshine, cheap land, varied landscapes for outdoor scenes and low wages. Also the openness of the city to novelty, aided by its remoteness and other-wordliness – 'Here it was possible to dream dreams, and to believe that anything was possible.'[9] Later, as the entertainment business expanded, much of the TV and music industry grew here too.

From the start LA filmed itself[10]. It wasn't just that the films were made there, either in studios, on backlots or on nearby locations. It was also that life in Los Angeles provided rich inspiration for their narratives and continues to do so. LA has become – through fiction, film, TV and popular music – probably the most 'mediated' city in the world, experienced at second hand by millions in both rich and poor countries. As such the city has been represented in various ways. The city's comfortable, consumerist lifestyle is often on display. In recent decades this has been more evident in TV series, like *90210* (the Beverly Hills zipcode), *The OC* (that is, Orange County), *Laguna Beach* and its spin-off *The Hills,* all named after parts of the city. Here, young people with money, cars, large homes and understanding parents have a good time while occasionally struggling to overcome the everyday crises of their suburban lives like flunking exams, unhappy relationships, getting in fights, doing drugs. Films in this genre include *Rebel Without a Cause* (1955) starring James Dean in what some call the first teenage movie, *Bob and Carol and Ted and Alice* (1969), a wife-swapping, bed-hopping foursome, *Pretty Woman* (1990) about a romantic fling between a rich man and a tart with a heart, and *Clueless* (1995) which updated Jane Austen's *Emma* to an LA high school. This hedonistic view of LA has been reinforced by pop music – especially the sun, sea and sand themes of many 1960s songs by the Beach Boys and others.

But writers and filmmakers have also portrayed another, tougher Los Angeles. One tradition is that of hard-boiled crime novels like James M Cain's *The Postman Always Rings Twice* (1934), *Double Indemnity* (1936) and *Mildred Pierce* (1941), in which white-walled, red-tiled bungalows conceal poisonous marriages. In the detective novels of Raymond Chandler like *The Big Sleep* (1939) and *Farewell my Lovely* (1940), private eye Philip Marlowe is locked in struggles with blackmailers, corrupt police and parasitic, rich families – the latter often being his clients. This tradition continued in the novels of Ross MacDonald, Walter Mosley and James Ellroy – the latter's four book *LA Quartet* (1987-92) presenting Los Angeles in the 1950s as a conundrum of sex crimes, satanic conspiracies, and political scandals. Then there are novels or films about moviemaking itself, often satirising its follies, deceits and extravagances: Nathanael West's novel *The Day of the Locust* (1939) set the trend, followed by others including Billy Wilder's film *Sunset Boulevard* (1950) and Robert Altman's *The Player (*1992).

Much of this work of fictionally portraying Los Angeles to the world, in books and songs and films, has been done by writers, musicians and filmmakers who came to the city from elsewhere in the USA, or from other parts of the world. Their work has been characterised as a migrant fiction – 'The distanced perspective of the outsider, marked by a sense of dislocation and estrangement, is the central and essential feature of the fiction of Los Angeles, distinguishing it from fiction about other American places.'[11] In fiction, as in fact, Los Angeles is a city largely created by immigrants.

LA's dark side[12]

Most city histories are of good times and bad, of golden ages alternating with periods of decline, of booms and busts. In contrast, Los Angeles' short history as an essentially 20th century city has been one of near continuous boom, but that prosperity has not been without its dark side. The city's development has often been scandalous. Automobile interests were active in the demise of the interurban streetcar system. The seizure in the 1910s of the water supply from the Owens Valley farmlands, north of the city, to serve the development of the San Fernando Valley involved venal politicians, greedy bankers and landowners and crooked developers – fictionalised in Roman Polanski's 1974 film *Chinatown*. Public housing ceased in the 1950s, denounced as socialistic. Redevelopment has often dislodged immigrant communities: parts of Chinatown were razed to make space for Union Station in the 1930s and the Hispanic community of Chavez Ravine was displaced to build a stadium for the Dodgers baseball team in the 1960s. Also in the 1960s Native Indian lands were corruptly taken for development in the Low Desert.

Successive waves of immigration did not go unchallenged by those who had arrived earlier. Exclusionary practices, designed to keep 'aliens' in their inferior place, have continued from the city's beginning. Local ordinances limiting rights of residence were common until ruled illegal and have been replaced by more indirect measures like street barriers, high user fees for local facilities, restrictions on access to public services and general disinvestment in schools, health and transport in immigrant neighbourhoods. Deportation of Mexicans as 'illegals' has continued intermittently. As has vigilantism. Asians have been the victims of oriental scares, culminating in the internment of Japanese-Americans in the Second World War. The largely Jewish elite of the film industry was hounded in the anti-Communist McCarthy witchhunt of the 1950s. Major riots have occurred from time to time: the Zoot Suit riots of 1943 (named after the clothes worn by the Hispanics beaten up by sailors on leave), the riots in Watts in 1965 and those following the acquittal of the police who beat up Rodney King in 1992 are only the most publicised in a long, shameful tradition. And there have been spectacular crimes, like the Black Dahlia case in 1947, the Manson murders of 1969, the O J Simpson case in 1994 and the 2009 death of Michael Jackson. Today gang warfare, much between Blacks and Hispanics contesting territory or drug trade, is rife and extends right across the city. Police corruption remains endemic.

Even the environment – so long the city's prime attraction – has seemingly become hostile. The earthquakes of the 1990s reminded LA that it sits on the San Andreas Fault. Mudslides and fires in the foothills have become regular occurrences through a combustible mix of land use, topography and timber construction; even the survivors find their gardens ruined and their swimming pools dirty. The city's air pollution is severe, the product of high transport and industrial emissions getting trapped by the city's surrounding mountains. (The term 'smog' was invented here.) Beyond these immediate restraints on the LA lifestyle, the city is a voracious consumer of water, energy and land.

Jan Morris on LA, 1976[13]

'Surveyed in the morning from one of its mountain belvederes, Los Angeles really does look one of the classic cities, one of the archetypes…Then it looks unmistakably a world city; and it will represent for ever, I think, the apogee of urban, mechanical, scientific man perhaps, before the gods returned. For it has lost its prime already. It has lost the exuberant certainty that made it seem, even when I first knew it, unarguably the City of the Future, the City That Knew How. None of us Know now, the machine has lost its promise of emancipation, and if LA then seemed a talisman of fulfilment, now it is tinged with disillusion. Those terrific roads, those thousands of cars, the sheen of jets screaming out of the airport, the magnificent efficiency of it all, the image building, the self-projection, the glamour, the fame – they were all false promises after all, and few of us see them now as the symptoms of redemption.'

Consequently, in recent decades the image of Los Angeles has lost some of its gloss. Once its prosperity, consumerism, mobility and openness were seen by some as the quintessence of 20th century urbanism, a model of city life offered by California to the rest of the world. Today, its wasteful consumption of resources, the air pollution, the wide gulf between rich and poor, the exploitation of cheap immigrant labour, ethnic chauvinism and prejudice, persistent violent crime, the increase of protective measures – walls, barriers, CCTV, private security and 'armed response' services – and its recent history of natural disasters, has made the city seem more of a warning than a promise. In 1976 the travel writer Jan Morris, commenting about the same time as Banham's and Webber's panegyrics, saw this writing on the wall. She found her feelings about 'this tremendous and always astonishing city' shot through with regret. It was still full of vitality, fun and wealth; brilliant people still flocked to it; but the dream had become tarnished. Written over thirty-five years ago, this now seems remarkably prescient.

15.

Growth and adaptation: cities as organisms

Hanoi 2007. Jetlagged and awake early, I gaze out from the eleventh floor of our hotel at the city starting its day. Below is a busy crossroads. The morning traffic is building up – children cycling to school; motorbikes with two, three, even four passengers; a few cars and vans; pedestrians; street traders carrying wares in flat baskets suspended front and back from a bamboo pole on their shoulder; the occasional lorry or bus. At the junction there are no signs, no traffic lights, no pedestrian crossings. Everyone must take their chance, negotiating their encounters with each other. They do so without ever stopping, slowing or swerving to get through the junction. From above, they look like ants, each busily and single-mindedly engaged in transporting some scrap of matter as its contribution towards building a new nest. And, like the ants, the walkers, riders and drivers at the junction never collide. In the mornings that I watch them there is never a crash.

Body parts and functions

We often feel that the city is like an ant heap; thick with people rushing hither and thither, each in pursuit of an individual task, while sharing a common purpose. As an image it is a commonplace of moviemaking, starting with the aerial shot of a city, the camera in the helicopter swooping above the dense buildings, streets, traffic and pedestrians, setting the scene of the teeming city world that the story's characters inhabit, before closing in on the action. In Alfred Hitchcock's *Psycho* (1960) the camera floats above Phoenix before zooming in on the adulterous lovers in the hotel room. In Mike Nichols' *Working Girl* (1988) it gazes down at the New York commuters pouring off the Staten Island ferry. In Michael Mann's *Heat* (1995) it tracks the cops chasing the robbers along the nighttime Los Angeles freeways.

Sometimes human rather than insect metaphors for the city are more descriptive. Body parts, functions and treatments all serve. So the city has *arteries* and *veins* through which people and vehicles *circulate*, its centre may be its *heart*, its parkland may serve as *lungs* for breathing fresh air. Some linear feature in its plan – maybe a long street or a river – may serve as a *spine,* supposedly giving it strength, and its outlying parts may be seen as *fingers*, reaching out into the surrounding countryside. Cities also have bodily functions. They *breathe* or not, their *pulse* may *beat* more or less strongly, their traffic may *roar*. They *eat* up land, *consume* other resources and *excrete* wastes of many forms – refuse, smoke, sewage. At worst they suffer from *sclerosis* or *cancerous growths*. They may *decay*. Malfunctions will require treatment: *surgery* is often recommended, otherwise *injections* of new *life blood* may be prescribed – in the form of investment, skills and ideas from new activities or people.

All these are simple organic metaphors. Some commentators have devised more sophisticated ones. It has been argued that a city has both *hard and soft body parts*: 'the hard is like the bone structure and skeleton, the soft the nervous system and its synapses, the connective tissue. One cannot exist without the other.'[1] Metaphorically, it may be psychological, as much as physiological, attributes that characterise the city: its *psyche, attitude, personality, soul* or *temperament*. The city has also been seen as a *monster*. This concept of the city as a human being underlies the fashion for writing 'biographies' of cities: London, Mumbai, Paris and Los Angeles have all had this treatment.[2]

City growth

Cities grow – as organisms do – and sometimes decline, even die. There are dead cities around the world, revealed by historians and archaeologists, and some – such as Carthage in present-day Tunisia, Macchu Pichu in the Peruvian Andes, Vijayanagar in south India – were large and important in their time[3]. Some dead cities have become mythic: Babylon and Pompeii, for example. But historically cities that died and disappeared are far outnumbered by cities that survived. Some of the world's present cities have great antiquity, reaching back into the millennium before Christ. Notable examples, rarely out of today's news, are the Middle East cities of Cairo, Damascus, Jerusalem, Jericho and Baghdad. Indeed, Damascus claims to be the oldest, most continuously occupied city in the world.

For both these old cities and for modern foundations, it is the last two centuries that have seen their really rapid growth[4]. In Europe the population of its main cities expanded between four and sixfold from 1800 to 1900: Hamburg from 130,000 to 706,000, Madrid from 160,000 to 540,000, Moscow from 250,000 to 990,000. In North America growth mostly came in the second half of that century: Chicago had a population of only 30,000 in 1850 but had grown to 1.7 million by 1900, St Louis from 78,000 to 575,000, Toronto from 31,000 to 219,000. Even more explosive growth in the cities of Asia, Africa and Latin America occurred in the 20th century, especially its second half: in 1900 Lima housed 130,000 people but had grown to 5.7 million by 1990; Dhaka from 104,000 to 6.1 million ; Kinshasa from 5000 (when it was called Leopoldville) to 3.8 million. In all cases, this growth was initially brought about by immigration into the cities, first from the surrounding countryside and then from further afield, finally in some cases from right across the world. Then, since immigrants tend to be young, high city birth rates added to the numbers.

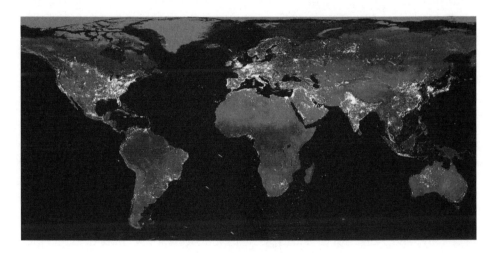

The world's cities at night

Big cities are not just populous; they are also extensive, spreading out to occupy a lot of territory. In 1800 London was about 10 kilometres across, walkable in an hour or two; by 1900 it was nearer 30 kilometres across; by 2000, 100 kilometres across. Today those cities of the world with a million and more people are thousands of square kilometres in extent. We can see them clearly on satellite images of the globe, especially at night when their lights are on. This spread happens in many ways. The city will claim open land for new activities: high-rises, improvised shanty towns, spacious villas, industrial plants,

241

sportsgrounds, shopping centres, public buildings like hospitals, schools and colleges, cemeteries, transport interchanges like bus and railway stations, shipyards, and airports. It may also absorb smaller surrounding towns and villages. Sometimes, neighbouring cities grow so much that they merge into each other to become vast conurbations. After a time and once the city has grown large, its existing populations or activities may move out to new suburban locations attracted by more space, cheaper property, less congestion and less pollution. New transport routes – roads, tramways, railways – connect them to the older parts of the city. Beyond that, these outer locations may themselves become attractive to new enterprises, like industrial parks, airports, office campuses and shopping centres – creating what have been called new 'edge cities.'[5] With this growth process you will commonly find on a city's fringes a scruffy mixture of isolated new buildings, construction sites, abandoned farmland, rubbish dumps and new roads leading nowhere at present – a 'no-man's-land'.

In parts of the world a new phenomenon is emerging that has been called the polycentric metropolis[6]. Here are clusters of towns and cities, even up to fifty in number, which may be physically separate but are functionally interrelated. Examples are the San Francisco Bay area, the eastern seaboard in the USA with Boston, New York and Washington at its core, South East England centred on Greater London, the lower Rhine valley in Germany and Holland, the Yangtse and Pearl River basins in China, the Tokyo-Osaka corridor in Japan; and incipiently Greater Jakarta in Indonesia, the Rio de Janeiro/Sao Paulo corridor in Brazil and the West African cities on the Gulf of Guinea between Accra and Lagos. The component towns or cities may be where most people live and work, but they are part of a wider, functional entity held together by dense flows of people, goods and information, carried along motorways, high speed rail lines, and telecommunication channels.

In many cities you can see the history of their growth written on them. Some ancient buildings survive – castles, palaces, mosques, exchanges, markets, theatres, stadia –because their functions persist or because they were built of masonry, rather than wood or mud, in the first place. Examples of adaptation can be found: warehouses converted to offices and flats, graveyards turned into parks, small dwellings extended and improved, large dwellings subdivided, rural tracks upgraded to city streets, rivers canalised. Some of these adaptations are extraordinary. In Syracuse in Sicily, you will see the Baroque facade of the cathedral, erected after the 1693 earthquake, fronting a Norman church from the 7th century, itself built within the Ionic columns of a Greek temple originating about 530 BC. In Cuzco in Peru, the churches and palaces built by the Spanish conquistadores of the 16th century incorporate massive masonry walls inherited from its time as the capital of the Inca Empire. Other cities retain traces of the past in their layout. The Piazza Navona in Rome, dominated by Bernini's sculptural *Fontana dei Quattro Fiumi* from the 17th century, takes its oval shape from an ancient stadium built in AD 86 by the Emperor Domitian. Broadway in New York City, which now cuts diagonally across the rectilinear street grid, originated as a trail that the settlers in the 1620s adopted as the main road north through Manhattan Island.

Jerusalem as palimpsest[7]

Looking out from the Temple Mount in Jerusalem you can see three historic sites: on the Mount itself stands the 7th century Dome of the Rock where, according to the Koran, Muhammad made his ascent to Heaven; tucked just below the Mount is a remnant of the great Second Temple of the Jews, destroyed by the Romans in AD 70 and today, as the Wailing Wall, still a sacred destination; and to the west is the Church of the Holy Sepulchre, where Jesus Christ was buried. These are remnants of the three religions – Islam, Judaism, Christianity – that venerate Jerusalem as a holy city. Politically the city has known even more rulers. Egyptians, Syrians, Greeks, Romans, Crusaders, Saladins, Mongols, Turks and the British have each wrested control of the city over its long history and left their mark on it. For many centuries it had four distinct quarters – Muslim, Jewish, Christian and Armenian – around their most important shrines and holy places. After the collapse of the United Nations' proposal to internationalise the city in 1949, it became spontaneously partitioned between a Jewish west and an Arab east with one crossing point at the Mandelbaum Gate. In 1967 the Israelis captured east Jerusalem and started its Jewish colonisation. They control the whole city to this day and the wall being built around the eastern parts of Jerusalem – ostensibly as a protection against Palestinian terrorists – is the physical expression of their dominance.

Cities that have been conquered, colonised or religiously converted more than once in their histories become a many layered palimpsest. Delhi, Istanbul and Jerusalem are classic cases where numerous palaces, walls and gates, and places of worship are left over from previous régimes. And there may be not just artefacts but also traditions carried over from the past, such as trades, ceremonies, myths and even cuisines – throughout Africa you can find, in the cities of the former European colonies, food inheritances that have survived the departure of the former rulers: German *Apfelstrudel* in Windhoek, Namibia; Italian *espresso* coffee in Asmara, Eritrea; French *patisserie* in Abidjan, Ivory Coast. Name changes through time often give the game away. In the Balkans many cities have had German, Turkish, Italian or Slav names as empires and faiths have come and gone. In Romania, today's Brasov, its name Hungarian, was formerly German Kronstadt; in Macedonia Skopje is the Cyrillic version of the former Serbian name of Skoplje which itself replaced the Turkish Ukub; and Dubrovnik, dubbed 'the Pearl of the Adriatic', originated as a medieval city state with the Italian name Ragusa.

Evolution and complexity

In these ways most large cities have today come to be multi-cellular, like plants and animals. Among my iconic cities this is truest of Tokyo and Los Angeles, both relatively modern foundations. It's unsurprising that over the last hundred years biological concepts have crept into expert theorising about city growth. The key figure here was Patrick Geddes. In the 1880s and 90s he had trained and worked as as a biologist. On moving to Edinburgh at the age of thirty-two he became involved in civic action and turned his thinking to cities. As the title of his major book *Cities in Evolution* (1915) suggests, he developed a biological take on cities. He invented the term 'conurbation' to describe the city regions that he saw emerging in Europe and North America, but deplored them 'as dissipating resources and energies, as depressing life, under the rule of machine and mammon.'[8] His answer was for cities to become more in tune with the environment. Although he admired Darwin as a naturalist, he was not attracted to Social Darwinism, the 'struggle for survival' analyses and *'laissez faire'* prescriptions that others at that time derived from the application of evolutionary thinking to human affairs. For 'Patrick Geddes believed passionately that, given reasonable social conditions, man is a co-operative animal. He also believed that, treated properly, the earth is fundamentally a co-operative planet on which to live. He aimed to find out how to achieve those reasonable social conditions and to teach people how their environment might be treated properly.'[9]

But Geddes was a poor communicator and not an easy read. It was left to Lewis Mumford, an American sociology-trained journalist, to bring a more coherent version of these views to a wider audience in his book *The City in History: Its origins, its transformations, and its prospects* (1961) and other writing. What Geddes and Mumford shared was a long historical view of the evolution (Geddes' chosen word) or transformation (Mumford's word) of cities since classical times. (It is essentially Western cities that was their focus.) In this they were both critical of the modern city as it had evolved through mechanisation, industrialisation and urbanisation to become wasteful of resources, oppressive of social life and overdependent on technology. To express this critique Mumford drew a distinction between what he called 'megatechnics', the dominant modern trend, and 'biotechnics', his proposed alternative. 'If we are to prevent megatechnics from further controlling and deforming every aspect of human culture, we shall be able to do so only with the aid of a radically different model derived directly, not from machines, but from living organisms and organic complexes (ecosystems)... As opposed to [megatechnics], an organic system directs itself to qualitative richness, amplitude, spaciousness, free from quantitative pressure and crowding, since self-regulation, self-correction, and self-propulsion are as much an integral property of organisms as nutrition, reproduction, growth, and repair.'[10] Or, in his elegant one-liner, the 'good life versus the goods life'.

Although she disliked Geddes' and Mumford's prescriptions for a more dispersed, less dense form of city, Jane Jacobs in *The Death and Life of Great American Cities* (1962) shared their organic perspective. She saw cities as an example of organised complexity, a concept derived from the life sciences, in which 'half a dozen or even several dozen quantities are all varying simultaneously and in subtly interconnected ways.'[11] From this perspective, she argued that the most important principles in dealing with cities are to seek out the 'unaverage' – that is individual cases, rather than overall patterns – as clues to what is going on; to think about processes rather than structures, focusing on how change happens rather than desired outcomes; and to work inductively, from the particular to the general rather than vice versa, not imposing universal solutions on differing circumstances. Such thinking underpinned her views on the role of pavements and parks as meeting places, on street layout to control traffic, on mixed property uses to generate liveliness throughout the day, and on renewing rather than rebuilding city neighbourhoods. These views influenced town planning practice enormously.

They also inspired the re-colonisation of inner city neighbourhoods by middle income families – so-called gentrification – in many Western cities in recent decades, a process that, ironically, has sometimes displaced people as much as her despised alternative of demolition and rebuilding.

SimCity

SimCity is a city building computer game designed in 1989 by Californian Will Wright. It was a new concept, a game that could be neither won nor lost, essentially for the single player. For this reason its designer initially found little support from the major games publishers. Then on its release it became the first commercially successful computer game and has spawned a range of successors and imitators. The objective of SimCity is to design, build and manage a city. The player can pursue any goals, or can explore some given scenarios, either based on real urban history (for example, the San Francisco earthquake 1906, crime and depression in Detroit 1972) or fictional (the Godzilla monster loose in Tokyo, a nuclear plant meltdown in Boston, Las Vegas attacked by aliens). Whatever the scenario, the rules of the game produce outcomes that are non-linear (with no simple input/output or cause/effect relationships), bottom-up rather than top-down (self-organising, nobody is in charge) and that proceed experimentally (by trial and error). With thousands of city blocks and dozens of variables there is a lot of complexity built into the software.

Jacobs' concept of organised complexity is captured well in the popular SimCity computer games. Here players run a city, using measures such as land zoning, tax rates, building infrastructure to achieve their objectives. Any choice will produce consequences – for example in traffic congestion, crime rates, property values, electoral results, recessions and booms – as the city self-organises in response. So that, as in real cities, adaptation to events progressively reshapes the city over time. A recent variant is the game Cityville.

Sustainability

Look in the indexes of Geddes' or Mumford's or Jacobs' book and you won't find the word 'sustainability'. Yet this is the dominant concept on which contemporary views of the city as an organism focus. It made a remarkable speedy transfer from science to politics. The key event was the publication in 1987 of the Brundtland Report *Our Common Future*[12]. It defined sustainable development as 'development that meets the needs of the present without compromising the ability of future generations to meet their own needs.' In essence this is about equity between generations. Sustainability requires the bequest from one generation to the next of those assets – environmental, economic, cultural and social – that are needed to meet the basic human needs of food supply, public health and economic livelihood. Morally, it argues, we should not beggar our successors any more than our neighbours.

In the twenty-five or so years since the Brundtland Report, the state of the global environment has become a dominant political concern. Threats to the planet's natural capital – its atmosphere, land, water, plants and animals – have become increasingly well-understood. Earthquakes, volcanoes, hurricanes, storms and floods, droughts – so-called Acts of God – have always impacted on human life. To these natural disasters are now added man-made disasters, arising from how human life is lived: air pollution, ozone depletion, infectious diseases like TB, malaria, gastroenteritis and HIV/Aids, climate change, water pollution, land erosion and the expansion of deserts, the destruction of forests and the extinction of animal and plant species. Such changes may seem less dramatic than natural disasters, but they are more insidious and far-reaching.

In early debates on sustainable development, cities were seen as both villains and victims. Their villainy lay in depleting assets through their role in consuming land, minerals and timber, destroying habitats, sucking in food, fibre, energy and water from distant sources, exporting and dumping their wastes on land, in rivers and the atmosphere. The wealth and sophisticated lifestyles of city dwellers – bigger consumers, more prone to fashion and competitive display, certainly in comparison with their rural cousins – were added to the charge sheet. But cities were also victims, at risk of disease and disorder, providing insecure livelihoods, overcrowded and congested, subject to power blackouts, prone to flooding, their air and water polluted. Both urban development and urban consumption were malign and human life in cities was the poorer for it. This was argued in relation to both the growth of Western cities from the 19th century onwards and of non-Western cities in the 20th century. There is truth in this condemnation as, just to take one example, the contemporary state of China's cities shows.

Cities on the Yangtse[13]

400 million people – one in fifteen of the world's population – live in the basin of China's Yangtze River. Along its middle and lower reaches, the cities of Shanghai, Chongqing, Wuhan and Nanjing are the powerhouses of China's economy accounting for 40% of national GDP. Until 1978 the size of Chinese cities was strictly controlled, in part to maintain rural populations, and city life was the privilege of a minority. But since then, under national policies of economic liberalisation, these and other Chinese cities have industrialised and urbanised at a phenomenal rate. And it shows. In the cities on the Yangtse all the negative impacts are apparent: overcrowding with one room per family, shared kitchens and toilets, insecure employment, child labour, ill health, great disparities of wealth, few public services, pollution, squalor and poor sanitation. In these respects these new cities are reminiscent of those of 19th century Europe and North America – for Chongqing, read Coketown. But there are important differences: the speed of industrialisation and urbanisation is far faster, consumption is growing rapidly alongside production, and the scale of development is bigger, with great investment in skyscraper offices, retail centres, freeways and monorails, all the trappings of the 21st century city. That brings additional, modern consequences: massive energy consumption, air pollution from road traffic as much as industry, water shortages, mountains of solid waste, often illegally dumped, and heavy pollution of the Yangtze river itself. There are national policies to achieve more sustainable development, but putting them into effect often falls short in the face of relentless growth and municipal corruption.

While cities occupy only about 2% of the world's surface, they use some 75% of the world's resources and release a similar percentage of wastes. The concept of an 'ecological footprint' provides a measure of a city's resource dependence: it is the land and water area needed to meet a population's food, fibre and mineral needs, to provide space for buildings and to absorb its wastes. Most cities have long since outgrown just satisfying these needs internally or from their immediate hinterland. So their footprint is large. An analysis for London in 2000[14] calculated that the city's 7.4 million people annually consumed 6.9 million tonnes of food (81% imported from abroad), travelled 64 billion passenger kilometres (69% by car), consumed 876,000 million litres of water, 154,400 gigawatts of energy (equivalent to 13 million tonnes of oil),

77 million tonnes of materials, and generated 296 million tonnes of solid waste and 41 million tonnes of CO_2. Its ecological footprint was estimated as 49 million global hectares[15], which is almost 300 times its geographical area, and indeed twice the size of the whole United Kingdom. The average footprint of each Londoner was 6.9 global hectares (including 0.32 for tourists) compared to an estimated global average of 2.18 per person.

Ecologically the world's cities may be villains and victims; but they may yet be saviours. They have to be, for they now accommodate half the world's population and they will not go away. Making cities sustainable requires changes in the investment, production and consumption processes that characterise them. It is essentially about metabolism – another organic concept. The metabolism of most present-day cities is essentially linear. Resources pass through without regard to their origins or to the destinations of their wastes, trees are felled for timber or pulp but forests are not replenished, distant food or clothing supplies are substituted for those more local by retailers to keep prices low, raw materials are extracted and processed into goods that are used briefly and then cast aside. In contrast, sustainability requires the substitution of a more circular metabolism whereby the outputs of one process become, whenever possible, the input for another. Urban life then sustains itself on fewer resources. An appropriate maxim is Reduce (consumption), Reuse (artefacts), Recycle (materials).

There are many options, some already practised somewhere, others just ideas at present. The familiar examples are improving the energy efficiency of buildings, vehicles and machinery; combined heat and power schemes, exploiting the waste heat from energy production to provide district heating; composting food waste; creating markets in pollution permits; shifting urban travel from cars to public transport, cycling and walking; planting more trees in cities to increase evaporation; recycling paper, glass, plastics, metal and cloth; adaptive reuse of buildings and products (at which poor city dwellers can teach much to the rich); and environmental taxes. Less familiar are such changes as better management of transport to increase capacities; reducing heat gain in buildings; decentralised energy production through local solar or wind energy; desalination to recycle waste water; reducing rain run-off by increasing the extent of permeable urban ground surfaces. More innovative ideas are shared, free or pay-as-you-go, cars and bikes; increased local food supply from farming within the city (in Cairo 20% of families keep livestock, often on roofs); and the trading of unwanted goods and services on an exchange basis, sometimes called 'freecycling'.

Living together at higher densities in cities is a necessary condition for achieving sustainability. Above all, high density cities make less claim on land: it is estimated that the entire urban population of the world could fit into an area of 200,000 square kilometres (roughly the size of the states of Senegal or Oman) if accommodated at densities similar to those found in high-class residential areas in European cities, like Kensington in London or Montparnasse in Paris[16]. High densities can also offer lower unit costs for services like piped water and telecommunications, waste disposal, health and education, and emergency services; the close location of production and consumption potentially reduces transport and favours recycling; terraced buildings can consume less energy; and walking, cycling and public transport become feasible travel choices for more residents.

New technologies can also help. So-called smart buildings can generate much of their own energy and water needs. Smart recycling plants can separate different wastes. Smart vehicles can reduce emissions – San Francisco's buses have been converted from petrol to electricity. But new technology alone will not suffice. Improving the energy efficiency or reducing the carbon emissions of vehicles can be nullified by greater travel distances; recycling more waste can be nullified by the endless growth of packaging; more efficient use of materials in construction can be nullified by the lower occupancy and growing size of dwellings as prosperity increases. So the design and regulation of cities, including the pricing of goods and services, is a necessary complement to technology. Beyond technology and regulation, the social mores that govern city behaviour will need strengthening, particularly the sociability, mutual respect and sense of shared fate that successful city living requires. A Slow Cities campaign, modelled on an earlier Slow (as against Fast) Food movement, was launched in Italy in 1999 and has spread to other countries[17]. It promotes less noise, shorter shopping hours, traffic calming, local trading, renovating buildings, less public advertising – though so far only in places with less than a 50,000 population.

In some cities around the world people are trying to put many of these precepts into effect. Curitiba in southern Brazil is an often quoted example. Now a city of nearly two million people, over three decades it has adopted policies for public transport, recycling, educational and cultural centres and housing that, in the words of a 2008 newspaper report, 'successfully transformed a congested, grimy, crime-ridden city into a world-renowned model of green living and social innovation.'[18] Freiburg in Germany and Portland, Oregon are other places frequently namechecked as 'ecocities.' Building sustainability into designs for new cities will always be an easier option. Architects are now keen on this. In the desert on the fringes of Abu Dhabi in the United Arab Emirates is the site for Masda, which it is claimed will be the world's first sustainable city, designed by British architect Norman Foster. Its design aims for a compact layout, low-rise buildings, 100% renewable energy, zero waste, all residents within 200 metres of public transport, recycled or sustainable certified building materials, 50% less than average water consumption – and fair wages for the workers who build the city. Dongtan in China, under development in the mouth of the Yangtse city, was another example, but its development has now stalled. Similar proposals are surfacing elsewhere. They may serve as inspirational exemplars and testbeds for innovation. But the real challenge, for urban designers, managers and rulers, is to retrofit the world's existing cities – as Jane Jacobs said 'Designing a dream city is easy; rebuilding a living one takes imagination.'[19]

Designing with nature

Mostly cities are built on, rather than in, the natural landscape. That is, they obliterate what was there before: woodland is uprooted, rivers are channelled, often disappearing into culverts, slopes are flattened. There are exceptions, cities where a strong topography still asserts itself in the shape and look of the city, as with the cities wrapped round natural harbours like Hong Kong or Sydney; or cities divided by numerous river courses like Stockholm and Bangkok or Lagos, built across islands and lagoons; or cities dominated by massive landforms like Table Mountain looming over Cape Town or Sugar Loaf Mountain over Rio de Janeiro. In San Francisco the city builders disregarded the hilly topography in imposing the standard rectilinear street grid upon it, thereby inadvertently creating in its combination of roller coaster streets and distant views a quite unique cityscape – famously on display in the car chase scene in the 1968 movie *Bullitt*. But, for most cities, their site has been treated like a blank canvas.

Bringing nature back into cities is a long held ambition of urban designers – *rus in urbe* is the common Latin slogan. One motive is practical: providing green spaces where city dwellers can exercise, breathe cleaner air, see plants and maybe some animals too, and thereby revive their otherwise jaded spirits. The provision of large parks in many 19th century European and North American

251

cities exemplified this belief. In some such places – like Central Park in New York, Hampstead Heath in London, the Bois de Boulogne in Paris or Phoenix Park in Dublin – the landscape is more rural than park-like, truly *rus in urbe*. There are other more localised practices, such as the creation of garden plots for growing produce; or the inclusion of garden squares or pocket parks in residential areas; or the planting of street trees and shrubs; or, more recently, the creation of community gardens and city farms in which people can experience working with plants and animals.

Designing with nature may also be a matter of aesthetics, incorporating natural motifs in the layouts and forms of city building. This reached an apotheosis in late 19th and early 20th century architectural trends, like the Arts and Crafts movement, *Art Nouveau*, the German *Werkbund*, the Vienna *Secession* and Catalan *Modernisma*. Antonio Gaudi was the most renowned exponent of this last style, creating in Barcelona curvaceous designs for the *Park G ell* gardens, the still unfinished cathedral of *La Sagrada Familia* and the *Casa Mila* apartment block. In time, variations on this aesthetic began to be applied to whole new city neighbourhoods. Curved streets were preferred to rectilinear grids, lots of room was left between buildings to let in the air and the sun, common spaces were provided for recreation, trees and shrubs were planted generously. This design concept has taken many forms in different cities: for example, in spacious public housing schemes within cities; in low density suburbs built by developers on the edge of cities; and in the garden cities and new towns built outside cities. We can see aspects of this aesthetic in architectural theories as different as those of Frank Lloyd Wright's 'Broadacre City' of low density, detached homesteads, in which every citizen was to be both an urbanite and a farmer, and Le Corbusier's 'Radiant City' of high-rise towers striding across an open landscape.

For other urban designers the organic quality of cities is a matter not of the structure and layout of buildings but of how they work and evolve – process rather than form. In the 1960s a group of Japanese architects founded a design movement called Metabolism. Its core idea was that the elements of the city change at different rates, some parts are quickly worn out, become inefficient and need replacement, while others have a longer, useful life. Whereas urban renewal tended to replace everything at once – that's why it was often called 'comprehensive redevelopment.' Similar concepts of the 'plug in' building or city were also developed outside Japan at this time, by the architect groups Archigram in Britain and Superstudio in Italy. None of these architects had many of their designs built. The most prominent exemplar of the idea came later in the Pompidou Centre in Paris, designed by Piano and Rogers and opened in 1977, with its vast open floors for changing exhibition space and the attachment of escalators and services to its façades.

The organic 'plug in' building: Pompidou Centre, Paris

The idea of changing the fabric of cities more organically did, though, achieve widespread acceptance in the final decades of the 20th century. Town planners have replaced the term 'redevelopment' with 'renewal' or 'regeneration', even 'renaissance', all implying more partial, incremental, adaptive approaches. Common characteristics are repairing and upgrading buildings; conversions to new uses; small scale clearances to let in air and light or to improve traffic circulation or create small squares or parks; retaining accommodation for local residents and businesses; repaving and new planting of public spaces; and

Its slogan was 'From the Age of the Machine to the Age of Life'. The Japanese Metabolist architects of the 1960s talked of designing buildings to provide 'dissectibility', separating permanent and impermanent elements, leaving them incomplete and open-ended, allowed to grow. To some extent Japanese cultural influences were at work here – a tradition of short-life wooden building, a view that man-made objects are an extension of nature, perhaps even a touch of Buddhist belief in the integration of dualities. None of this had much widespread influence on real city building. Its influence was apparent in various unrealised urban design projects, notably Kurokawa's 1961 Helix City and Kenzo Tange's 1964 Tokyo Bay scheme, and in pavilions at Expo '70 in Osaka. There was one exception: the Nakagin Capsule Tower built in Ginza, Tokyo in 1972 in the form of a thirteen storey concrete service core to which were attached, with just four strong bolts each, 140 prefabricated studio apartments, complete with built-in furniture and designed to be replaceable. However no units have been replaced since its original construction. It is still standing, though in disrepair, full of asbestos and not very earthquake-proof. One commentator sees it as 'a preview of those dwellings which typify the late twentieth century city: the disposable homes of the homeless, cobbled together from paper, plastic and canvas.'[21]

inserting new buildings that are sympathetic in scale and style to the existing cityscape. In most Western cities this is now the orthodoxy. In the USA it goes under the name of the 'new urbanism'.

Resilience

Metaphorically cities as organisms can experience birth, growth, maturity, decay and death. They can also be reborn. In 1945, at the close of World War Two, the cities of Hiroshima, Nagasaki, Tokyo, Manila, Hamburg, Dresden, Berlin, Kiel, Warsaw, Rotterdam and Coventry lay in ruins, many of their residents dead, their livelihoods destroyed, their surviving populations often starving and sick. But these cities were not abandoned. Within a decade their populations – even in Hiroshima – had returned to pre-war levels. Within two decades they had regained much of their pre-war vitality. This was most evident in their rebuilding. Some cities seized the opportunity for major replanning with new layouts, new activities, a new style. Rotterdam and Coventry took this path. Others were more concerned to restore what was there before and reconstructed, on the old pattern, the major buildings and places that characterised parts of the city before their destruction. This happened in Warsaw and in Dresden. In all cases the cities came back to life.

Seemingly, the organic dynamism that makes cities grow and flourish also often enables them to outlast violence pitted against them, making them resilient. In time, even Baghdad and Basra in Iraq, Kabul and Kandahar in Afghanistan may likewise recover from the effects of the wars recently fought across and around them. Cities that have been subject to fire, earthquake, flood or disease also show this natural capacity for recovery. In all these cases it is not just the physical city that needs to recover; it is also a matter of renewing the institutions of its economy, society and politics where these had been damaged or destroyed.

What comes after disaster is unlikely to be a complete restoration of any *status quo ante,* because the recovery will involve different agents in a different context. This may be because those active in the life of the city before the disaster have left the scene. Some may indeed have fled or been driven out as culprits in the disaster that overtook the place, even imprisoned or executed. Or they may have left the city in its hard times, pursued their lives elsewhere and not returned. There will usually be new entrepreneurs seeing opportunities for good returns from investing time, effort and money in city renewal. A potent example of this subtle shift within urban resilience is New Orleans. Hurricane Katrina hit the city in July 2005. When the levees were breached, 80% of the city was flooded and at least 700 people died. Most of the city's population of 480,000 left. A year later only about 200,000 had returned, but numbers have increased in subsequent years. But the lower lying areas, most damaged by the flooding, were predominantly where black people lived and they resettled in lesser numbers. It may be that the 'new' New Orleans comes to be a smaller, whiter, richer city than the 'old' New Orleans.

16.

Getting by: city life

Stellenbosch 2001. Visiting Cape Town we decide to have a day out in the Winelands. We end up in Stellenbosch, founded in 1679, second in age only to Cape Town itself. It is a handsome city of about 100,000 inhabitants, its centre laid out round a large green, its streets flanked by oak trees, with many white-timbered buildings reminiscent of colonial architecture elsewhere. Its university was fiercely Afrikaan in apartheid days. Now black, mixed race and white people mingle in the streets, shops and cafes. At the end of the day, driving out of the place back to Cape Town we notice hundreds of people, now almost entirely black, walking alongside the road in our direction. "There must be a football match or something tonight," I remark to my companion. A few miles on we realise our mistake. For here is another, parallel Stellenbosch of shacks and shanties, with a few new matchbox houses, where these people live – they were commuting home, by foot, the only mode they could afford. This parallel 'informal' city is quite as populous as the 'formal' city.

Surprises and secrets

Everyday city life is full of surprises like this, occasions when things turn out different than expected, are not as they first appear, or remain ambiguous. Those of us who live in cities know this better than others. We – as much as analysts, artists or rulers – have our particular perspective. Ours is the view of the city from the street, rather than the view of cities from the corporate office tower of government, business or media, or from the artist's studio or the academic library. It is a personal view, maybe shared with a few others such as family, neighbours, workmates, friends or people with common interests. This everyday life of cities may be noted in personal diaries, letters and emails, and is the subject of much ephemeral conversation – 'How was your day?' 'What have you been up to lately?' 'Why did it take so long to get here?' 'Did you see...?'

But it is rarely documented for posterity, though there are exceptions when the everyday event becomes, albeit briefly, newsworthy; or even exceptionally memorialised.

Heroes and heroines

Near St Paul's Cathedral in London is a small park fringed by office buildings, known as Postman's Park because it was the regular lunchtime hangout of workers at the former General Post Office nearby. The Victorian painter and philanthropist George Watts promoted the erection here of a memorial to otherwise forgotten Londoners who had given their lives attempting to save others. His idea failed to find any backers, so he created the memorial himself in the form of a 50 foot long open gallery. Along the walls of the gallery Watts placed Doulton pottery tablets commemorating the acts of bravery. Among them are:

'*David Selves*, aged 12, Off Woolwich supported his drowning playfellow and sank with him clasped in his arms. September 12 1886.'

'*Sarah Smith*, Pantomime artiste at Prince's Theatre, died of terrible injuries received when attempting in her dress to extinguish the flames which had enveloped her companion. January 24 1863.'

'*William Drake*, Lost his life in averting a serious accident to a lady in Hyde Park whose horses were unmanageable through the breaking of the carriage pole. April 2 1869.'

'*Samuel Rabbeth*, Medical Officer of the Royal Free Hospital, who tried to save a child suffering from diphtheria at the cost of his own life. October 26 1884.'

Cities are also full of secret places, known only to a few, kept away from the public gaze. Children may know more of such places than adults, seeking them out as play spaces. Equally dropouts, dissidents and criminals may find there the safe havens they need. An internet-based movement for urban exploration was started in Toronto in the 1990s by Jeff Chapman aka Ninjalicious. (Ninjas are found in Japanese folklore and have legendary abilities including control over natural elements). Its commitment is to access those spaces in the city that are formally off-limits, like stormdrains, tunnels, vacant lots, abandoned buildings, rooftops. They claim a long tradition, including the exploits of Philibert Aspairt, lost while exploring the Parisian catacombs in 1793; Harry H

Gardiner's first external ascent of a skyscraper in Detroit in 1916; the founding of Cave Clans in Melbourne and other Australian cities in the 1980s; and the 1994 rediscovery of Moscow's Metro 2 subway system designed in the Stalin era for a quick escape from the city. Chapman's guide to such urban exploration includes advice on stealth and concealment, useful equipment, ethics and manners[1].

Assaults on the senses

Cities are noisy, dazzling, odorous places, crowded with people, buildings and vehicles. They assault our senses of hearing, sight, smell and touch, even taste. Some of this is unpleasant: the smell of drains, sweat, exhaust fumes; the push and shove of crowds in the street, in shops or on buses; the cacophony of traffic horns, shouts, sirens, squealing brakes and occasional crashes. But we may find other sensual experiences in cities delightful: the smile from a neighbour, the sight of handsome buildings, the smell of tree blossom, the sound of church bells or of muezzins, even for some the rattle of an elevated railway or the rumble of a tram. The pleasant and unpleasant can be linked – witness the glorious sunsets that air pollution can cause. Or the same experience may produce ambivalent reactions: being in a crowd may induce claustrophobia and fear or a sense of solidarity and elation; eye contact with a stranger may seem friendly or hostile.

Those aspects of city life that assault our senses vary from time to time and from place to place. Take smell. In most cities of the North and in parts of some cities of the South, underground sewage pipes now carry human and industrial effluent away for processing and disposal, so that its smell – and its heath risks – are rare. In other places, such effluent may run down streets, in open ditches, discharge directly into rivers, its smell ever-present; the stench from animal or human shit in the streets may add to the stink and mess. On top of this may be the smells from industrial emissions, from food preparation in or off the streets, from rotting garbage, from traffic fumes. In response we may just hold our nose. But bike and motorbike riders increasingly feel the need to wear masks in urban traffic.

Take the lighting of cities. Today shop windows, headlights and rearlights on vehicles, advertising, floodlit buildings and streetlights illuminate our night-time city. Until the last 200 years, most cities were routinely pitch-dark after sundown. Public lighting, with candles, began in a small way in London in the late 18th century. About that time a minor European princeling, arriving and finding streetlamps and shop lighting, assumed that the metropolis had been lit up just for him. It was gas, later replaced by electricity, that brought street lighting to parts of most Western cities by the end of the 19th century. It enhanced the scope for nocturnal street life and it also provided better opportunity for its supervision by the police – a German advertisement for Osram of this period shows a light bulb decked out as a constable arresting a burglar. Since then, the internal and external lighting of city buildings and neon advertising have raised city lights to new heights of intensity and artistry. Challenging this today is a 'dark sky movement' campaigning against light pollution, wanting to 'reclaim the night sky' so city people can see the stars.

Or take graffiti. Writing, drawing or painting illicitly on walls or other surfaces in a public place has a long history. It is there in the ruins of Ephesus, Pompeii and Rome. Modern graffiti originated in New York in the 1970s, associated with an emergent hiphop culture and with the availability of spraycan paints. It is now found in most cities. Typically it will mark a presence ('X was here'), express an opinion ('Your war, our dead'), celebrate achievement (Read less, live more) and advertise the artist through the attached nicknames, called 'tags'. Motivations are partly aesthetic and graffiti is treated seriously as public art by some critics and collectors. One curious aspect is how universal are some of its stylistic conventions, particularly the riotous colour mix, the thick lettering, often with a black outline, the crowded juxtaposition of words and images. Above all, graffiti is subversive: explicitly or implicitly, its verbal or visual message is usually an assertion of values in opposition to established authority. In Prague, following John Lennon's death in 1980, young people smothered a wall in graffiti as a shrine that, through the subsequent decades of Communist and then post-Communist rule, has been fought over by the artists, residents and the police; it still survives.

Then, there is the noise in cities. In public spaces traffic noise is its most apparent source, for across the world motor transport has increasingly taken over from the quiet modes of walking and cycling in getting about cities. Apart from the sound of engines running, brakes squealing and tyres scraping road surfaces that is found everywhere, an energetic use of horns by some drivers characterises some cities. Aside from the street noise of traffic, there is increasingly an ambient noise of music, TV or advertising piped into the city's semi-public spaces like stores, foyers, stations and forecourts. Building works

The John Lennon memorial graffiti, Prague

– demolition and construction – are also permanent in cities. As well, cities hum with the talk of their occupants as they go about their daily lives. The phenomenal growth in the ownership of mobile phones in the last decade has added to the cacophony of talk. Walk down a city street anywhere in the world and you'll find people clutching phones to their ear, often speaking at high volume, uninhibited in what is said ('For Christ's sake, just buy some bananas', 'He's so gross', 'I hardly know her and I certainly haven't slept with her'), seemingly oblivious of any willing or unwilling listeners.

Finally, the sense of touch has its city uses. Obviously, city people perform everyday tasks with their hands like other people. But cities are becoming more tactile as transactions become mechanised: typing on a keypad to gain entrance to a building, swiping a card to pay a bus or train fare, using a PIN to validate a credit card purchase, texting on a mobile phone. Increasingly we do not just look, listen and smell but also feel our way around the city.

In these and other ways, as city inhabitants our senses are assaulted daily. In consequence there is a long tradition of diagnosing a psychopathology of urban life. In the Bible's Old Testament Babylon exemplifies such a mental and behavioural disorder. Juvenal's *Satires* present the teeming life of Rome as a place of flattery and bribery, noise and traffic, morally and mentally unhealthy. The classic modern treatise is Georg Simmel's 1903 essay *The Metropolis and Mental Life*. Observing the Berlin of the early 20th century, he argued that the modern city made unprecedented demands on the subjective resources of its residents, producing an endemic crisis of inner life. This problem was greatest for the many new immigrants to the city, familiar with the slower, more regular rhythm of rural daily life. The response to this intensity of stimulus was typically for city dwellers to retreat into individualism and a blasé and expedient relationship to others, minimising contact, even eye contact in crowds, preferring impersonal transactions to personal dealings, remaining indifferent to others' misfortunes, vigorously defending their personal space[2]. Today country people still lay such charges against city life.

In the streets

Talk of street life evokes an attractive sense of liveliness: being part of the crowd, with lots going on, the stimulus of new sounds and sights, children at play, the opportunity to follow impulses, in and out of shops, bazaars and cafes, people watching, displaying new outfits, maybe basking in nice weather. The ultimate expression of this street liveliness is the *passeggiata*, the custom of the daily stroll in many Mediterranean cities. But such liveliness is in part the product of others' livelihoods. And for them – for street traders, entertainers, taxi drivers and rickshaw men, fast food sellers, even beggars and thieves – making a living on the street can be tough, scraping an uncertain income from few sales and low margins, overworked, underpaid, often abused by employers or customers, chased by police. Contrast the description of the charm of the contemporary *passeggiata* in L'Aquila with a grim account of the Naples street scene a century ago. The latter description might have equally fitted Dublin, London's East End, or New York's Lower East Side at that time. Today it is in Lima, Kinshasa, Calcutta and the other cities of the South that such street scenes are to be found.

In all cities a lot goes on in the streets. Street life is at its most active where people are thickest on the ground, in the parts of cities where buildings are packed closely, activity is intense, traffic movement is strong, pedestrians dominate vehicles. In contrast the streets in low density, peripheral parts are altogether less busy; indeed in some strongly motorised cities being on foot in the street in suburban areas can mark you out as an object of suspicion. The

Street life Italian style

L'Aquila 1970s. 'This section of the Corso and the cafes are important socially as the setting for the *passeggiata*. This takes place every evening during the hour before supper, and on Sundays and feast days at midday, after people have been to Mass and before they return home to dinner, when it is the custom to take a walk under the colonnades. The purpose of this outing, the *passeggiata*, is to see friends and to be seen, and everyone dresses very smartly. Couples and groups of friends with arms linked walk up and down very slowly: university students, self-conscious national servicemen in uniforms from the nearly military barracks, family groups, groups of girls and groups of young men – people of all ages. From time to time groups converge to stand and talk, or adjourn to a café for an aperitif, and so it continues for an hour or so, after which the colonnades are deserted. The *passeggiata* is an event, rather like a large cocktail party, and open to all strata of society.'[3]

Naples 1880s. 'It was characteristic of the ailing local economy that tens of thousands of people subsisted by peddling their wares amidst the filth of the city lanes and alleys. It was these impoverished entrepreneurs who gave Naples its feverish activity as a great emporium…The elite of the streets were newspaper vendors who practiced only one trade year-round and enjoyed a stable remuneration. The other huxters were 'gypsy merchants', authentic nomads of the marketplace who moved from activity to activity as opportunity dictated. There were sellers of vegetables, chestnuts and shoe laces; purveyors of pizzas, mussels and recycled clothes; vendors of mineral water, corn cobs and candy. Some of the men completed their activity by acting as messenger boys, distributors of commercial leaflets or private dustmen who emptied cesspits or removed domestic waste for a few *centisimi* a week. Others acted as professional mourners paid to follow the hearses bearing the bodies of substantial citizens to the cemetery at Poggioreale. By their presence, hired paupers swelled the attendance, allowing the genteel classes to confirm their popularity and their sense of power.'[4]

throng of people creates the customers or audience for what street entrepreneurs of many kinds – traders, entertainers, proselytisers – offer to the passers-by.

Everywhere there is trading in city streets. There are permanent kiosks on the pavement; there are temporary stalls erected or cloths spread on the ground each day, chairs set out for personal services, pavement cafes; and there are mobile traders pushing carts or riding bikes, carrying trays or baskets with their goods. Accosting prospective punters, even people in vehicles temporarily stopped at traffic lights or people on buses and trains, is part of the sales technique. Any goods that are portable are sold in the street – newspapers, magazines, lottery tickets, cigarettes, bus and metro tickets, small furniture, stationery, fish, meat, fruit and vegetables, clothes, kitchenware, petrol, leather

---

Street food

Every city has food sold and consumed on its streets. The essence of street food is to be low tech: it must be prepared simply, usually by frying, boiling, grilling or liquidising unless it comes ready made like ice cream, be served with just a paper napkin or plate, carried by hand and eaten with fingers or disposable cutlery like chopsticks or forks. Above all, it must be fast and cheap. Burgers (from Hamburg, via North America), pizza (originally from Naples), croissants from France (with a Turkish Muslim origin – the crescent shape is the clue) and kebabs (from the Middle East) are the near universal, modern street foods. But there are still lots of local specialities, such as

fish sandwiches in Istanbul
roasted chestnuts in London
tortillas in Mexican cities
bhelpuri and coconut juice in Indian cities
dodo (fried plantain) in Lagos
crepes in Paris and blinis in Moscow
falafel in Middle East cities
takoyaki (octopus dumplings) in Tokyo
pad thai (noodles with garnish) in Bangkok
fruit juices in many tropical cities
sausage or steak sandwiches in Australia
fries with mayonnaise in Brussels
meat patties in Kingston, Jamaica

Street food is not just for snacking. It can be the main meal of the day, eaten at a pavement café. Some city families use it as take-aways for home consumption – in Bangkok parlance, a woman who feeds her family with street food is known as a 'plastic bag housewife.'

263

goods, souvenirs and more. Street trade is where counterfeit Rolexes, perfumes or trainers are on sale – 'genuine fakes' as their vendors often slyly declare. Services may also be on offer: letter writing, repair work, haircuts and shaves, healing, shoe shining, fortune telling, mobile phone use (on a per call change basis), vehicle minding (usually carrying as much threat as promise), goods delivery, card and board games. People wait and queue in the streets. It is in the street that you hail transport. Always there is fast food on offer.

In city streets someone is somehow always claiming your attention, even your support. Advertisements are the most obvious case, on billboards, on hoardings round buildings, in neon signs, on the sides of buses and taxis, on the metro ticket, even attached to people as with so-called sandwich board men. Shop signs and shop windows add their messages. Traders shout their sales pitches. Campaigners seek to waylay you, grab your attention, get you to sign their petition or make a donation to their cause. Tarts and pimps may solicit you, beggars may harangue you, pickpockets may rob you, at worst muggers may assault you. Occasionally more organised campaigning takes over the street as mass demonstrations march in support of some political cause; this may go off peacefully or may sometimes turn into a riot. At times the police or army or vigilantes may be a threatening presence on the streets.

But street life can also be entertaining. People socialise there, hanging out with friends. Streetside bars and cafes provide the venue for those who can afford the cost of a drink or meal; otherwise benches, walls or the ground must serve. Children may play in the street. Across the world young skateboarders have colonised city spaces, testing their skills against walls, steps and street furniture. Freerunning – vaulting, spinning and flipping acrobatically over and through buildings – also has its youthful exponents. You see football played in the streets of every city in the world. Then there are more formal street entertainments. Street theatre ranges from individual performers through small groups to large productions like carnivals, parades, fairs and circuses. Mostly entertainments are very local, though some are reproduced around the world: one example is the human statue who stands, often painted silver all over, immobile for hours on end; another is the Andean pipe band playing arrangements of pop standards. There is also unintended entertainment from the hustlers, eccentrics and exhibitionists that no city is without.

Street life is not exclusive to city streets. There are also squares and piazzas where trading, campaigning, entertainment and socialising go on. Some cities have one space that pre-eminently serves this purpose. As are

264

Krakow's central market square Rynek Glowny, reputedly the largest in Europe, occupied by exhibits and entertainers and market stalls, fronted by cafes and restaurants; the Djemaa El Fna in the heart of Marrakesh where a nightly carnival of herb doctors, acrobats, trained monkeys, charmed snakes, storytellers, musicians and food stalls is illuminated by butane lamps; and the many central *Plazas,* often flanked by cathedral and palace, like the Plaza Major in Madrid and those created by the conquistadors in Latin American cities, of which Zocalo in Mexico City is the most renowned. In other cities it is park life or beach life that draws the crowds. Climate may mark the distinction: in temperate zones city parks are where people often congregate;

Mardi Gras, New Orleans

in tropical zones beaches are the equivalent. Copacabana in Rio de Janeiro may be the most famous beach in the world. It is 4 kilometres long, backed by the ocean-side drive and high-rise buildings of downtown Rio. Here you sunbathe and swim but also walk, jog, cycle, make sand sculptures, play handball, eat, drink, sleep, perform, buy and sell, talk, rant and flirt, pausing for only a few hours every night for the beach to be cleaned up and made ready for the next day. On New Year's Eve you cast white flowers into the ocean and wish for good fortune.

These squares, parks and beaches are vast, popular, lightly regulated spaces where city people can express themselves spontaneously. They and the adjoining streets are also frequently the sites of collective celebrations like New Orleans' Mardi Gras, Munich's Oktoberfest, Siena's Palio horse race, the bull running in Pamplona and Edinburgh's Hogmanay. These are massive events attracting millions of participants, but there are also smaller festivities in other cities around the world. This is a long tradition with roots in religious observances that then spilled out of the churches, mosques and temples into the city streets. To acts of worship were added feasting and drinking, games and sports, dressing up, drama and dance, markets and fairs. Some festivals stretched from days to weeks. From time to time government or faith leaders have sought to ban such public celebrations or curb their excesses, not least from a political fear of the crowd. But the urge to 'dance in the streets' has proved remarkably resilient, not just in the persistence of traditional faith-linked festivities but also in the constant emergence of new forms, like open-air concerts, firework displays and marathons, the latter now annual in over a hundred cities of the world[5].

Life skills

Living in cities you must acquire certain skills: finding your way around the place, coping with the looks and words and touch of your fellows, provisioning yourself with necessary goods and services for survival, maintaining good relations with neighbours, protecting yourself from annoyance and danger. These are skills learned on the job, as it were, as city children grow up or newcomers to the city settle down. To complement these skills we carry daily in our pockets or bags items like keys, money, cash and credit cards, maybe other kinds of ID, a notebook, pen or pencil, a city map, diary, mobile phone, lip salve, paper tissues, a travel card, maybe an iPod with earphones plugged in and a watch on the wrist. These portable skills and tools enable us to deal with city life day by day. There are also less tangible aids to city living. Images and understandings of the city can be created that shape our daily choices of how to spend time and money, even though most of us may hardly be aware of them. Our journey to that shop to make that purchase is not just determined by a straight calculation of need and money; it is also guided by a working knowledge of the temporal and spatial patterns that characterise daily city lives.

These patterns express themselves in a number of ways. One is the rhythms of city life, played out at different scales. Most obviously there are the continuous movements of people in the city, in and out of buses, taxis and train stations, crossing streets at junctions, traffic accelerating and braking (regulated in part by the red, amber, green sequence of traffic lights), the interweaving of individuals in crowds. Then there are other recurrent rhythms: daily rhythms of workers commuting, children going to and from school, shoppers getting out and about, people going to lunch or supper or entertainment; weekly rhythms of workdays, leisure time, market days or religious observances like the Muslim Friday, the Jewish Saturday or the Christian Sunday; and seasonal rhythms of vegetation, climate, local festivals, family celebrations and holidays including the now universal Christmas.

There are also the mental maps that we craft to help us navigate our way around the city. Taxi drivers are the people most in need of such maps – among London taxi drivers it is known as 'The Knowledge' and to get a licence you must be tested on it and accurately describe a chosen route in the city. For the rest of us these mental maps are created over time and are under constant revision as we walk, drive or ride through the city, noting familiar sights, sounds and smells, connecting them up topographically. Such mental maps serve not just to get us broadly from place to place, but also in the detailed negotiations of crossing streets safely, avoiding congestion, keeping in the sun or shade, knowing the least busy bus stops, or which side of the street has the more interesting shopwindows. The resultant map is then stored in our mind, to act mostly as an autopilot directing us towards a chosen destination. How this 'image of the city' works in practice was explored by the American urban planner Kevin Lynch.

Another pattern is in the narratives located in the city. Most are personal: where we went to school, places we have worked, that concert in the park, where we visited the hospital. These experiences accumulate day by day, year by year and mean that our mental map of the city is also marked with memories,

Kevin Lynch's *The Image of the City*[6]

In the 1960s Kevin Lynch explored how people found their way around cities, by asking residents of Boston, Jersey City and Los Angeles to give directions to a stranger about getting from A to B, D to F, Q to X and so on. What emerged from their descriptions was a schema which distinguished five elements in their mental image of the city: *paths* for movement; *nodes* where paths intersect or activity intensifies; *edges* where two elements join, providing discontinuities, possibly barriers; *districts* of distinct character; and *landmarks* serving as markers, either close or distant. This feels right. Common instructions might be 'keep the park on your left' (edge), 'you'll know you're heading in the right direction when you see the radio mast' (landmark), 'turn left at the busy junction' (node) and 'then go through an industrial zone' (district). Sadly, this profoundly humane approach has had little impact on city design.

which may encourage us to favour some districts or routes and shun others. Some memories will be individual, others will be shared with friends or family and can serve as points of reference – 'It's in that street where Cousin Jamal once lived…' or 'It's where the cinema used to be…' Other narratives may be shared more widely by people with common perspectives of gender, faith, ethnicity, sexuality, for example. As a generality, for women the city will be less extensive, more home-centred, structured around daily and weekly routines. People of particular faiths or ethnicities may have ties to particular city neighbourhoods in which they feel at home with their fellows, seeing other parts of the city as different, even alien. Gay or lesbian districts within the city, where these perspectives and behaviours are the norm rather than the exception, are now widely found.

Past public events commonly leave their trace on the contemporary city. Every city has street or building names that relate to historic persons or events, though the reference may often be lost on current residents. Memorials or plaques may sometimes spell it out. In ex-colonial cities the former governing power may still be present in place names. In Hong Kong, mostly forgotten sons and daughters of empire are still there in great numbers in place names, not eradicated since the city reverted to China: just in the Central District are Connaught Road, Des Voeux Road, Stanley Street, Wyndham Street as well as

Queen's Road and Upper and Lower Albert Road. These histories have often become the basis of the group walks that tourist guides offer: visiting the sites of past ghost sightings, murders, fires and street battles are popular offers.

Consumers and citizens

Much of our energy spent on getting by and getting on in a city casts us as consumers. We must supply ourselves and our households with goods and services. Some of this is necessary to survival: food, shelter, learning, health most basically. But, beyond that, for city people who live above subsistence level there is a vast array of goods, services and experiences on offer, more so than in small towns or the countryside. Fashion dictates these choices to some degree and people in cities are blasted with adverts, promotions and word of mouth recommendation for new products, new shops, new styles unrelentingly – Available Now! 0% credit! Open till Ten Tonight! Easy Parking! Modern cities have become sites of consumption, most evidently in the shopping malls, the superstores, the multiplex cinemas and the sports stadia that attract large numbers of people to them and often operate 24/7.

But we inhabit cities not just as consumers but also as citizens. The concept of citizenship has urban origins: the word was used from the Middle Ages in Europe to refer to an inhabitant of a town. Only later, particularly from the rhetoric of the American and French revolutions, did it also acquire the wider association of citizens of the state or even citizens of the world. Even so, citizenship remains important in modern city life. Cities' demographic diversity creates a need for engagement between people of different faiths, classes, ethnicities and nationalities. Their size and density enforce numerous and frequent interactions between people crowded together. The chances they give people to improve their lot – through learning, rewarding work, better health, improved housing – are competed over. For all these reasons city rulers legislate our rights and responsibilities as citizens. But apart from such top-down measures, citizenship also requires opportunities for us to take bottom-up initiatives independently of rulers. Our role as consumers, freely choosing among the goods and services on offer in the city, must be complemented by our choices as citizens of actions to take, individually or collectively, to secure fairness or justice, sometimes by challenging the policies or authority of rulers.

Important here is the maintenance of what is often called a city's public

269

realm, that is, the streets, squares and parks that are open to all. They are distinct from the private realms of homes, workplaces, commerce, governments or faiths, to which access is more or less restricted to those who have a reason to be there. A generous public realm has long been an urban tradition. The Agora of classical Athens and the Forum of classical Rome were prototypes. Today, those city spaces that are used for demonstrations and protests – like The Mall in Washington, Trafalgar Square in London, Tarir Square in Cairo– are heirs to this tradition. In some cities attempts have been made through urban renewal to extend the public realm by creating new squares, cultural centres, parks, and watersides. Some are successful in attracting usage, as has been the Rockefeller Centre Plaza in New York or Place Beauborg fronted by the Pompidou Centre in Paris. Others have failed to secure the loyalty of citizens.

7.

Postscript: cities as Heaven and Hell

Throughout history, in all parts of the world, cities have been regarded as either heaven or hell. On the one hand, the sites of glorious human achievements, the product of human creativity in aesthetics, technology and social organisation, places where people can live fulfilling lives. On the other, sordid, unhealthy, ugly places, the sites of human misery and poverty, both material and spiritual. The range of common descriptors for cities in phrase and fable illustrate this ambivalence.

The City – popular North American term for the centre of major urban areas, as in 'We're going into the city tonight.' Also 'The City' is shorthand for London's financial centre (the administrative district of the City of London) and, as a metonym, its businesses.

City of the Dead (or Necropolis) – common term for a large cemetery in many cities, and most particularly the City of the Dead in eastern Cairo, where 800,000 squatters now live among the tombs and mausoleums.

City of Dreadful Night – used to describe the Victorian city, originating as the title of a book of doggerel verse by James Thomson published in London in 1880. Subsequently adopted by Rudyard Kipling in his 1888 narrative on Calcutta.

City of Light – used widely and loosely for cities in periods of artistic and intellectual creativity, for example, Baghdad of the Caliphate from the 8th-12th centuries or Paris in the 19th century: perhaps 'light' refers to 'enlightenment.'

The City Beautiful – the name given to an urban design movement of the late 19th and early 20th century that sought to bring order and grandeur in rebuilding cities; it was largely practised in North American cities but had both European precursors, in the work of Haussmann in Paris and his imitators, and successors, in the grandiose plans for their capitals of Mussolini, Hitler and Stalin.

City of God – title of a 5ᵗʰ century tract by St Augustine; also the name of a modern day Rio de Janeiro *favela* and of a book and film about life there.

City on a Hill – an eulogistic metaphor for the US nation first proposed by John Winthrop in a 1630 speech to the Massachusetts Bay Company; Ronald Reagan later added the adjective 'shining.' It has a precursor in St Matthew's Gospel: 'Ye are the light of the world. A city that is set on an hill cannot be hid.'

Cities of the Plain – Sodom and Gomorrah, cities on the plain of the River Jordan, destroyed by brimstone and fire for the wickedness of their inhabitants, as recounted in the Book of Genesis; subsequently a metaphor for sinfulness and deviant behaviour, used as such for the title of Volume Four of Proust's *Remembrance of Times Past*.

The two uses of the term 'City of God' make the point sharply. St Augustine wrote his tract *The City of God* soon after Rome had been sacked by the Visigoths in 410. For him this was just the latest in a succession of disasters to bring down – through slaughter, pestilence, fire, siege, sacking and plunder – the City of Man. Babylon, Troy and Athens had gone that way before. He set out to provide consolation in the spiritual triumph of Christianity. So his 'City of God' was to be inhabited by people who forgo the earthly pleasures of the City of Man and dedicate themselves to Christian values. Fifteen centuries later, naming the Rio de Janeiro housing project *Cidade de Deus* ('City of God' in Portuguese), when it was built in 1966 on a drained mangrove swamp in the south of the city, may or may not have been a conscious theological reference, may or may not have been intentionally ironic. The subsequent 1997 *City of God* novel by Paulo Lins and 2002 *City of God* film by Fernando Meirelles tell the story of young boys growing up in the *favela*, first joining and later running gangs involved in robbery and drug dealing, defending their trade and their territory quite ruthlessly and mostly getting killed by rivals or the police.

The contrast here is between the city as a place of hope or of despair. Universally both are true. The writer Jonathan Raban in his 1974 book *Soft City* argued that 'Finding the city irredeemable is only the other side of the coin to expecting it to be Paradise: utopias and dystopias go, of necessity, hand in hand.'[1] Of necessity, rather than just in reality, for it is the tension between the good and the bad in city worlds and its occasional resolution, that makes the world's cities such astonishing places.

Notes and references

1. Introduction: making sense of cities

1. *New Oxford Dictionary of English* (1998), Clarendon Press, Oxford
2. See entry for *Metaphor* in H W Fowler, *A Dictionary of Modern Usage* (1965), Oxford University Press, London
3. Jeremy Seabrook, *In the Cities of the South: Scenes from a Developing World* (1996), Verso, London, p.86
4. See UN Habitat, *State of the World's Cities 2008/2009: Harmonious Cities* (2008), , Earthscan, London
5. Quoted in Roy Porter, *Madness*, in eds Steve Pile and Nigel Thrift, *City A-Z* (2000), Routledge, London, p.137
6. Lewis Mumford, *The City in History: its origins, its transformations, and its prospects* (1961), Secker and Warburg, London, Preface
7. Hugh Stretton, *Urban Planning in Rich and Poor Countries* (1978), Oxford University Press, Oxford
8. Italo Calvino, *Invisible Cities* (1974), Secker and Warburg, London, p.42 for Chloe, p.61 for Ersilia, p.101 for Thekla
9. Italo Calvino, *Invisible Cities* (1974), Secker and Warburg, London, p.36

2. Living together: cities as communities

1. Lewis Mumford, *The City in History: its origins, its transformations, and its prospects* (1961), Secker and Warburg, London, p.148
2. See ed. John Carey, *The Faber Book of Utopias* (1999), Faber and Faber, London
3. See Geoffrey Parker, *Sovereign City: The City-State through History* (2005), Reaktion Books, London
4. Fernand Braudel, *The Mediterranean and the Mediterranean World in the Age of Philip II, Vol 2,* (1973), Collins, London, p.473
5. See Mark Mazower, *Salonica: City of Ghosts* (2004), HarperCollins, London

6. See Leonie Sandercock, *Cosmopolis II: Mongrel Cities in the 21ˢᵗ Century* (2003) Continuum, London and New York

7. *The Economist*, 20 December 2003, p.43

8. Quoted in Peter Hall, *Cities of Tomorrow: An Intellectual History of Urban Planning and Design in the Twentieth Century* (1988), Basil Blackwell, Oxford, p.126

9. Peter Hall, *Cities of Tomorrow: An Intellectual History of Urban Planning and Design in the Twentieth Century* (1988), Basil Blackwell, Oxford, p.170

10. R D Putnam, *Bowling Alone: The collapse and revival of American community* (2000), Simon & Schuster, New York, p.664

11. Raymond Williams, *Keywords: a Vocabulary of Culture and Society* (1976), Fontana/Croom Helm, London, p.65

3. Legacy: Venice past and present

1. James Morris, *Venice* (1960), Faber and Faber, London, p.29

2. See Deborah Howard, *Venice and the East* (2000), Yale University Press, New Haven

3. Henry James, *Italian Hours* (1909), William Heinemann, London, p.7

4. John Pemble, *Venice Rediscovered* (1996), Oxford University Press, Oxford, p.47

5. Fernand Braudel, *Civilisation and Capitalism, 15ᵗʰ-18ᵗʰ century, Volume III, The Perspective of the World* (2002), Phoenix Press, London, p.49

6. Robert C Davis and Garry R Marvin, *Venice, the Tourist Maze* (2004), University of California Press, Berkeley, California, p98ff

7. James Morris, *Venice* (1960), Faber and Faber, London, p.325

8. Henry James, *Italian Hours* (1909), William Heinemann, London, p.190

9. Régis Debray, *Against Venice* (2002), Pushkin Press, London, p.58

4. Conflict: cities as battlegrounds

1. UN Habitat, *State of the World's Cities 2008/2009: Harmonious Cities* (2008), Earthscan, London, p.141

2. Stephen Graham, Introduction: Cities, Warfare, and States of Emergency, in ed Stephen Graham, *Cities, War and Terrorism: Towards an Urban Geopolitics* (2004), Blackwell Publishing, Oxford, p.25

3. Revelations, 18.

4. Lewis Mumford, *The City in History: its origins, its transformations, and its prospects* (1961), Secker and Warburg, London, p.90

5. Rob Humphreys, *Prague: the Rough Guide* (1995), Rough Guides, London, p167; W G Sebald, *Austerlitz* (2002), Penguin Books, London, p.63

6. The story of District Six is recorded in the District Six Museum in Cape Town: see www.districtsix.co.za (accessed 22 March 2013)

7. See eds Jane Schneider and Ida Susser, *Wounded Cities: Destruction and Reconstruction in a Globalized World* (2003), Berg, Oxford

8. Eric Hobsbawm, *The Age of Revolution: Europe 1789-1848* (1962), Weidenfeld and Nicholson, London, p.112

9. Eric Hobsbawm, *Age of Extremes: The Short Twentieth Century 1914-1991*, Michael Joseph, London, p.458

10. Quoted in Mike Davis, *Planet of Slums* (2006), Verso, London, p.203

11. Jeremy Seabrook, *In the Cities of the South: Scenes from a Developing World* (1996), Verso, London, p.80, p.89, p.140

12. William Blake, *London*, in Songs of Innocence and Experience (1967), Oxford University Press, Oxford, plate 46

13. Peter Ackroyd, *Blake* (1995), Sinclair-Stevenson, London, p.157

5. Transformation: Mumbai's many worlds.

1. Suketu Mehta, *Maximum City: Bombay Lost and Found* (2005), Headline Review, London, p.3

2. Gillian Tindall, *City of Gold: The Biography of Bombay* (1982), Temple Smith, London, p.129

3. Ed Leo Mirani, *Time Out: Mumbai & Goa* (2008), Time Out Guides, London, p.59

4. Gillian Tindall, *City of Gold: The Biography of Bombay* (1982), Temple Smith, London, p.219

5. Suketu Mehta, *Maximum City: Bombay Lost and Found* (2005), Headline Review, London, p.79

6. Sharada Dwivedi and Rahul Mehrotra, *Bombay: The Cities Within* (1995), India Book House PVT Ltd, Bombay, p.311

7. The Guardian, *Welcome to the world's first billion-dollar home* (14 October 2010), London

8. Suketu Mehta, *Maximum City: Bombay Lost and Found* (2005), Headline Review, London, p.284

9. Soutik Biswas, *Mumbai: The Indian writer's New York* (19 July 2010), on www.bbc.co.uk/news/world-south-asia-10645880, (accessed 22 March 2013)

10. PricewaterhouseCoopers, 'Which are the largest city economies in the world and how might this change by 2025?', *Economic Outlook* (November 2009), London, Tables 3.1 and 3.6

6. Images and narratives: artists' cities

1. Horace Engdahl, Presentation speech for Orhan Pamuk's Nobel Prize for Literature 2006, The Swedish Academy, on: http://www.nobelprize.org/nobel_prizes/literature/laureates/2006/announcement.htm (accessed 22 March 2013)

2. Norbert Wolf, *Expressionism* (undated), Taschen, Hong Kong, p.56

3. Walter Benjamin, quoted in James Donald, 'Cinema' in eds Steve Pile and Nigel Thrift, *City A-Z* (2000), Routledge, London and New York, p.41

4. Tony Reeves,*The Worldwide Guide to Movie Locations* (2001), Titan Books, London

5. Jean Baudrillard, *America* (1988), Verso, p56

6. Raymond Chandler, 'The Simple Art of Murder', in *The Second Chandler Omnibus* (1962), Hamish Hamilton, London, p.14

7. Peter Hall, *Cities in Civilisation: Culture, Innovation and Urban Order* (1998), Weidenfeld and Nicholson, London, p.553

8. Jeff Vandermeer, *Veniss Underground* (2003), Prime Books, Canton, p.11

9. See Merlin Coverley, *Psychogeography* (2006), Pocket Essentials, Harpenden

10. Jonathan Raban, *Soft City* (1974), Hamish Hamilton, London, p.2

11. See Michael Haag, *Alexandria: City of Memory* (2004), Yale

12. Lawrence Durrell, *Balthazar* (1958), Faber and Faber, London, p.2

13. Constantine Cavafy, *The City*, as translated in Lawrence Durrell, Justine (1957), Faber and Faber, p.221

14. Edward El-Kharrat, quoted in ed Malcolm Bradbury, *The Atlas of Literature* (1996), De Agostini Editions, London, p.292

15. Edmund Keeley, *Cavafy's Alexandria* (1996), Princeton University Press, Princeton, New Jersey, p.6

7. Energy: novelty and excess in New York

1. See Risa Mickenberg, *Taxi Driver Wisdom* (1996), Chronicle Books, San Francisco

2. Peter Hall, *Cities in Civilisation: Culture, Innovation and Urban Order* (1998), Weidenfeld and Nicholson, London, p.746

3. Eric Homberger, *The Historical Atlas of New York City* (1996), Henry Holt, New York, p.3

4. Ed Cyndi Stivers, *Time Out: New York* (2004), Penguin, London, p.19

5. Jan Morris, *A Writer's World: Travels 1950-2000* (2003), Faber and Faber, London, p.238

6. Jan Morris, *A Writer's World: Travels 1950-2000* (2003), Faber and Faber, London, p.245

7. A.M.Schlesinger, quoted on page 34, Peter Hall, *Cities of Tomorrow: An Intellectual History of Urban Planning and Design in the Twentieth Century* (1988), Basil Blackwell, Oxford, p34

8. Eric Homberger, (1996), *The Historical Atlas of New York City (1996)*, Henry Holt, New York, p.68

9. New York Times, *Record immigration changing New York's neighbourhoods* (24 January 2005), New York

10. See entries in ed Kenneth T Jackson, *The Encyclopaedia of New York City* (1995), Yale University Press, New Haven and London

11. Adam Gopnik, *Through the Children's Gate: A Home in New York* (2006), Alfred A Knopf, New York, p.101

12. The conceit of Wall Street high-flyers as 'Masters of the Universe' was offered in Tom Wolfe, *The Bonfire of the Vanities* (1987), Jonathan Cape, London

13. Graham Clarke, 'A 'Sublime and Atrocious' Spectacle: New York and the Iconography of Manhattan Island', in ed Graham Clarke, *The American City: Literary and Cultural Perspectives* (1988), Vision Press, London, p.55

14. Peter Conrad, *Modern Times, Modern Places* (1998), Thames and Hudson, London, p.58

15. Ed Malcolm Bradbury, *The Atlas of Literature* (1996), De Agostini Editions, London, p.193

16. Tom Wolfe, *The Bonfire of the Vanities* (1998), Jonathan Cape, London, p.77

8. Transactions: cities as marketplaces

1. Jan Dodd and Mark Lewis, *The Rough Guide to Vietnam* (2003), Penguin, London, p.374

2. The sources for 'Some kinds of business in Baltimore, Bahrain and Brisbane' are local *Yellow Pages* publications.

3. This distinction comes from Rosabeth Moss Kanter, *World Class: thriving locally in the global economy* (1996), Simon and Schuster, New York

4. Alfred Marshall, *Principles of Economics* (1920), Macmillan, London, p.271

5. Lewis Mumford, *The City in History: its origins, its transformations, and its prospects* (1961), Secker and Warburg, London, p.254

6. Jane Jacobs, *The Economy of Cities* (1970), Jonathan Cape, London, p.49

7. Alfred Marshall, *Principles of Economics* (1920), Macmillan, London, p.271

8. Cushman & Wakefied, *European Cities Monitor 2010* (2010), Cushman & Wakefield, London

9. Edward Glaeser, *The Triumph of the City* (2011), Macmillan, London, p.41

10. David Drakakis-Smith, *Third World Cities* (2000), Routledge, London, p.120

11. David Drakakis-Smith, *Third World Cities* (2000), Routledge, London, p.134

12. Mike Davis, *Planet of Slums* (2006), Verso, London, p.87

13. Friedrich Engels, *The Condition of the Working Class in England* (2009), Penguin, London, p.68

14. Garth Myers, *African Cities: Alternative Visions of Urban Theory and Practice* (2011), Zed Books, London, p.70

9. Space and time: analysts' cities

1. J B Harley, 'Deconstructing the Map', *The New Nature of Maps* (2001), The Johns Hopkins University Press, London, p.158

2. See Sarah Hartley, *Mrs P's journey: the remarkable story of the woman who created the A-Z map* (2001), Simon and Schuster, London

3. See Mark Ovenden, *Metro Maps of the World* (2003), Capital Transport Publishing, London

4. Ken Garland, *Mr Beck's Underground Map* (1994), Capital Transport Publishing, London, p.7

5. Peter Haggett, *Locational Analysis in Human Geography* (1965), Edward Arnold, London, p.395

6. Friedrich Engels, *The Condition of the Working Class in England* (2009), Penguin, London, p.18

7. Jan Morris, *A Writer's World, Travels 1950-2000* (2003), Faber and Faber, London, p.86, p.262, p.436

8. See Janet L Abu-Lughod, *Before European Hegemony: The World System AD 1250-1350* (1989), Oxford University Press, Oxford
9. Mike Davis, *Planet of Slums* (2006), Verso, London, p.19
10. Fernand Braudel, *Civilisation and Capitalism, 15ᵗʰ-18ᵗʰ century, Volume III, The Perspective of the World* (2002), Phoenix Press, London, Part 2
11. UN-Habitat, *Cities in a Globalising World: Global Report on Human Settlements 2001* (2001), Earthscan Publications Ltd, London and Sterling, p.34

10. Metamorphosis: Tokyo's renewals and reinventions

1. Jan Dodd and Simon Richmond, *The Rough Guide to Tokyo* (2005), Rough Guides, New York, p.70
2. Donald Richie, *Tokyo: A View of the City* (1999), Reaktion Books, London, p.84
3. Foreign Policy, *The Global Cities Index 2010* on http://www.foreignpolicy.com/articles/2010/08/11/the_global_cities_index_2010 (accessed 22 March 2013)
4. Edward Seidensticker, *Low City, High City: Tokyo from Edo to the Earthquake* (1991), Harvard University Press, Cambridge, p.90
5. Ian Buruma, *Inventing Japan: From Empire to Economic Miracle* (2005), Phoenix, London, p.vii
6. Edward Seidensticker, *Low City, High City: Tokyo from Edo to the Earthquake* (1991), Harvard University Press, Cambridge
7. Roland Barthes, *Empire of Signs* (1983), Jonathan Cape, London, p.30
8. Jan Dodd and Simon Richmond, *The Rough Guide to Tokyo* (2005), Rough Guides, New York, p.25
9. Donald Richie, *Tokyo: A View of the City* (1999), Reaktion Books, London, p.132
10. Donald Richie, *Tokyo: A View of the City* (1999), Reaktion Books, London, p.64
11. William Gibson, *Modern boys and mobile girls*, on: www.guardian.co.uk/books/2001/apr/01/sciencefictionfantasyandhorror.features (accessed 22 March 2013)

11. Efficiency and order: cities as machines

1. Thomas Carlyle, *Signs of the Times*, Edinburgh Review No 98, reprinted

in *Critical and Miscellaneous Essays* (1869), Chapman and Hall, London, p.317

2. Peter Conrad, *Modern Times, Modern Places* (1998), Thames and Hudson, London, p.93

3. Translated quotes from Filippo Tommaso Marinetti, *Manifeste du Futurisme*, Le Figaro, Paris, 20 February 1909

4. See J R Kenworthy, *Transport Energy Use and Greenhouse Gases in Urban Passenger Transport Systems: A Study of 84 Global Cities* (2003), on http://cst.uwinnipeg.ca/documents/Transport_Greenhouse.pdf (accessed 22 March 2013)

5. Tom Vanderbilt, *Traffic: Why We Drive the Way We Do (and What It Says About Us)* (2008), Allen Lane, London, p.212

6. John Reader, *Cities* (2004), William Heinemann, London, p.56

7. Brian Appleyard, *Understanding the Present: Science and the Soul of Modern Man* (1993), Picador, London, p.42

8. Quoted on page 210, Peter Hall, *Cities of Tomorrow: An Intellectual History of Urban Planning and Design in the Twentieth Century* (1988), Basil Blackwell, Oxford, p.210

12. Variety: the contradictions of Paris

1. Norman Davies, *Europe: A History* (1997), Pimlico, London, p.803

2. Quoted in Peter Hall, *Cities in Civilisation: Culture, Innovation and Urban Order* (1998), Weidenfeld and Nicholson, London, p.202

3. Quoted in Norma Evenson, *Paris: A Century of Change 1878-1978* (1979), Yale University Press, New Haven and London, p.130

4. Definitions mostly from *The New Oxford Dictionary of English* (1978), Clarendon Press, Oxford

5. Quoted in Colin Jones, *Paris: Biography of a City* (2004), Allen Lane, London, p.320

6. Tony Judt, *Postwar: A History of Europe since 1945* (2005), Heinemann, London, p.210

7. Jan Morris, *Locations* (1993), Oxford University Press, Oxford, p.18

8. Cole Porter, *I love Paris*, words and music from Can-can 1953, (C) 1952 (Renewed) Chappell & Co., Inc. (ASCAP)

9. Adam Gopnik, *Americans in Paris: A Literary Anthology* (2004), Literary Classics of the United States, New York, p.xv

13. Power: rulers' cities

1. Deyan Sudjic, *The Edifice Complex: How the Rich and Powerful Shape the World* (2005), Allen Lane, London
2. Peter Hall, *Cities of Tomorrow: An Intellectual History of Urban Planning and Design in the Twentieth Century* (1988), Basil Blackwell, Oxford, p.216
3. Peter Hall, *Cities of Tomorrow: An Intellectual History of Urban Planning and Design in the Twentieth Century* (1988), Basil Blackwell, Oxford, p.216
4. Time Out, *Rome* (2001), Penguin, London, p.62
5. Donald J Olsen, *The City as a Work of Art: London, Paris, Vienna* (1986), Yale University Press, New Haven and London, p.9
6. See Alexandra Richie, *Faust's Metropolis: a history of Berlin* (1998), HarperCollins, London.
7. Philip Mansel, *Constantinople: City of the World's Desire 1453-1924* (1995), John Murray, London, p.xi
8. Mike Davis, *Planet of Slums* (2006), Verso, London, p.104
9. Peter Ackroyd, *London: The Biography* (2000), Chatto and Windus, London, p.103
10. F J Popper, quoted in Peter Hall, *Cities of Tomorrow: An Intellectual History of Urban Planning and Design in the Twentieth Century* (1988), Blackwell, Oxford, p.60
11. Machiavelli, *The Prince* (1961), Penguin, London, p.68
12. Alexandra Richie, *Faust's Metropolis: a history of Berlin (1998),* Collins, London.

14. Modernity: Los Angeles' rise and fall

1. See David Brodsly, *LA Freeway: An Appreciative Essay* (1981), University of California Press, Berkeley, California
2. Quoted in Richard Longstreth, *The Drive-in, the Supermarket and the Transformation of Commercial Space* (1999), MIT Press, Boston, p.13
3. Peter Hall, *Cities in Civilisation: Culture, Innovation and Urban Order* (1998), Weidenfeld and Nicholson, London, p.832
4. Quoted in ed. Nikos Stangos, *David Hockney by David Hockney* (1976), Thames and Hudson, London, p.104
5. See Melvin Webber, 'The Urban Place and the Non-Place Urban Realm',

in Melvin Webber et al, *Explorations into Urban Structure* (1964), University of Pennsylvania Press, Philadelphia.

6. Reyner Banham, *Los Angeles: The Architecture of Four Ecologies* (1971), Allen Lane The Penguin Press, London, p.23

7. Jan Morris, *A Writer's World, Travels 1950-2000* (2003), Faber and Faber, London. p.227

8. *Hooray for Hollywood* is a 1937 song about the movie business, still played each year at the Academy Awards ceremony

9. Peter Hall (1998), *Cities in Civilisation: Culture, Innovation and Urban Order* (1998), Weidenfeld and Nicholson, London, p.552

10. See Thom Anderson's film *Los Angeles Plays Itself* (2003), a narrated collage of over 200 film clips examining the city as background and character in the movies made there.

11. David Fine, *Imagining Los Angeles: A City in Fiction* (2000), University of New Mexico Press, Albuquerque, p.13

12. The modern chronicler of Los Angeles' dark side is Mike Davis, *City of Quartz: Excavating the Future in Los Angeles* (1990), Verso, London.

13. Jan Morris, *A Writer's World, Travels 1950-2000* (2003), Faber and Faber, London, p.236

15. Growth and adaptation: cities as organisms

1. Charles Landry *The art of city making*, RSA Journal, (October 2005), Royal Society of Arts, London, p.52

2. See Peter Ackroyd, *London: The Biography* (2000), Chatto and Windus, London; Gillian Tindall, *City of Gold: the biography of Bombay* (1982), Temple Smith, London; Colin Jones, *Paris: Biography of a City* (2004), Allen Lane, London; John and Laree Caughey, *Los Angeles: Biography of a City* (1992), University of California Press, London

3. See Vittoria Calvani, *Lost Cities* (1976), Minerva, Geneva

4. Population growth statistics from B R Mitchell, *International Historical Statistics 1750 to 1993* (1998), Macmillan Reference, London

5. See Joel Jarreau, *Edge City: Life on the New Frontier* (1991), Doubleday, New York

6. See Peter Hall and Kathy Pain, *The Polycentric Metropolis: Learning from Mega-City Regions in Europe* (2006), Earthscan, Sterling VA.

7. See Bernard Wasserstein, *Divided Jerusalem: The Struggle for the Holy City* (2001), Profile Books, London

8. Patrick Geddes, *Cities in Evolution* (1915), Williams and Norgate, London, p.86

9. Paddy Kitchen, *A Most Unsettling Person: An Introduction to the Ideas and Life of Patrick Geddes* (1975), Victor Gollancz, London, p.15

10. Lewis Mumford, *The Myth of the Machine: The Pentagon of Power* (1964), Secker and Warburg, London, p.395

11. Jane Jacobs, *The Death and Life of Great American Cities* (1962), Jonathan Cape, London, p.433

12. World Commission on Environment and Development, *Our Common Future: Report of the World Commission on Environment and Development* (1987), Oxford University Press, Oxford. (Known as The Brundtland Report after the Commission's Chair, Norwegian Gro Harlem Brundtland.)

13. See Organisation for Economic Cooperation and Development, *Environmental Performance Reviews: China* (2007), OECD, Paris

14. See City Limits, *A Resource Flow and Ecological Footprint Analysis of Greater London (2002),* at http://www.citylimitslondon.com/ (accessed 22 March 2013)

15. A global hectare is one hectare of biologically productive space with world average productivity and so comparable between economies.

16. UN-Habitat, *An Urbanizing World: Global Report on Human Settlements 1996* (1996), Oxford University Press, Oxford, p.418

17. See http://www.slowmovement.com/slow_cities.php (accessed 22 March 2013)

18. Tom Phillip, *Quiet revolution* (26 March 2008), The Guardian, London

19. Jane Jacobs, *The Death and Life of Great American Cities* (1962), Jonathan Cape, London, p.97

20. See Kisho Kurokawa, ed Dennis Sharp, *Metabolism and Symbiosis: From the Age of the Machine to the Age of Life* (1998), BookART, London

21. Peter Conrad, *Modern Times, Modern Places* (1998), Thames and Hudson, London, p.298

16. Getting by: city life

1. See Ninjalicious, *Access All Areas: A User's Guide to Urban Exploration* (2005), Infilpress, Toronto

2. Georg Simmel, *The Metropolis and Mental Life* (1971), University of Chicago Press, Chicago

3. Stephanie Lindsay Thompson, *Australia Through Italian Eyes: A study of settlers returning from Australia to Italy* (1980), Oxford University Press, Oxford, p.8

4. Frank Snowden, *Naples in the Time of Cholera 1884-1911* (1995), Cambridge University Press, Cambridge, p.35

5. See Barbara Ehrenreich, *Dancing in the Streets: A History of Collective Joy* (2007), Granta Books, London

6. Kevin Lynch, *The Image of the City* (1960), MIT Press, Cambridge, Massachusetts

17. Postscript: cities as Heaven and Hell

1. Jonathan Raban, *Soft City* (1974), Hamish Hamilton, London, p.11

Image Sources

- Saul Steinberg's *View of the World from 9th Avenue*
  The Saul Steinberg Foundation
- Ebenezer Howard's Three Magnets
  http://architectureandurbanism.blogspot.co.uk/2010/10/ebenezer-howard-garden-cities-of-to.html
- de Barbari's view of Venice 1500
  http://commons.wikimedia.org/wiki/File:Jacopo_de'_Barbari_-_Plan_of_Venice_-_WGA01270.jpg
- The Grand Canal – like a watery motorway
  Thinkstock
- The Ghetto
  Thinkstock
- Dresden 1945
  CORBIS
- Walls without, walls within the city: Mannheim 1695 and Venice's ghetto 1500
  Mannheim is Anonymous print; Venice is extract from de Barbari (as above)
- Train travel in Mumbai
  Author's photo
- Mumbai's dhobi laundries
  Author's photo
- Ernst Ludwig Kirchner's *Potsdamer Platz* 1914.
  Norbert Wolf, *Expressionism* (undated), Taschen, Hong Kong,
- Sci-fi city of the future
  Frank R Paul, City of the Future, cover illustration, Amazing Stories, April 1942
- Marilyn in New York – in neon
  Thinkstock
- Third Avenue, Manhattan – glitz and grot
  Author's photo

- Istanbul's Grand Bazaar
  Author's photo
- Abandoned car factory, Detroit
  Thinkstock
- Hillside favela in Rio de Janeiro
  Thinkstock
- Flows (A), networks (B), nodes (C), hierarchies (D) and surfaces (E)
  Fig 1.5 in Peter Haggett, Locational Analysis in Human Geography (1965), Edward Arnold, London
- Hokusai's *The Great Wave* – a foresight of Tokyo's traumas
  Bridgeman Art Library
- Tokyo's metro system
  Tokyo Tourist Information Centre
- Night-time Tokyo – ablaze with light
  Author's photo
- Boccioni's *The City Rises* 1910
  The Bridgeman Art Library
- Le Corbusier's Plan Voisin for Paris
  FLC/ADAGP, Paris and DACS, London
- Haussmann boulevard
  Thinkstock
- The master plan of Brasilia
  Casa de Lucio Costa
- Chicago's elevated railroad
  Thinkstock
- LA's freeways
  Thinkstock
- Night-time view of LA from Griffith Park
  Thinkstock
- The world's cities at night
  NASA
- The organic 'plug in' building: Pompidou Centre, Paris
  Thinkstock
- The John Lennon memorial graffiti, Prague
  Thinkstock
- Street festivities – Mardi Gras, New Orleans
  Thinkstock

Thanks

Explorers need back-up: others who provide support, advice and encouragement. So it is, with these explorations of cities through icons, metaphors and perspectives, that there are people who have helped me on my way. Some have pointed me in new directions, others have debated my observations about places we both know, yet others have helped me to achieve greater clarity in getting across my ideas; and the unknown contributors to Wikipedia have verified many facts. In particular I thank Ruth Levitt, Patsy Healey, Alan Ritch, Brian Hudson, Anne-Marie Varigault, Jeremy Turk, the late Derek Stroud, Romek Delimata and Harry Bingham for their comments and contributions at various stages. Also Jennifer Liptrot and colleagues at Troubador Publishing for getting the book to its destination. Above all, I thank Felicity Solesbury as my companion on many of my travels to cities, and for challenging my tendency to make lists.

Index of cities

Aberdeen 128
Abidjan 244
Abuja 206
Accra 93, 242
Aleppo 26
Alexandria 23, 26, 28, 37, 86, 97
Algiers 60, 63, 186
Amsterdam 24, 28, 31, 86, 127, 152, 157
Ankara 209
Antwerp 125, 149, 152
Asmara 244
Astana 206
Athens 13, 19, 23
Auckland 185
Avignon 128
Babylon 8, 52, 119, 207, 240, 260
Baghdad 60, 63, 210, 213, 271
Bahia 93
Bahrain 25, 124, 129
Baku 128
Baltimore 58, 90, 124, 177
Bangalore 81, 126, 129
Bangkok 14, 65, 120, 123, 144, 179, 212
Barcelona 120, 127, 217, 252
Basra 255
Beijing 63, 123, 218
Beirut 8, 26, 60, 125
Belfast 31, 60, 125
Benares 149

Benghazi 63
Bergamo 40
Berkeley 170
Berlin 6, 11, 22, 59, 62, 87, 127, 147, 182, 204, 205, 211, 223, 261
Birmingham 28
Bogota 8, 60, 63
Bombay (see also Mumbai) 209
Bonn 129
Boston 58, 90, 268
Bradford 125
Brasilia 61, 187, 206, 207, 208
Brasov 244
Brazzaville 138
Bremen 24
Brescia 40
Brisbane 124
Bruges 149
Brussels 127, 153
Bucharest 8, 63, 215
Budapest 8
Buenos Aires 19, 186, 223
Bukhara 149
Cairo 6, 8, 9, 22, 37, 62, 63, 136, 149, 180, 210, 271
Calcutta (see also Kolkata) 81, 271
Calicut 149
Cambridge 17
Canberra 11, 206
Canton 149
Cape Town 59, 79, 136, 217

Caracas 135
Carthage 23, 240
Casablanca 215
Cayman Islands 153
Chandighar 187, 206
Chenzou 185
Chicago 8, 9, 58, 90, 126, 145, 215, 216, 241
Chongqing 248
Constantinople (see also Istanbul) 8, 9, 24, 26, 37, 92, 205, 211
Cordoba 213
Cork 120
Coventry 276
Curitiba 250
Cuzco 243
Dadaab 135
Damascus 9, 125, 149
Danzig (see also Gdansk) 24
Delft 86
Delhi 52, 71, 81, 136, 138, 180, 181, 206, 208
Detroit 58, 93, 126, 257
Dhaka 136, 241
Dodoma 206
Dongtan 250
Dresden 52
Dubai 19, 83, 123, 129, 151, 213
Dublin 63, 85, 89, 108, 122, 125, 184
Dubrovnik 244
Düsseldorf 127
Edinburgh 8, 31, 90, 126, 266
Ephesus 259
Essen 217
Florence 13, 24, 46, 120
Fordlandia 151

Frankfurt 22, 28, 58, 127
Freetown 60
Freiburg 250
Gabarone 128
Gaza 23, 52, 60, 135
Gdansk (see also Danzig) 63
Genoa 24, 39, 152
Glasgow 125
Goa 26
Granada 210
Grozny 60
Guernica 51
Guernsey 153
Guimarães 217
Haarlem 86
Hamburg 24, 52, 108, 241
Hangchow 149
Hanoi 122, 212, 239
Harare 60
Havana 136, 179
Herat 23
Hiroshima 52, 161
Hong Kong 13, 18, 26, 123, 126, 129, 136, 148, 153, 268
Houston 54
Hue 62
Isfahan 121
Islamabad 206
Istanbul (see also Constantinople) 85, 120, 217
Izmir (see also Smyrna) 28
Jaffa 26, 28
Jakarta 5, 65, 138, 242
Jericho 8, 240
Jerusalem 24, 26, 60, 140, 243
Jersey City 105, 268
Johannesburg 129

Kabul 60

Kampala 28, 60

Kandahar 24, 83, 129

Kansas City 123

Karachi 24, 83, 129

Khartoum 52, 135

Kiel 276

Kiev 207

Kinshasa 60, 138, 241

Kingston 60, 93

Kinshasa 136

Kobe 51

Kolkata (see also Calcutta) 209

Königsberg 24, 143

Krakow 22, 24, 58, 149, 265

Kuala Lumpur 19

Kuwait 25

Lagos 138, 242

La Paz 120

L'Aquila 262

Las Vegas 9, 129

Leipzig 63

Leningrad (see also St Petersburg) 52

Liechtenstein 25

Lima 119, 144, 241

Linz 211

Lisbon 51, 179

Liverpool 17, 71, 93

Lodz 58

London 1, 8, 9, 12, 28, 29,51, 52, 66, 79, 86,89, 96, 127, 140, 141, 142, 147, 149,154, 173, 177, 181, 215, 219

Los Angeles 8, 9, 12, 13, 28, 63, 79, 89, 90, 225ff, 239, 241, 257, 268

Luanda 135

Lübeck 24

Luxembourg 25

Lvov 58

Macau 26

Macchu Pichu 240

Madrid 51, 52, 127, 149, 207, 241

Manaus 128

Manchester 3, 71, 125, 135, 146

Manila 63, 123, 178, 211, 219

Maribor 217

Marrakesh 85, 265

Marseille 147

Masda 250

Medellin 179

Melbourne 28, 144, 257

Memphis 93, 123

Mestre 49

Mexico City 3, 9, 22, 51, 67, 135, 180, 265

Miami 94, 153

Milan 24

Milton Keynes 22

Minsk 58

Mogadishu 60, 61

Monrovia 138

Monte Carlo 25

Montreal 179

Moscow 9, 90, 120, 123, 145,147, 151, 207, 241, 257

Mumbai (see also Bombay) 9, 22, 31, 52, 65, 67ff, 86, 90, 135, 153

Munich 17, 127, 211, 266

Nagasaki 52, 161

Nairobi 52

Nanjing 248

Naples 49, 108, 147, 262

Nashville 8, 125

Naypyidaw 206
Newcastle 122
New Orleans 51, 255
New York 1, 8, 9, 11, 16, 28, 31, 52, 67, 79, 88, 89, 90, 93, 101*ff*, 123,147, 177, 178, 185, 204
Nicosia 59, 60
Nottingham 125
Novgorod 207
Novosibirsk 151
Odessa 26
Oman 129
Oxford 9, 90
Padua 24, 40
Palermo 60
Panama City 60, 62
Paris 6, 8, 9, 11, 12, 13, 22, 28, 31, 63, 79, 85, 88, 89, 90, 96, 112, 125, 127, 147, 149, 175, 177, 179, 187, 190*ff*, 214, 271
Perugia 179
Phnom Penh 120, 223
Phoenix 239
Pompeii 119, 240, 259
Pondicherry 26
Port-au-Prince 51, 60
Portland 250
Prague 9, 58, 62, 63, 86, 89, 259
Pyongyang 211
Qatar 25
Rangoon 213
Riga 24, 58
Rio de Janeiro 8, 9, 19, 93, 185, 186, 266, 272
Rome 9, 51, 58, 140, 180, 183, 205, 209, 243, 260
Rostock 24

Rotterdam 31
Saigon 8, 62, 180, 215
Salonika (see also Thessaloniki) 26, 27
Salt Lake City 150
Salzburg 46
Samarkand 8, 149, 209
San Francisco 19, 28, 51, 129, 215
San Marino 25
Santa Domingo 62, 219
Santiago 223
Sao Paulo 136, 178, 185
Sarajevo 52, 177
Seattle 39
Shanghai 5, 8, 9, 75, 90, 136, 154, 210, 213, 248
Sheffield 125
Shenzen 151
Shiraz 121
Sienna 266
Silicon Valley 126, 153
Singapore 25, 123, 153, 212, 220
Skopje 244
Smyrna (see also Izmir) 26, 27
Soweto 63, 148
Stalingrad (see also Volgograd) 209
Stellenbosch 256
St Louis 58, 241
Stockholm 8, 22, 120
St Petersburg (see also Leningrad) 8, 63, 85, 139, 151, 206, 219, 221,
Sydney 9, 19, 28, 145, 148, 153, 288
Syracuse 242
Tabriz 121
Taipei 129
Tallinn 24, 217

Tangier 24

Teheran 63, 120, 211

Tel Aviv 150

Theresienstadt 57

Thessaloniki (see also Salonika) 27

Timbuktu 8

Tokyo 8, 9, 51, 52, 123, 156*ff*, 179,
204, 254

Toronto 28, 241, 257

Trieste 24, 58

Tunis 63

Turku 217

Tuzla 62

Tyre 23

Valparaiso 179

Vancouver 28

Vatican City 25

Venice 8, 9, 13, 24, 44*ff*, 57, 86, 90,
149, 152, 204

Verona 24, 40

Vienna 9, 13, 92

Vijayanagar 240

Volgograd (see also Stalingrad) 209

Warsaw 63, 108

Washington 11, 28, 58, 208

Watford 125

Windhoek 244

Wolfsburg 151

Wuhan 248

Yimu 126

Zurich 153